Race, masculinity and schooling

EDUCATING BOYS, LEARNING GENDER

Series editor: Debbie Epstein and Máirtín Mac an Ghaill

This timely series provides a well articulated response to the current concerns about boys in schools. Drawing upon a wide range of contemporary theorizing, the series authors debate questions of masculinities and highlight the changing nature of gender and sexual interactions in educational institutions. The aim throughout is to offer teachers and other practitioners grounded support and new insights into the changing demands of teaching boys and girls.

Current and Forthcoming titles:

Race, masculinity and schooling:
Muslim boys and education

Louise Archer

Open University Press

Open University Press
McGraw-Hill Education
McGraw-Hill House
Shoppenhangers Road
Maidenhead, Berkshire
England SL6 2QL

email: enquiries@openup.co.uk
world wide web: www.openup.co.uk

First published 2003

A catalogue record for this book is available from the British Library.

ISBN 0 335 210627 (pb)   0 335 210635 (hb)

Library of Congress Cataloging-in-Publication Data
CIP data applied for

Typeset by YHT Ltd, London
Printed in Great Britain by Bell and Bain Ltd, Glasgow

For Lesley and John Archer

Contents

Series editors' preface

Educating boys is currently seen – both – globally and locally – to be in crisis. In fact, there is a long history to the question: what about the boys? However, it was not until the 1990s that the question of boys' education became a matter of public and political concern in a large number of countries around the world, most notably the UK, the USA and Australia.

There are a number of different approaches to troubling questions about boys in schools to be found in the literature. The questions concern the behaviours and identities of boys in schools, covering areas such as school violence and bullying, homophobia, sexism and racism, through to those about boys' perceived underachievement. In *Failing Boys? Issues in Gender and Achievement,* Epstein and her colleagues (1998) identify three specific discourses that are called upon in popular and political discussions of the schooling of boys: 'poor boys'; 'failing schools, failing boys'; and 'boys will be boys'. They suggest that it might be useful to draw, instead, on feminist and profeminist insights in order to understand what is going on in terms of gender relations between boys and girls and amongst boys. Important questions, they suggest, are: what kind of masculinities are being produced in schools, in what ways, and how do they impact upon the education of boys? In other words, there is an urgent need to place boys' educational experiences within the wider gender relations within the institution and beyond.

Despite the plethora of rather simplistic and often counter-productive 'solutions' (such as making classrooms more 'boy-friendly' in macho ways) that are coming from governments in different part of the English-speaking world and from some of the more populist writers in the area (e.g. Steve Biddulph), there is a real necessity for a more thoughtful approach to the issues raised by what are quite long-standing problems in the schooling of boys. Approaches for advice to researcher in the field of 'boys' under-achievement' by policy makers and by teachers and principals responsible for staff development in their schools are an almost daily event, and many have already tried the more simplistic approaches and found them wanting. There is, therefore, an urgent demand for more along the lines suggested here.

This not a series of 'how to do it' handbooks for working with boys. Rather, the series draws upon a wide range of contemporary theorising that is rethinking gender relations. While, as editors, we would argue strongly that the issues under discussion here require theorising, it is equally important that books in the area address the real needs of practitioners as they struggle with day-to-day life in schools and other places where professionals meet and must deal with the varied, often troubling, masculinities of boys. Teachers, youth workers and policy makers (not to mention parents of boys – and girls!) are challenged by questions of masculinity. While many, perhaps most, boys are not particularly happy inhabiting the space of the boy who is rough, tough and dangerous to know, the bullying of boys who present themselves as more thoughtful and gentle can be problematic in the extreme. We see a need, then, for a series of books located within institutions, such as education, the family and training/workplace and grounded in practitioners' everyday experiences. These will be explored from new perspectives that encourage a more reflexive approach to teaching and learning with reference to boys and girls.

We aim, in this series, to bring together the best work in the area of masculinity and education from a range of countries. There are obvious differences in education systems and forms of available masculinity, even between English-speaking countries, as well as significant commonalities. We can learn from both of these, not in the sense of saying 'oh, they do that in Australia, so let's do it in the UK' (or vice versa), but rather by comparing and contrasting in order to develop deeper understandings both of the masculinities of boys and of the ways adults, especially professionals, can work with boys and girls in order to reduce those ways of 'doing boy' which seem problematic, and encourage those that are more sustainable (by the boys themselves now and in later life). Thus books in the series address a number of key questions: How can we make sense of the identities and behaviours of those boys who achieve popularity and dominance by behaving in violent ways in school, and who are likely to find themselves in trouble when they are young men on the streets? How can we address key practitioners concerns about how to teach these boys? What do we need to understand about the experiences of girls as well as boys in order to intervene effectively and in ways which do not put boys down or lead them to reject our approaches to their education? What do we need to understand about gender relations in order to teach both boys and girls more effectively? How can we make sense of masculinities in schools through multi-dimensional explanations, which take into account the overlapping social and cultural differences (of, for example, class, ethnicity, dis/ability and sexuality), as well as those of gender? What are the impacts of larger changes to patterns of employment and globalisation on the lives of teacher and students in particular schools and locations? The series, as a whole, aims to provide practitioners with new insight into the changing demands of teaching boys and girls in response to these questions.

As editors, we have been fortunate to be able to attract authors from a number of different countries to contribute to our series. We are very pleased to publish Louise Archer's work on this key educational issue. Much of the work currently being carried out on boys and schooling, because of its simplicity, fails to explore both practitioners' concerns and academic insights. What is original about Louise's work is that she describes in detail the social world that young people inhabit, while suggesting explanations of a more complex nature. She achieves this at a number of levels. Her discussion is located within a weaving together of theoretical and policy debates. This enables her to provide productive frameworks that suggest the kind of questions that Muslim boys and girls would like policy makers and practitioners to address. At the same time, she captures the contemporary complexity of the generational experiences of what it means for Muslim boys and girls to grow up in England. She wonderfully juxtaposes the media representation that sensationalises and demonises Muslim masculinity with young Muslims' own accounts. The latter, contributes to a part of a rich, diverse map of post-colonial ethnicities, as they make a diverse engagement with do-it-yourself biographies, drawing upon cultural, religious, national and gender resources in their coming-of-age in late modernity. A further level of complexity is added to her discussion of the young people's identity formations, by returning us to the issue of social inequalities. This linking of identities and inequalities is most important in illustrating the commonalities (with other social groups) and specificities of young Muslim life within a key institution, that of schooling. Louise provides a highly accessible text to a broad audience, offering some ways of thinking through these issues, as well as practical ideas for educators.

Máirtín Mac an Ghaill
Debbie Epstein

Acknowledgements

It is difficult adequately to thank all the people who have contributed in so many different ways towards this book – the following does not really do justice to the task.

The primary data that I have drawn upon in the book came originally from my PhD study, for which I am indebted to the pupils and teachers at the four schools for their generous time and cooperation. It is impossible to thank my friend Tamar Dutt enough for her wonderful interviewing work and for her endless interest, discussions and comments in relation to this research. Many thanks are also due to Nessa Sarwar for stepping in at such short notice to conduct interviews in one of the schools. In relation to my PhD, I would also like to acknowledge my supervisor Pam Maras and numerous other Greenwich colleagues and friends who helped me immensely to survive those difficult years. The family of my former partner, Neelam Visana (who died just as I started the PhD), also deserve exceptional recognition for their strength and love during this time. I would also like to express my thanks to Nira Yuval-Davis and Ann Phoenix for giving me such a hard, but rewarding, viva, which spurred me on long after the actual event.

I would like to express my sincere thanks to Becky Francis, Chris Skelton and Máirtín Mac an Ghaill for their initial ideas, support and influence in relation to giving me the impetus and the opportunity to write the book. Thanks also to Debbie Epstein and Shona Mullen for supporting me in this venture.

Some of the data and arguments in Chapters 2, 3 and 7 have been published in journal articles. I am grateful to Taylor and Francis (*Race, Ethnicity and Education*), Sage (*Feminism and Psychology*) and Palgrave (*Feminist Review*) publishers for allowing me to reproduce material here.

My colleagues at the Institute for Policy Studies in Education have been a wonderful source of support throughout the writing of this book. I am grateful for being given the 'flexibility' of time to write and I thank everyone who patiently allowed me to bend their ears along the way. In particular, I offer my warmest gratitude to Barbara Read and Carole Leathwood for diligently reading the manuscript and for offering such inspired thoughts and comments, and to Lindsay Melling for her excellent assistance with compiling the References.

Last, but by no means least, I would like to thank all my family and friends for their unwavering love and support over the years. My husband Matthew has been particularly wonderful, providing not only a top-notch proof-reading service, but endless glasses of wine and cooked dinners to ease the writing process (not to mention putting up with my need to offload and discuss every minute detail along the way). I am also sincerely grateful to my mum and dad for all their very many different investments in my life and for working so hard to enable me to be in the position I am today. It's not much to offer back, but I dedicate this book to them as a small token of my deepest thanks.

Introduction

The start of the twenty-first century has witnessed a widespread popular fascination with Muslim masculinity. At the time of writing, there seem to be almost daily reports in the newspapers and television about Islamic fundamentalist terrorist threats, coupled with speculation (both alarmist and 'reassuring') about the allegiances and loyalties of Britain's mainstream Muslim communities. In the aftermath of the attacks of 11 September 2001, and the US/UK war on Iraq, the news has been peppered with 'dangerous Muslim men', such as Saddam Hussain, Osama Bin Laden and, closer to home, Abu Hamza (the London-based Muslim cleric who has been accused of terrorist links). Balanced and positive images of 'normal' Muslim masculinity appear to be rather thin on the ground.

Young Muslim men have occupied a sensationalized and demonized position, at the forefront of the British popular imagination, for a number of years now and few would disagree that they are currently regarded as national 'folk devils'. Since the publication of Salman Rushdie's *The Satanic Verses* in 1988, young Muslim men have been represented as book-burning, angry youths rioting on the streets of Britain's cities. Over the years, images of angry Muslim young men have also been placed centre stage within reporting of the 'riots' in northern towns, such as Bradford and Oldham, where racial divides between white and Asian communities have been brought to the fore. The high-profile al Qaeda terrorist attacks this century have further fuelled the popular fascination, and fear, of 'dangerous', 'angry' Muslim masculinity.

Muslim masculinity has not only been associated with global terrorism, fundamentalism and urban unrest. In educational terms, Muslim boys have been identified as under-achieving and problematic pupils, suffering high rates of school exclusion and low rates of post-16 progression. In short, it is fair to say that Muslim boys are indeed 'hot topics' of social and educational debate.

In contrast to these sensationalized and negative stereotypical representations of Muslim masculinity, relatively little work has attempted to address British Muslim boys' own views and experiences. In one sense this is unsurprising because dominant social and educational discourses have always tended to treat young men from minority ethnic groups as a 'unified lump' (Sewell 1998: 124). However, a body of sociological and feminist educational research has begun to emerge that critically engages with issues of masculinity, 'race'/ethnicity and social class. For example, consideration has been given to the ways in which black (and white) working class boys negotiate and 'survive' schooling. Attention has also been drawn to the variety of ways in which black British Caribbean boys construct their identities within schools, but very little attention has been given specifically to British Muslim boys' identities and experiences in relation to schooling. This book represents an attempt to address this gap.

Issues of 'race', ethnicity and equality have always occupied a marginal space within educational discourses. To use an anecdotal illustration, I am frequently asked (predominantly by white people) *why* I research issues of 'race' and racism. It is almost always assumed that there must be some personal reason that explains why I am working within this specific field. Of course these assumptions are partly correct – my academic interests developed initially from personal relationships and circumstances. But it is interesting that I have never been asked this question in relation to other aspects of my research, for example, about widening participation in higher education (HE) issues, or work in relation to gender and schooling. In other words, while it is generally agreed that they are important issues, 'race' and racism are still largely represented as 'specialist' (not mainstream) educational issues.

The aim of this book is to locate issues concerning Muslim boys within wider debates around 'race', racism, masculinity and schooling. The questions, dilemmas and debates raised are not only specific to Muslim boys – they are integrally linked to the wider production, and representation, of minority ethnic masculinities within educational discourses. In particular, the book attempts to 'open up' the ways in which themes of 'ethnicity', 'gender' and 'culture' are addressed within schools. I also write as a feminist researcher, and consequently the book is centrally concerned with challenging (with the goal of addressing) inequalities.

The data reported here are drawn from an earlier larger study that was conducted with Muslim boys and girls from four schools. This research examined the ways in which Muslim pupils understood and constructed their ethnic and gender identities in relation to home and school. The project asked about experiences of racism and sexism, views on what the causes and 'solutions' might be, and explored variations within the pupils' responses. A focus was made upon the various ways in which Muslim young people represent *themselves*, and the ways in which they resist and challenge dominant popular representations of, for example, Muslim masculinity.

The book is organized into three main sections. The first section, Part I, sets out current theoretical and educational policy debates and issues in relation to Muslim boys. This provides an overview of relevant literature and policy developments and introduces the main concepts. This section forms a supporting framework for the issues, and may be of particular interest to students and researchers. Chapter 1 reviews the popular 'boys in crisis' debate and discusses different approaches and ways of theorizing masculinity. It traces the ways in which race and ethnicity have been conceptualized within both academic theory and educational policy and practice, and details my own theoretical approach. Chapter 2 charts changing public and educational representations of Asian and Muslim pupils. It examines the shift in views of Asian pupils from being 'behavers and achievers' to more recent distinctions between 'achievers' and 'believers' and associated public concerns and 'Islamaphobia'. The benefits of pursuing a critical feminist approach to the study of Muslim masculinity in schools are highlighted.

The second section, Part II, of the book provides a detailed examination of identity issues, looking at how Muslim boys conceptualize racial, ethnic and religious identities at home and at school. Chapter 3 examines the various means through which boys construct 'Muslim' and 'black' ethnic/ racial and religious identities. The notion of 'gangsta' masculinity is also discussed. In Chapter 4 attention is given to boys' constructions of gender identities, examining, for example, the boys' performance of 'laddish' identities within schools. Particular attention is also given to the ways in which the boys attempt to regulate Muslim girls' identities through discourses of 'culture' and tradition. Chapter 5 addresses the relationship between boys' identities inside and outside of school. Consideration is given to the importance of leisure interests and activities and the role of 'home' and family relations in relation to boys' identities.

The final section, Part III, of the book addresses the link between identities and inequalities, focusing in particular on Muslim boys' accounts of racism, schooling and their educational aspirations. Chapter 6 reviews the ways in which the boys understood and experienced racism, both within and outside of school. It details boys' views on the different potential causes of racism and its solutions, such as 'fighting back' or 'ignoring it'. Chapter 7 looks at Muslim boys' educational and occupational preferences and aspirations and their views of schooling. It also examines the ways in which the boys talk about Muslim girls' post-16 options, demonstrating an important link between identities and educational choices. Themes are drawn together in the final chapter, where recommendations are made for theory and practice, including practical ideas for educators.

Part I

Debates and issues

chapter one

Gender, ethnicity and education: the theoretical and policy context

This chapter sets out the theoretical and policy context of the book, introducing readers to literature and debates pertaining to boys, 'race', ethnicity and schooling. The chapter is organized into four main parts. The first part reviews the 'boys in crisis' debate, concentrating on feminist critiques of these issues and highlighting the ways in which minority ethnic boys have been sidelined within wider concerns about boys' under-achievement. The second part discusses how issues of masculinity might be conceptualized, with particular attention drawn to how we might theorize 'hegemonic masculinity' and black masculinity/masculinities. The third part of the chapter examines the conceptualizations of 'race' and ethnicity within academic theory, while the final part traces the ways in which issues of 'race' and ethnicity have been addressed within educational policy and practice.

The 'boys in crisis' debate

It is difficult to avoid media panics and public debates portraying boys as currently 'in crisis'. Such concerns were (in)famously encapsulated in the BBC1 current affairs programme *Panorama*, entitled 'Is the Future Female?' (transmission date, 24 October 1994), and they have endured since then as fuel for discussion across both the popular and educational media. The issue of male educational 'under-achievement' and the related male 'crisis of confidence' (*The Times*, 5 September 1998: 7) thus remains a priority on the agendas of academics, policy-makers and practitioners. Indeed, fears about 'masculinity in crisis' and boys' under-attainment are common throughout western industrialized countries (Francis 1999), but it is worth noting that concerns about boys (particularly working class boys) and schooling are not really a new phenomenon. Indeed, they have been aired for over one hundred years (Delamont 2000), although the current interest in 'masculinity' has only featured within mainstream academic research since the 1970s (Mac an Ghaill 1996). There are various feminist accounts and perspectives on boys' schooling (for example, Kenway 1995; Weiner *et al.* 1997), but Skelton (2001) provides a particularly useful and accessible overview and analysis of the issues within the context of the United Kingdom.

Numerous explanations have been offered for the (supposed) crisis in modern-day masculinity (see, for example, Newton 1998). One line of argument has proposed that the rise of feminism, and challenges to the dominance of traditionally male forms of thought (such as rationality and positivism) by post-structuralism, have negatively impacted upon men's sense of identity. A reactive men's movement has emerged, arguing that boys and men are effectively 'losing', and thus need to 'regain' their masculinity in the face of such changes (for example, Bly 1990).

One of the major factors that has been identified as contributing to 'boys in crisis' relates to the changes brought about by the changing nature of work/employment through post-industrialization (namely the collapse of 'traditional men's work' following the decline of heavy industry and the rise of the service economy). It has been suggested that these changing social and economic relations have left young men increasingly confused about their role in society and their personal, sexual and work-related identities because 'the surrounding images of masculinity are complex and confused' (Frosh *et al.* 2002: 1). Some commentators fear, therefore, that modern men experience increased identity confusion due to the lack of consensus in society over what it means to be a man and what constitutes acceptable masculinity. This perceived identity confusion has been linked to an increase in young male depression and suicide rates and criminal/anti-social behaviour (Lloyd 1999).

Men from working class backgrounds have been identified as particularly suffering from the changing economic conditions described. The decline of Britain's heavy industrial manufacturing base has increased the threat of unemployment among working class men, and this has entailed a range of negative psychic and material consequences, particularly because work is often a central pillar of masculine identity. 'As the 1997 hit film *The Full Monty* made clear, men who formerly worked in factories are struggling to reinvent themselves in the light of a new economy in which some women have the economic power they have lost' (Walkerdine *et al.* 2001: 1). However, many feminists differ from proponents of the 'masculinity in crisis' view in their interpretations of these issues. For example, it could be argued that the difficulties encountered by working class men reflect wider class inequalities rather than an essential crisis in masculinity per se.

The popularity of the notion of 'masculinity in crisis' has been reinforced, however, by concerns about boys' educational 'under-achievement'. Statistics suggest that, on the whole, girls are obtaining better results than boys in key public examinations. Although the accuracy of these figures is a matter of debate, they have been interpreted by proponents of the 'boys in crisis' debate as evidence that girls' 'over-achievement' is reinforcing and causing male 'under-achievement'. For example, in August 2000 David Blunkett (then British Secretary of State for Education) spoke critically about girls' overly aggressive assertiveness which, he suggested, not only improved girls' levels of attainment but also disadvantaged men and boys. Within the British press, such fears about boys' under-performance have become recurring features in the reporting of GCSE and A Level examination results each summer. It is notable, however, that the lack of achievement of *some* boys (particularly white, working class boys) has been singled out as a greater cause for concern than that of others.

The widespread concern about boys' academic under-achievement also extends into the post-compulsory sector, exemplified by worries about (working class) men's 'absence' from post-compulsory education and training (McGivney 1999: 1). Educational policy goals of 'widening participation' in higher education and promoting 'lifelong learning' within 'the learning society' are now common within industrialized societies. Within these policy discourses, working class men (particularly those from African/ Caribbean, Pakistani and Bangladeshi backgrounds, see CVCP 1998a) constitute a key target group due to their low rates of participation in higher education. These policy concerns seem rather blinkered, however, when viewed in light of evidence indicating that working class women are equally under-represented in higher education and that many men, namely white, middle class men, continue to participate and achieve very highly (see Archer *et al.* 2003).

In recent years a substantial, and growing, body of feminist critique has developed in opposition to the 'boys in crisis'/boys' under-achievement discourses outlined above. This feminist critique has suggested that the crisis has been sensationalized and exaggerated (see the key critical examinations by Kenway 1995 and Weiner *et al.* 1997). It also maintains that popular notions of 'masculinity in crisis' and 'boys' under-achievement' tend to be over-simplistic and derive from particular (sexist and racist) assumptions. For example, feminists have argued that the debate is underpinned by gendered assumptions about the 'natural' division of labour in society. These assumptions are revealed by the lack of comparable policy concern regarding *women*'s responses to the uncertainties of modernity and 'flexible', insecure new modes of employment.[1]

Some of the key feminist criticisms of the 'boys in crisis' debate are brought together by Epstein *et al.* in their book *Failing Boys?* (1998). The authors argue that the debate has been framed in particular, narrow, masculinist terms and they argue instead for a relational and balanced view of the issues around gender and schooling. For example, they suggest that it is unhelpful to view girls' and boys' achievement in binary terms (whereby the assumption is that if one group wins the other loses). Instead they argue that 'questions around equity and differences among boys and among girls as well as between boys and girls are key to understanding what is happening in schools' (Epstein *et al.* 1998: 4).

Failing Boys? outlines and critiques popular understandings of both the 'causes' of male under-achievement and the range of measures that have been proposed in response. The authors identify three main perspectives within the debate on boys' under-achievement and trace the implications of each. First, they examine the '*poor boys*' perspective, in which boys are understood to be the victims of education injustices. Within this discourse, men are assumed to have lost control of their lives due to the rise of feminism and the increasing feminization of schools and education. Such accounts are exemplified by the work of Robert Bly (1990), Steve Biddulph (1994) and Neil Lydon (1996), and are criticized by Epstein *et al.* (1988) for being reactionary discourses that attempt to bolster particular dominant forms of masculinity. The second perspective identified is entitled '*failing schools failing boys*'. This perspective is rooted within the current school effectiveness movement, a worldwide trend utilizing 'new managerial' (Trow 1994; Clarke and Newman 1997) and masculinist discourses that blame boys' failures upon 'under-performing' institutions (see Rassool and Morley 2000 for a critique). As Davies (2003) notes, new managerialism is a form of governance characterized by ever increasing, centralized administrative and managerial control. New managerialist practices shift power away from professionals, like teachers, through cultures of surveillance and audit. These cultures are both externally imposed upon and internalized by those working within new managerial regimes. Epstein *et al.* (1998) express their concern that, in effect, this discourse further marginalizes and suppresses anti-sexist work within schools, with financially poorer schools being particularly targeted and disadvantaged.

The third perspective identified, termed '*boys will be boys*', draws upon essentialist, biologically based conceptualizations of masculinity to suggest that boys are not 'naturally' predisposed to doing school work (despite their supposedly superior intellects) and are thus prevented from achieving by their biology. Epstein *et al.* (1998) criticize this final perspective for its flawed biological assumptions and for its implicit heterosexualization of schools and its advocation of the use of girls to police boys' behaviour.

An additional key flaw that the authors identify within 'boys' under-achievement' and 'masculinity in crisis' discourses is the assumption that all girls perform academically well and all boys do not. These discourses ignore the considerable differences in achievement between boys and girls from different social classes and ethnic backgrounds. Epstein *et al.* (1998) criticize proponents of the 'boys in crisis' debate for portraying a general pattern of under-achievement and crisis among *all* boys (and a converse picture of attainment and unproblematic identities among all girls). They argue that this generalization (of male under-achievement versus female success) glosses over complex differences in attainment and experience between, and within, different groups of boys and girls according to social class, sexuality and ethnicity. As Raphael Reed (1999) notes, even though 'full' national data on achievement by 'race', social class and gender remain unavailable, it is clear that pupils' academic achievement varies considerably across social class (middle class boys achieve more highly on average than working class boys) and between ethnic groups. To some extent, the strength of social class differences in achievement has masked issues of 'race' and ethnicity; indeed, some researchers have even proposed that it is possible to subsume and reduce issues of 'race' to those of social class (Furlong and Cartmel 1997). However, important and complex patterns of achievement have been identified across class, gender and ethnicity (Murphy and Elwood 1998). For example, Bangladeshi/Pakistani and African/Caribbean boys have low rates of attainment and high rates of exclusion (Marland 1995; West and Lyons 1995; Gillborn and Gipps 1996; Watkins 1998) as well as low rates of progression into further/higher education (NCIHE 1997; DfEE 1999).

The feminist critique of the boys' under-achievement and 'masculinity in crisis' debates is detailed, convincing and robust, and yet such discourses continue to exert influence within educational policy and practice. In some respects, the issue of whether (and to what extent) male under-achievement really 'exists' or not is immaterial because the myth has numerous, 'real' consequences. As Lynn Raphael Reed explains:

> deconstructing the subject of the underachieving boy is not to engage in an argument about whether male under-achievement exists: its 'reality' is a measure of its productivity in shaping educational policies and practices and there is considerable evidence of its current effects
>
> (Raphael Reed 1999: 60)

The power of the 'masculinity in crisis' discourse is also reflected by the uneven attention given to different sides of the debate in the media. As Skelton indicates, it is disheartening to note that within popular and media spheres, critical accounts and more balanced investigations of the 'under-achievement' phenomenon (such as by Francis 2000a) 'do not seem to have attracted the same publicity' as sensationalized accounts of masculinity in 'crisis' (Skelton 2001: 32).

Minority ethnic boys and the 'boys in crisis' debate

Boys from minority ethnic backgrounds have been largely absent from the 'boys in crisis' debate, reflecting their more general invisibility within educational policy and within academic texts and theorizing. Early seminal sociological studies of boys and schooling focused exclusively on white working class boys (for example, Willis 1977; Corrigan 1979), but this bias continues through to the present day in both research and policy. This prioritization of white masculinity is problematic on a number of levels. The early studies mentioned above attracted criticisms from feminists for their narrow, normative focus and for their potential contribution to a romanticization of (white, heterosexual) working class boys and their 'anti-school' cultures. More recently, criticisms have focused on the assumption that white boys' 'failure' is somehow *more* problematic and abnormal, and thus is more deserving of attention and intervention, than low levels of attainment among other groups of pupils. Arnot *et al.* (1998) suggest that this situation has arisen because white boys constitute a sizeable proportion of the school population and consequently their relatively low levels of average performance render them highly visible. But this bias towards white masculinity may also reflect the powerful positions of white middle class parents, who are more able to get their voices heard in policy and practice, and who do not want their sons to be educationally 'outclassed' (see Skelton 2001 and Ball 2003). Consequently, minority ethnic boys – and issues associated with black masculinity – are often marginalized and hidden within academic research and writing (Mirza 1999).

In the few spaces where they have been addressed, minority ethnic boys and issues of 'black masculinity' have been negatively represented and conceptualized within dominant social and educational discourses. Minority ethnic boys thus occupy contradictory positions, being both invisible *and* hyper-visible, represented as both outside of/exceptions to 'normal' masculinity and also the epitome, or source, of particular anti-social problems. For example, Mama (1995) draws attention to popular racist discourses in which black men are represented as inherently 'stupid' and 'problematic', due to being stereotyped as aggressive, criminal, highly sexed and poorly educated. As I detail in Chapter 2, Muslim boys and men have been similarly subject to a barrage of negative stereotypes and representations, although the content of these discourses has been somewhat different. Consequently, as Mirza argues, it is somewhat ironic that the 'academic silence on the subject of black masculinity is matched by a consuming daily presence' (Mirza 1999: 137). This notion is explored further below in relation to academic conceptualizations of masculinity.

Conceptualizing masculinity

The question of what is meant by the term 'masculinity' can be related to wider academic debates about the theorization and conceptualization of identity. These debates are ongoing both across and within different disciplines, but they can be crudely categorized into 'positivist' and 'post-structuralist' traditions. Positivist approaches treat identity in terms of individual psychology. That is, identity is assumed to be relatively stable and fixed, holding the potential to be measured and/or observed through scientific methods. Gender and ethnic/cultural identities are understood to be displayable through an individual's conformity to particular sets of stereotypical views, attitudes, behaviours and practices, which can be measured and assessed by researchers (for example, Phinney 1990; Betancourt and Regeser Lopez 1993). Thus from a positivist position, masculinity is assumed to be a consistent aspect of gender identity, which can be measured (for example, through the use of specially designed attitude scales or questionnaires).

The growth of post-structuralist approaches within the social sciences has challenged these positivistic assumptions by questioning the scientific principles of objectivity and rationality. Within post-structuralist perspectives, identity is understood to be shifting and multi-faceted (for example, Bhavnani and Phoenix 1994), constantly evolving and 'in process' (Hall 1996). Hall describes identity as constituted, and re-made in a never-ending process of 'becoming', such that identities are never 'achieved' (completed or finished), rather, they are formed through their continual construction, negotiation, contestation and assertion. In other words, a person constructs and asserts their identity in different ways, across different contexts and time, and in relation to shifting social structures and divisions of 'race', gender, class, sexuality, dis/ability and so on. Thus there may be various different gender identities and forms of masculinity available to an individual, and these will reflect and be formed in relation to a wide range of other social positions and discourses.

These different epistemological approaches are mirrored to some extent by various different socio-political perspectives on masculinity. I do not intend to rehearse the details of these perspectives here (rather, see Skelton 2001 and Coltrane 1994 for overviews); instead I would like to draw attention to Gough's (1998) simple, yet useful, theoretical distinction between two broad socio-political approaches to masculinity, the 'celebratory' and the 'critical'. Within celebratory conceptualizations of masculinity (for example, Bly 1990), men are perceived to be victims (within education and society) of modern changes, who require help to regain their lost or damaged senses of self and power. Such perspectives may assume particular gender roles and relations to be 'natural' and may tend to homogenize men as a social group beneath the banner of 'masculinity'.

In comparison, critical approaches (many of which would fall beneath the banners of feminist and post-structuralist theories) aim to disrupt and dismantle common sense notions of masculinity, showing how patriarchal power and privilege operates (Wetherell 1993). Critical theorists attempt to highlight differences in power and experience between groups of men, examining the construction of various competing forms of 'masculinities'. From a feminist post-structuralist perspective, masculinity can be interrogated as a discursive practice so that 'men become gendered and questionable, no longer synonymous with the human and the normal' (Wetherell 1993: 2). The political aim of such analyses is to contribute to 'unmasking and depowering men's pretence to objectivity' (Brod 1994: 84), and to therefore identify opportunities for intervening in the reproduction of inequalities. Feminist post-structuralist perspectives have criticized positivistic identity theorizing and research for pathologizing women's identities and development in relation to an assumed male norm (for example, Gilligan 1982; Mies 1993). It has also been shown, for example, how the use of masculinity and femininity scales within social psychology provides scientific reinforcement of sex role stereotypes (Duelli Klein 1983).

Critical approaches have drawn attention to the ways in which masculinities are socially and historically situated. As will be argued within this book, masculinities need to be understood as being located within complex, unequal power relations and structural inequalities. Structural inequalities are socially and historically positioned and can be both material and discursive in their form (that is, they can operate on a range of economic, social, emotional and psychic levels). As I have written with colleagues elsewhere (Archer *et al.* 2001), structural inequalities do not operate in a 'one way' fashion upon individuals or groups, but can be met by resistance. These inequalities, while shifting in their specific form and articulation, can also be broadly durable and persistent, with patterns of inequality being reproduced across shifting times and contexts 'within a network of multiple, unequal power relations' (Archer *et al.* 2001: 46).

In this book I conceptualize masculinity as entailing individual and collective agency, 'performance' (Butler 1990) and resistance within a framework of structural inequalities (see also Archer *et al.* 2001a). Masculinities are understood to be relational identities that are constructed in various ways through everyday talk (Edley and Wetherell 1997). Boys and men, as social actors, actively construct a range of different masculinities (Mac an Ghaill 1994) by drawing on available *discourses* of masculinity. Discourses can be defined as broad, shared patterns of understanding and language. As Wetherell and Potter (1992) point out, discourses are not merely descriptive, rather they can have 'real' effects within the world. This is because talk is an ideological, constitutive (never neutral) activity. Through language we put together and construct identity positions and understandings of the world. These constructions must be constantly re-made, argued for and

defended through negotiations with others and against competing discourses and understandings (see Wetherell and Potter 1986, 1992;
Wetherell 1987, 1993, 1994; Billig 1988, 1991).

The theoretical viewpoint taken within this book is thus one in which
individuals have agency and can negotiate identity positions, albeit within
the constraints of inequalities that limit and position them as social actors.
Social actors are not just rationalistic beings, but also are driven and guided
by powerful emotional and psychic factors (see, for example, Lucey *et al.*
2003). This renders analysis of masculinities within the classroom (or
anywhere else) a highly complex task, since the researcher must engage
with boys' multiple, shifting and subjectively experienced identities while
also locating these issues within broader material structures (Mahony and
Zmroczek 1997).

Hegemonic masculinity

Issues of power are key to critical analyses of masculinity, and in this
respect the concept of *hegemonic masculinity* is a useful theoretical tool. As
Brittan (1989) notes, much recent theorizing of masculinity utilizes the
concepts of 'hegemony' and multiple identities/masculinities. This body of
work has been strongly influenced by the seminal work of Connell (1987,
1995, 1997) and his colleagues (Carrigan *et al.* 1985) who introduced the
concept of 'hegemonic masculinity' to refer to the most powerful forms of
masculinity operating within a culture at any one time. Hegemonic masculinity thus entails the existence of numerous competing masculinities, and
describes 'those dominant and dominating modes of masculinity which
claim the highest status and exercise the greatest influence and authority'
(Skelton 2001: 50).

Hegemonic forms of masculinities are not fixed, enduring structures, nor
are they consistently asserted by all men. Carrigan *et al.* (1985) identify
additional categories of masculinity, such as complicitous masculinities
whereby men may benefit from patriarchy through the general subordination of women (the 'patriarchal dividend', Connell 1995: 79), without
actively endorsing hegemonic masculinities. They also point to power differences between men, whereby some men are more advantaged by dominant forms of masculinity than others. This is because, as Gramsci (1971)
proposed, hegemony is never complete or absolute, needing instead to be
reworked and defended against alternatives. Thus manliness is 'a contested
territory ... an ideological battlefield' (Edley and Wetherell 1995: 17), the
site of struggles between different groups of men (socially and historically)
over the symbols (Gilroy 1993) and meanings of 'being a man'.

Consequently, there is no single form of 'hegemonic masculinity', but
rather a range of possible 'hegemonic masculinities' which can be drawn
upon, aligned with or shifted between ('mobilised around', as Kenway and

Fitzclarence 1997 put it). Within this process, some less powerful forms of masculinity are subordinated and marginalized (Carrigan *et al.* 1985). This is not a random process, but is often structured along lines of 'race', ethnicity, sexuality and social class. A common feature of hegemonic masculinities is their organization around the discursive subordination of Others, particularly women and gay men (Connell 1989; Edley and Wetherell 1995; Gough 1998; Paechter 1998). White masculinities are also defined against racial others (Cohen 1988; Wetherell and Potter 1992; Kimmel 1994; Gough 1998; Gough and Edwards 1998). Thus dominant forms of masculinity tend to share some broad characteristics and ways of being. For example, in the classroom Frosh *et al.* (2002) identified 'popular' masculinities as involving ' "hardness", sporting prowess, "coolness", casual treatment of schoolwork and being adept at "cussing" ' (Frosh *et al.* 2002: 10). Becky Francis has also discussed the notion of laddishness as incorporating 'hedonistic practices popularly associated with [young male peer groups] for example "having a laugh", alcohol consumption, disruptive behaviour, objectifying women, and an interest in pastimes and subjects constructed as masculine' (Francis 1999: 357). The centrality and function of male peer groups to the construction of laddish identities is also underlined by Head as being to 'reward the macho qualities of being cool, hard and risk-taking' (Head 1999: 36).

While these approaches to the study of masculinity/masculinities have continued to gain momentum within educational and sociological research, some concerns have been raised that 'masculinity' remains an imprecisely defined, 'catch-all' term, which may be too broad and fuzzy to be useful (see Hearn 1996). The utility of the concept of hegemonic masculinity has also been questioned by Francis (1998, 2000a) and Whitehead (1999). Both of these writers suggest that current definitions may be too limited and conceptually restricted:

> the concept of hegemonic masculinity goes little way towards revealing the complex patterns of inculcation and resistance which constitute everyday social interaction. Furthermore, it is unable to explain the variant identity meanings attached to the concept of masculinity at this particular moment in the social history of Euro/American/Australasian countries
>
> (Whitehead 1999: 58)

Thus the concept of hegemonic masculinities is used with caution within this book. Instead, a more specific notion of 'local hegemony' is developed and utilized to account for the ways in which particular discourses may be powerful, or hegemonic, within highly localized instances. For example, the concept is used to describe moments in schools where Muslim boys may assert patriarchal, racialized masculinities that marginalize, or exert power, in relation to Muslim femininity, but which do not carry the same 'weight' in relation to white femininity or masculinity. Caution is also exercised in theorizing hegemony to avoid simplistic or unidimensional analyses and understandings of Muslim masculinity. As Walkerdine *et al.* suggest, attending to the combined intersection of the social, cultural and psychic dimensions of subjectivity is a vital aspect of feminist critique (Walkerdine *et al.* 2001: 15). They argue that an understanding of how young people *live* subjectivity is crucial to understanding how class and gender (and 'race') operate in the present. Similarly, there have been recommendations for more work exploring masculinities as complex, multiple and variant across context (Connell 1996; Davies 1997). As will be discussed below, these concerns relate particularly to the ways in which 'other', minority ethnic boys have been conceptualized within academic theories.

Theorizing black masculinities

In addition to the argument that academic research on masculinity has tended to privilege the study of white boys and men, Alexander (2000) has also suggested that critical analyses of gender and ethnicity have tended to concentrate on black women. As a result, concerns have been expressed that there has been rather little critical and/or feminist theorizing of *black masculinity* (Mirza 1999; Alexander 2000).

Within the work of Connell (1995), boys from 'other' (minority) ethnic groups are identified in terms of their subordinated and marginalized forms of masculinity, that is, forms of masculinity that are suppressed/repressed and oppressed by hegemonic masculinity. Some researchers have identified particular features of minority ethnic masculinities as entailing forms of resistance to racism, for example, Ross (1998) has suggested that some African/Caribbean male cultures operate as defensive responses to white racism. Brod (1994) has also talked about 'the tensions and trade-offs' in Jewish men's constructions of masculine identities, suggesting that they use racialized sexism and patriarchy as a means for resisting racism. The idea that minority ethnic masculinity can constitute a form of resistance is developed further by Hearn and Collinson (1994). They suggest that masculinity can provide a site from which to engage with other social inequalities: 'Masculinities may be simultaneously an *assertion* of a particular social location (sometimes of more than one such location simultaneously) and a form of *resistance* of one social division to another' (Hearn and Collinson 1994: 110, original emphasis).

However, Alexander (1996) argues that black masculinities should not be understood as merely responses or reactions to white racism and feelings of powerlessness. Instead, she suggests that black masculinities should be conceptualized as extensions of male power: 'Black masculinity is ... perhaps best understood as an articulated response to structural inequality, enacting and subverting dominant definitions of power and control, rather than substituting for them' (Alexander 1996: 137). She proposes that Muslim masculinities have been represented as 'failed' masculinities (Alexander 2000: 235), and in the next chapter popular constructions of Asian and Muslim masculinities will be examined in greater detail. Subsequent chapters will expand upon the various ways through which Muslim boys enact and subvert dominant discourses in order to assert distinctive ('racialized') masculinities within the school context. But first I would like to review how issues of 'race' and ethnicity have been approached and treated within schools and in educational policy.

Conceptualizing 'race', culture and ethnicity

In this section I will consider the various ways that notions of 'race', 'ethnicity' and culture have been conceptualized in academic theory and I propose that masculinity can be usefully theorized as both a 'racialized' and a 'classed' identity. I hope to demonstrate that these questions of conceptualization and terminology are not merely a matter of academic interest – but that they are important issues for all who work within schools and education. As Werbner (1996) suggests, the language and assumptions that we use to name social phenomena is highly powerful and can entail a range of inclusionary and exclusionary effects. Thus, the terminology which teachers, policy-makers and researchers adopt in their work will have ramifications and consequences for the lives of those subsumed within it.

The use of the term 'black' has caused considerable controversy with regard to the minority ethnic groups its usage includes or excludes. In the 1960s and 1970s, a common 'black' political identity was proposed as a useful banner for diverse minority ethnic groups to rally beneath in order to politically resist and struggle against colour based racism. However, it became clear during the 1980s that not all minority ethnic groups felt equally well represented by the term 'black'; in particular, Modood (1994) drew attention to the ways in which the interests of Asian groups were obscured and subsumed by those of Caribbean and African groups.

The term 'Asian', however, is an equally problematic term. Its common sense usage (to denote people from South Asian subcontinent countries of India, Pakistan, Bangladesh and Sri Lanka) has been criticized for excluding groups from other parts of Asia and for glossing over many national, linguistic, regional and religious differences between those it encompasses.[2] In this book, the more specific terminology of 'Muslim' or 'Asian Muslim' is used most frequently as a pragmatic means for referring to the boys who came from differing South Asian backgrounds. In certain circumstances it is used in conjunction with national descriptors (for example, Pakistani, Kashmiri, Bangladeshi) where it is judged to be appropriate. Although, as detailed in Chapter 3 and elsewhere (Archer 2001), the boys most often referred to themselves simply as 'Muslim'.

These debates about terminology reflect the wider sociological discussions in which conceptualizations of race and ethnicity have been contested. For example, a strong critique has been made of 'traditional'/common sense definitions of race which treat it as a biological or physiological 'fact'. Such assumptions have been criticized for being both 'incorrect' and for bolstering racist discourses. As Donald and Rattansi argue:

> in genetic terms, the physical or biological differences between groups defined as 'races' have been shown to be trivial [and] [n]o persuasive empirical case has been made for ascribing common psychological, intellectual or moral capacities or characteristics to individuals on the basis of skin colour or physiognomy
>
> (Donald and Rattansi 1992: 1)

I would agree, however, that because racism remains a powerful force within society, we still need a way to engage with racial issues and the effects of racism while simultaneously recognizing that the concept of race itself is socially constructed and is not a natural or biological phenomenon. The meaning(s) of race are socially and historically specific and are formed through discourse – these meanings are not fixed but are 'unstable and "decentred" [and are] constantly being transformed by political struggle' (Omi and Winant 1986: 68). Therefore a circumscribed usage of the term (denoted by quote marks, hence 'race') is useful. In this way, we can draw upon a notion of provisionality, or *strategic essentialism*,[3] to engage with the lived consequences and effects of racial inequalities while also recognizing that race is a fiction (in other words, it is not grounded in any objective, essential biological reality). This notion of 'race' can then be mobilized to examine racial inequalities, to consider, for example, 'how racial logics and racial frames of reference are articulated and deployed, and with what consequences' (Donald and Rattansi 1992: 1).

The conceptualization and definition of ethnicity has been debated with equal fervour (May and Modood 2001). Stuart Hall's seminal work forms the key texts on theorizing ethnicity (for example, 1992, 1993a,b, 1996). Hall proposed a new conceptualization of ethnicity which resisted and challenged the narrow, racist and imperialist notions of ethnicity that were predominant in public (New Right and Thatcherite) discourses at the time of his writing. He developed a conception of ethnicity that acknowledged the importance of 'history, language and culture in the construction of subjectivity and identity, as well as the fact that all discourse is placed, positioned, situated, and all knowledge is contextual' (Hall 1992: 257). In other words, like 'race', ethnicity was shown to be socially constructed and produced through interactions and across public and private discourses – it is not 'natural', pre-given or pre-existing.

Similarly, the boundaries of ethnic groups – defining who 'belongs to' or 'has' a particular 'ethnicity' – are constructed and negotiable/negotiated. These boundaries change over time according to prevailing economic, political and ideological conditions (Anthias and Yuval-Davis 1992; Yuval-Davis and Anthias 1989). Thus ethnic groups are not biological, cultural or natural phenomena – they are loosely bounded, ever-shifting collectivities whose membership is subject to continual re/construction and contest. Gender plays an important role within the construction of the ethnic group boundaries, in particular 'women are constructed as representing and reproducing collectivities and their boundaries biologically, culturally and symbolically' (Yuval-Davis 2001: 12). In other words, ethnicity is often constructed in relation to particular notions of masculinity and femininity and these ideals are used to create, regulate and maintain particular ethnic group identities.

In addition to gender, it is widely agreed within critical, feminist/ sociological thinking that social class and other social identities and categorizations also impact upon, and interact with, racial and ethnic identities and inequalities (see Archer *et al.* 2001b). However, there is less consensus in relation to the question of how we might conceptualize and describe these inter-relationships between 'race', ethnicity, gender and social class. Various terms have been proposed, for example, these relationships have been described as 'cross-cutting' or 'intersecting' categories and have also been called 'fractured' and/or 'hybrid' identities (for example, Bradley 1996).

As Francis (2001) discusses however, all these notions remain problematic. 'Cross-cutting' and 'intersecting' identities are inadequate terms because, first, they imply a fixed, observable reality and, second, they assume that social categories are homogenous. This latter assumption also implies that inequalities can be 'added on' to one another, such that a person with membership of two or more minority groups (for example black women and working class lesbian women) might be considered 'doubly' or 'triply' oppressed. Such conceptualizations ignore 'the simultaneity of oppression and resistance' (Brewer 1993: 28) that is experienced by many people and fail to engage with the ways in which identities and inequalities can be multi-constitutive of one another. The notion of 'cross-cutting' and 'intersecting' identities and inequalities also raises the question of whether all categories are treated as being equally important at all times, or whether particular identities might be more important than others – and if so, how, where, why and under what circumstances? As Cealey Harrison and Hood-Williams (1998) also discuss, the idea of multiple cross-cutting and interacting/intersecting social categories becomes 'ultimately unworkable' because there are simply too many possible category combinations to analyse simultaneously – and there is no theoretical justification for focusing on just one or two particular variables.

The notion of 'hybridity' is also somewhat inadequate for conceptualizing multiple social identities (for example, Solomos and Back 1995; Werbner and Modood 1997; Yuval-Davis 1997; Anthias 2001). For example, Yuval-Davis points out that notions of hybridity reflect essentialist notions of fixed/homogenous identities because they imply a joining together of distinct entities to produce a new hybrid identity. Instead, I suggest that social identities might be conceptualized as integrally intermeshed and inter-related – such that axes of 'race', ethnicity, social class and gender cannot be easily separated out from one another because they are combined in such a way that they 'flavour' and give meaning to each other. Thus, 'the black subject cannot be represented without reference to the dimensions of class, gender, sexuality and ethnicity' (Hall 1992: 255) and 'gender as a category of analysis cannot be understood decontextualised from race and class' (Brewer 1993: 17). In this respect, a conceptualization of 'racialized masculinity' is a useful theoretical tool because it can help us to keep such inter-relationships at the forefront of our thinking.

Addressing 'race' in educational policy and practice

Issues of conceptualization are not merely academic – they can affect the lives and experiences of pupils within schools. As Ali Rattansi (1992) comprehensively details, the specific conceptualizations of 'race' and ethnicity that prevail within educational policy at any particular time will directly influence and shape the forms of practice that are subsequently undertaken within schools.

Rattansi records how, during the 1960s, hostility grew among some teachers and local education authorities (LEAs) towards the increasing presence of minority ethnic children within schools. This hostility expressed itself in the form of negative stereotyping of minority ethnic pupils and their communities, and by the refusal of some headteachers to admit additional black pupils into their schools (Rattansi 1992). Educational policies at this time focused strongly upon issues of language (for example, English for immigrants, 1963), and Asian pupils were prime targets and recipients of these policies. As Rattansi details, these educational policies were orientated towards encouraging assimilation and persuading minority ethnic groups to 'give up' their alien customs and language. These discourses constituted a 'compensatory' approach to schooling minority ethnic pupils – that is, they treated such pupils as educationally problematic, lacking in key skills and abilities, and so sought to compensate for these deficiencies (Mullard 1985). These views were underpinned by a notion that minority ethnic cultures are homogenous, discrete, definable and essentially different from mainstream culture, whereas white/British culture was regarded as unproblematic and 'normal'. In 1966, however, the debate shifted when the Home Secretary, Roy Jenkins, made a landmark call for 'equal opportunity' and 'cultural diversity' within schools. This action brought about an important change in emphasis, in that (white) racism (rather than 'other cultures') was finally accepted as constituting a potential source of problems in relation to issues of difference.

During the 1970s and 1980s educational policy was characterized by discourses of 'multiculturalism' and 'anti-racism'. In 1979, Anthony Rampton presided over an investigation into causes of 'West Indian underachievement' but, as detailed by Rattansi (1992), this investigation developed and was eventually published as the Swann Report (DES 1985). The Swann Report introduced a discourse of multiculturalism, arguing that 'race' was an issue for all schools, not just those with substantial minority ethnic populations. Subsequent multiculturalist educational approaches were characterized by a focus on the 'celebration of difference', the intention of which was to promote an equal valuing of different cultures. According to Rattansi, the multicultural movement was successful to some extent because it opened up new cultural and political spaces, but it also attracted strong criticisms. In particular, multiculturalism's strategy of *celebration of difference* was targeted for reproducing stereotypical views of minority ethnic groups due to its focus on specific, simplistic cultural symbols (the 'Saris, samosas and steel bands syndrome', Donald and Rattansi 1992: 2). These approaches also treated ethnic groups as homogenous entities by ignoring the complexity of attainment (for example, in terms of class and gender) among pupils from similar ethnic backgrounds. Multiculturalism also failed to engage with, or challenge, existing power relations and inequalities between ethnic groups, for example, defining Other cultures in terms of their difference from an English/British norm. Multicultural discourses have therefore been largely dismissed by feminists and other critical thinkers because they reify, homogenize and 'fix' ethnic group boundaries, perpetuating, rather than challenging, inequalities (Yuval-Davis 1997).

The 'anti-racist' critique developed in response to the shortcomings of multiculturalism, and attempted in particular to redress multiculturalism's over-emphasis upon a de-politicized notion of 'culture'. Proponents of the anti-racist approach attempted to shift attention on to the structures of power, that is, on to the institutions and practices that produce racism and racial inequalities. However, the implementation of anti-racist policies and initiatives met with a number of difficulties and, as Rattansi (1992) cogently argues, anti-racist approaches were similarly critiqued for utilizing simplistic understandings of racism. For example, anti-racist thinking failed to take account of the contradictions, ambivalences and resistances that characterize racist ideologies and practices. Neither could it account for the complex intermeshing of racism with other identities and inequalities, such as gender and social class.

In 1988, the Education Reform Act and the development of a national curriculum further changed the ways in which issues of 'race' and ethnicity were approached within schools. Critics suggested that the new standardized national curriculum attempted to impose a notion of national unity and identity, contradicting the previous focus upon ethnic differences, and thus represented a 'typical tactic of modern statecraft and modern nation formation' (Donald and Rattansi 1992: 5). These changes contributed to a 'dropping off', or silencing, of race/ethnicity from the educational agenda.

From the 1990s through to the present day, there has been a subtle eradication of 'race' from the educational policy agenda. As argued by critics such as Gewirtz (2000), current New Labour government rhetoric normalizes and promotes particular white, middle class values in relation to schooling (illustrated, for example, in its publications that advise parents on the 'best' ways to support their children). It has also been noted that issues of 'race' and ethnicity are now more likely to be subsumed within current policy concerns about *social exclusion* (Lewis 2000). As Munt (2000) suggests, this recent policy focus upon social inclusion/exclusion prioritizes ideals of commonality and assimilation over issues of difference and injustice. In other words, policies aim to include those who are 'excluded' into the dominant framework/state of being, rather than challenging existing inequalities within the mainstream system, or encouraging alternative ways of being. Thus, the achievement of 'inclusion' is prioritized as more important than addressing the reasons through which people become 'excluded' or, as Munt (2000: 3) puts it, 'the seductive promise of belonging seems to supersede the experience of estrangement'. Once again within educational policies, it seems that 'race' is being framed as merely a minority ethnic (not a mainstream) issue (Phoenix 2000). Contemporary policy discourses largely dismiss the role of structural inequalities, focusing instead on problems within groups, to explain and tackle the educational and social difficulties facing minority ethnic groups. For example, a plethora of current policies and strategies seek to address patterns of low attainment and poor educational progression among 'socially excluded' groups by targeting their 'low aspirations' and 'faulty' attitudes/behaviours.

Issues of 'race' and ethnicity have dropped even further down the educational policy agenda since being overtaken by panics about masculinity (particularly the boys' under-achievement debate, as detailed at the beginning of this chapter). Working class 'black' boys however have been singled out as a particular cause for concern due to their lack of achievement and their association with behavioural, disruptive problems. Yet, whereas problems of (white) masculinity have been located in terms of external factors (for example, changing employment conditions, the rise of feminism, improving girls' attainment), the problems associated with minority ethnic young men have been framed in terms of their 'race' and culture. This point will be further explored in the next chapter.

It is also notable that within academic literature and educational policy, issues of 'race' and gender have been mostly addressed as separate, unrelated matters. Gilroy (1993) argues against the collapse of gender and race within policy and theory, and Mirza (1992) explicitly criticizes the ways in which educational discourses have treated 'race' as a 'male issue' and gender as a white issue. The next chapter will give further consideration to the ways in which black masculinities have been addressed and conceptualized within schools, with specific reference to the history of Asian and Muslim boys in British education.

Summary

This chapter has discussed the popular view that boys are suffering from a 'crisis of masculinity' and that they are under-achieving in school examinations. A feminist critique was brought to bear upon these 'boys in crisis' and 'male under-achievement' discourses, arguing that, first, they are not new concerns and, second, they tend to be too simplistic and are underpinned by particular assumptions that reproduce gendered, classed and racialized inequalities. I also explored some of the different approaches that have been proposed in relation to the study, and conceptualization, of masculinity, outlining the benefits of addressing issues of power and plurality within such attempts. Consideration was given to the contradictory positioning of minority ethnic men within academic and public discourses: issues of black masculinity have been mostly invisible at the level of theory and they remain hyper-visible within popular thinking and media reports.

I have attempted to convey how issues of 'race' and ethnicity, and the terminology of 'Asian' and 'black' identities, might be more usefully conceptualized and used within educational discourses. It has been argued that 'race', gender and social class are inter-linked social categories and within this chapter I have questioned how this relationship might be best described in order to capture the complexity of these social identities and inequalities. The final section of the chapter discussed developments in the treatment of race and ethnicity in British educational policies and discourses: from compensatory approaches, to 'multiculturalist' and 'anti-racist' movements, through to the contemporary focus upon social exclusion. I tried to tease out some of the consequences of these different discourses for minority ethnic pupils, illustrating, for example, the various ways in which such policies treat disadvantaged groups as the source of their own problems. The next chapter will consider the changing ways in which Muslim pupils have been represented within educational theory and policy. It will also describe the study on which subsequent data chapters are based.

Notes

1 The excellent feminist study by Walkerdine *et al.* (2001) does attempt to redress such assumptions, however, highlighting the range of problems posed to young working class and middle class women, and detailing the women's agency, adaption and resistance to modern societal changes.
2 It is interesting to note, however, that a circumscribed political usage of 'Asian' identity has recently been proposed by Shain (2000).
3 This term was proposed by Spivak and is detailed in Landry, D. and Maclean, G. (eds) (1996) *The Spivak Reader*. New York: Routledge.

chapter two

Muslim pupils: current debates and issues

Introduction

The presence of the Asian diaspora in Britain is often thought of as being a relatively recent phenomenon, but South Asian migrants arrived as early as the seventeenth century, when Indian adventurers travelled to Britain (see Ballard 1994). This small Asian population developed with the settlement of Indian sailors in the nineteenth century and then underwent a period of considerable growth and expansion between the 1950s to 1970s, as policies were developed to encourage mass migration from South Asia (and the Caribbean) to supplement British labour shortages. Many of the early migrants originally envisaged returning to their countries of origin, but it has been noted that this 'myth of return' (Anwar 1979) is now in steep decline among many British Pakistani (Shaw 1994), Bangladeshi (Gardner and Shukur 1994), Sikh (Ghuman 1991) and other Asian communities and families.

In contradiction to popular racist discourses, which decry the 'swamping' of Britain by Asian and other minority ethnic groups, the overall numbers of South Asians remain small, accounting for just under 4 percent of the total UK population, as the 2001 census records.[1] However, South Asian groups do remain heavily concentrated in particular geographical areas (predominantly towns and cities) of the UK. The current British South Asian population is heavily skewed towards younger generations, particularly the increasing 'second generation' of children who are born in Britain, so continued growth is predicted, even though tight immigration controls since the mid-1960s have severely restricted the inflow of South Asian migrants.

This chapter charts some of the dominant changing public perceptions and stereotypes of the British Asian presence. Contrasts are drawn between academic and media views of British Asians from before and after the Salman Rushdie affair. Thus the chapter begins by examining and critiquing 'pre-Rushdie' academic conceptualizations of second generation young Asians which focused on notions of culture, conflict and identity crisis. I also argue against the widespread conceptualizations of Asian pupils as 'behavers and achievers' which predominated at this time. Attention is then given to the 'post-Rushdie' situation, in which differences between Muslim and (other) Asian young people have been privileged. Popular discourses of 'Islamaphobia' are examined, including the current public preoccupation with fundamentalism. The chapter concludes by detailing how a critical, feminist approach might be taken in order to explore issues of Muslim masculinity within schools.

'Pre-Rushdie' constructions of Asian pupils: culture, conflict and identity crisis

Within mainstream social psychological theories, general issues of 'identity' have largely been conceptualized without explicit reference to race or ethnicity although, as critics note, such theories have been based upon the assumption of a white norm. These positivistic social psychological theories have addressed issues of *ethnic* identity almost exclusively through a focus upon *minority* ethnic identities. In other words, majority group, white identities have remained relatively unexamined within this paradigm, and attention has been directed instead to the social and cognitive formation (and development, for example Aboud 1988) of minority ethnic identities (for example, Phinney 1989, 1990; Hutnik 1991). These theories sought to apply general principles of identity development to minority groups, often subsuming all ethnic groups within a broad brush 'majority' versus 'minority' binary approach.

Theorists such as Marcia (1980), Berry *et al.* (1987), Phinney (1990) and Hutnik (1991) produced 'quadri-polar' conceptualizations of ethnic minority (sic) identity, proposing that an individual can be located in relation to two main axes of identification. Within these approaches it is assumed that the minority ethnic subject can be placed within a particular section of a quadrangle relating to their expression of either a high or low identification with 'mainstream' and 'minority group' axes of identification. The four sections of the quadrangle represent: an acculturated identity (high on both axes), an assimilated identity (high mainstream; low minority group identifications), a marginalized identity (low on both axes) or a resistant identity (low mainstream and high minority group identification).

From this perspective it has been assumed that, for most minority groups, acculturation and assimilation orientations are the most beneficial to mental health and 'good' psychological adjustment (for example, Phinney and Alipuria 1990). Indeed, within such models, rejection of majority culture and/or 'clinging' to minority ethnic customs, beliefs and culture are positioned as psychologically detrimental and have been associated with problems of 'culture clash' and 'identity crisis'. Second generation young people from minority ethnic backgrounds have been closely associated with this notion of 'identity crisis', which is assumed to arise from their location 'between two worlds' and it has been suggested that Asian young people are particularly 'confused and culturally ambiguous' (Hiro 1991: 151). Muslim young people have been additionally singled out as special cases within these research traditions. Muslim identity orientations have been classed as either 'orthodox'/'traditional' or 'progressive', depending upon (the researcher's perception of) the individual's relationship to majority and minority cultures (for example, Weinreich 1983; Ellis 1991). Such research has suggested that the benefits of an acculturated identity orientation may be tempered by strict (gendered) minority cultural norms. In other words, researchers have suggested that identity conflict and psychological problems are highest among 'progressive' Muslim women, who are attracted to, but who cannot easily achieve, a 'less restrictive' way of life (Kelly 1989; Ghuman 1991).

These models can be criticized for assuming a rather fixed, static and highly individualized notion of ethnic identity, and for their unproblematized assumptions of two distinct, homogenous cultures forming the axes of identification. Instead, feminists and critical sociologists have argued that communities and cultures are not static and ahistorical, nor are they mutually exclusive to other cultures, including 'mainstream' society (Yuval-Davis 1994: 185). These models have also attracted criticism due to the normative assumptions that underpin which forms of identification are valued as more 'psychologically beneficial' identity orientations. For example, as mentioned above, positivistic social psychological theories assume that assimilated and acculturated orientations are the most psychologically beneficial forms of identity (for example, Phinney 1989; Phinney *et al.* 1992). These assumptions can be criticized for their unequal privileging of mainstream culture and derision of minority group identifications. In other words, these models naturalize the assimilation/acculturation of minority groups into (an uncritically examined notion of) majority culture and they pathologize those individuals and groups who do not appear to melt into the societal 'melting pot'. As Rattansi (1992) has indicated, proponents of 'melting pot' discourses of assimilation and acculturation overwhelmingly fail to recognize that it is predominantly *white* interests that are presented as the universal interests of all ethnic groups within such appeals to common (national) identities.

These positivistic approaches also place a specific emphasis on the identities of *minority* ethnic groups, to the neglect of majority groups and the comparable search for, and 'achievement' of, white identities. For example, it is often implied, or assumed, that the process of 'finding' and 'achieving' an ethnic identity is inherently more conflictual and problematic for minority, as opposed to majority, group members (for example, Padilla *et al.* 1986; Stopes-Roe and Cochrane 1990; Ghuman 1991). This again indicates that there are particular normative assumptions underpinning these models. Additionally, there has been strong criticism of the proposal that Muslim families, individuals or groups are 'special cases' who can be categorized as having progressive or traditional/orthodox identities (for example, Shaw 1994; Ahmed 1996).

In contrast to the picture painted by the broad-brush approaches described above, the Asian diaspora in Britain can be seen to comprise a diverse and heterogeneous group of people. People who identify as 'Asian' may be differentiated in terms of national heritage, region, language, religion and caste (to number but a few distinctions). This heterogeneity of Asian 'communities' is illustrated in the book edited by Ballard (1994) where attention is drawn to the difficulty of making even broad generalizations about particular Asian 'groups'. For example, Ballard argues that even national identities, such as 'Indian' or 'Bangladeshi', are partial identifications that mask a vast array of internal differences:

> while most people will fairly willingly identify themselves as either 'Indians', 'Pakistanis' or 'Bangladeshis' when asked to do so, it would be a great mistake to assume that those so identified will show any great degree of commonality among themselves, or that they will ever interact in a sufficiently coherent way to merit being described as a community
>
> (Ballard 1994: 4)

Nevertheless, the common valency of the term 'Asian' is self-evident within academic, popular and educational discourses and, as will now be discussed, 'Asians' in Britain have been subject to various homogenizing stereotypes and assumptions.

Asians and 'culture'

Dominant and popular discourses have assumed, and perpetuated, a close association between 'Asians' and 'culture'. As Benson (1996) cogently discusses in her critique, Asians have been assumed to be 'culture-rich' communities. Asian culture has been ambivalently represented within the popular imagination, as both a (positive) source of strength and cohesion, and a source of restriction and oppression. As Rattansi (1992) points out, the Swann Report

> slid into the trap of singling out 'Asian' culture and especially its main bearer, 'the Asian family', to explain the contrast with West Indians.

Asians 'kept their heads down', a strategy supposedly more likely to succeed in a 'hostile' (read 'racist') environment

(Rattansi 1992: 18)

The popular association between Asians and culture is encapsulated within the image of the Asian family/community. In relation to schooling and education, the supposedly 'tightly knit' Asian family and community have been held up as supporting pupils' educational achievement and producing 'good' pupils, yet it has simultaneously been blamed for restricting and oppressing children. Such stereotypes have been widely noted within schools:

> multicultural handbooks and official reports such as Rampton and Swann warn against the common teacher stereotypes of Afro-Caribbean ('disruptive', 'lazy') and Asian ('industrious', 'passive', 'over-ambitious') students which are also documented in academic research on teachers' attitudes
>
> (Rattansi, 1992: 25)

The characterization of Asian pupils as 'industrious, passive and over-ambitious' reflects the complex, and sometimes ambivalent, content of racial and ethnic stereotypes. The stereotype contains both 'positive' and negative elements: being 'industrious' might be generally viewed as a useful, positive trait whereas being 'passive' or 'over-ambitious' are less favourable descriptors. However, these seemingly positive elements may hide deeper resentments or complaints, for example, as (Rattansi 1992: 27) suggests, 'Asians in Britain have been regarded both as scroungers and as so industrious that they are taking over jobs and businesses, as both thrifty and flashy'. Similarly, 'Indians' are described within one social psychological text book as a 'commercially successful' but 'subordinate' group that has 'a culture that is relatively inward looking' (Hogg *et al.* 1988: 493). Commenting upon an article in the *Daily Mail* (28 July 1993: 'Can Asians recivilise our inner cities?), Claire Alexander reiterates the inherent ambivalence and contradictions within such popular views of Asians, drawing attention to the role of 'culture' in these discourses:

> On the one hand, the invocation of strong cultural values and traditions are seen as a positive contribution to society, overtly challenging wider social decay, whereas on the other, they are seen as constituting a source of internal oppression for the young
>
> (Alexander 2000: 5)

Thus within such stereotypes, Asian 'culture' may be both resented (for promoting mobility) and pathologized (as restrictive and unfair), while also being admired (for example, for promoting 'family values', and 'respect' for the elderly and/or authority).

The stereotype of Asian culture as both supportive and oppressive/restrictive remains potent within contemporary public and educational discourse. For example, research has suggested that teachers often assume that Asian pupils experience a clash between their home and school cultures (Kitwood and Borrill 1980; McKellar 1994). The following excerpt is taken from a social psychological text on inter-group relations, and it reveals some of the common assumptions that are made about 'Asian culture' in relation to schooling: 'The Asian girl in a British school, forbidden by her parents to go swimming because of cultural taboos ... cannot simply be regarded as "one of the others" when it comes to swimming lessons' (Brown 1988: 217–18). Brown negatively represents Asian 'culture' as characterized by oppressive gender relations (exemplified by the restriction of girls) which, he suggests, raises issues of difference in relation to (white British) educational values and discourses. As this example indicates, issues of culture conflict have been primarily rehearsed in relation to gender, and specifically in relation to girls. Research suggests that many school teachers assume that Asian girls experience a conflict between the worlds of school and home because school constitutes a place of freedom where repressive family relations are escaped (Ballard 1994; Verma *et al.* 1994). In other words, it is widely believed that Asian culture (but specifically 'the family') is responsible for any problems experienced by Asian girls in relation to issues of identity and schooling. Thus girls are thought to be subjected to 'the malaise of being caught between two cultures' and 'identity crisis', a form of individual splitting between two essentialized cultural forms, 'Asian' and 'British-Western' (Rattansi 1992: 19).

It has been noted that Pakistani and Bangladeshi families are publicly perceived to be highly resistant to assimilation, with an adherence to particular attitudes, codes of dress and behaviour and in relation to issues of language (Shaw 1994). Within schools, issues of dress and clothing have often formed the symbols around which arguments over culture and ethnicity are conducted. For example, fierce debates have occurred over whether Asian and Muslim girls should be allowed to wear trousers and/or head scarves to school. Concerns have thus been expressed that Asian girls' lack of participation in 'normal' school practices reflects the influence of an oppressive and 'backwards' home culture. Within such discourses, the 'Asian girl' is thus particularly negatively represented as the repository of difference and the marker of cultural boundaries. Indeed, research has shown that Muslim girls' generally lower levels of participation in extra-curricular activities may be blamed by some school staff for creating cultural divisions between pupils and for 'lessen[ing] the impact of attempts to develop a whole school response to cultural diversity' (Verma *et al.* 1994: 81). Many educational authorities have responded to these concerns by attempting to develop and strengthen home–school links (Deshpande and Rashid 1993) to encourage integration and cooperation between Asian communities and schools.

In academic circles, a small number of (predominantly) feminist researchers and academics have attempted to dismantle the various myths surrounding Asian families and issues of culture in relation to girls. For example, they have drawn attention to the ways in which Asian girls construct and negotiate their identities, arguing that girls experience greater problems due to racism and schooling than from their families (for example, Brah and Minhas 1986; Shaw 1994; Basit 1996, 1997b; Brah 1996; Archer 1998; Shain, 2000). However, comparatively little attention has been paid specifically to Asian boys' constructions of identities and negotiations of culture (see Alexander 2000), a situation that this book aims to address.

Asian pupils as 'behavers and achievers'

Within schools, Asian pupils have been generally stereotyped as being well behaved and high-achieving pupils, or 'behavers and achievers' (Mac an Ghaill 1988). Comparisons have been made primarily between Asian and African/Caribbean groups, as Gillborn notes, 'the two most common beliefs which are held concerning pupils of South Asian ethnic origin [are] that they both behave and achieve more positively than their Afro-Caribbean peers' (Gillborn 1990: 72).

The reality of Asian pupils' 'achievement' is, however, questionable because attainment seems to vary across gender and between different Asian 'groups', and is still generally lower on average than for comparative white groups of pupils (Kysel 1988; Rattansi 1992; Cheng and Heath 1993). This myth of universal high achievement has persisted despite evidence of the high achievement of Indian pupils as opposed to the very low attainment of Bangladeshi pupils (for example, House of Commons 1986).

In terms of post-compulsory educational participation, the representation of Asian groups is improving on the whole (Modood 1993), but there are differential rates of entry between groups, with Bangladeshi and Pakistani groups faring worse than others (Modood and Shiner 1994). Indeed, even for those who do enter HE, entry to the 'best' universities is unequally spread, and minority ethnic students remain concentrated in less prestigious, mostly post-1992, inner city institutions (Bird 1996). In other words, minority ethnic groups, but particularly Asian Muslim (Bangladeshi, Pakistani) groups, have still not achieved an equality of access in relation to further and higher education.

The stereotype of high achieving and well behaved Asian pupils can be traced to the popular assumption that Asian families place a high value on their children's education (Afshar 1989; Rattansi 1992) and have high expectations of the system (Tomlinson 1984). But, as various critical researchers have pointed out (for example, Cohen 1988; Gilroy and Lawrence 1988; Mac an Ghaill 1994; Gillborn 1990; Rattansi 1992;

Connolly 1998), Asian 'model pupils' are also regarded as 'passive' and (in the case of males) 'effeminate', due to dominant associations between education and femininity. Paul Connolly (1998) conducted research in a multi-ethnic primary school and found that teachers made different interpretations of the 'silly' behaviours of boys from different ethnic backgrounds. The behaviours of 5–6-year-old African/Caribbean boys were regarded as threatening control and order within the school, whereas the silly behaviours of Asian boys were dismissed. Instead teachers associated these behaviours with the boys' immaturity, and Connolly found that such behaviours were interpreted within stereotypes of Asian boys as 'hardworking and helpful' and 'quiet and little' (1998: 119, 121).

To summarize, dominant public and educational discourses have closely associated Asian pupils with 'culture'. 'Asian culture' has been represented within the popular imagination as both the source of Asian groups' educational 'success' and the source of Asian pupils' problems at school. Asian pupils have been popularly identified both as passive 'behavers' and 'achievers' and as suffering from culture conflict and repressive cultural values. These constructions are problematic on a number of levels. For example, they have been criticized for sharing a simplistic understanding of culture and identity and for being predicated upon normalized white British dominant values and practices that consequently pathologize Asians as 'Others'. These popular constructions also hide issues of racism and cultural imperialism, deny the agency of Asian groups and individuals through the promotion of sweeping assumptions and generalizations about Asian groups, and gloss over complex patterns of educational achievement and participation.

'Post-Rushdie' constructions: 'Muslim' boys and fundamentalism

It is interesting to note that prior to particular world events, relatively little academic attention was paid to Asian boys. It was not until the 1990s that this group became regarded as particularly educationally and socially problematic, as stereotypes of 'good', passive, hardworking 'Asian' pupils were superseded by increasing moral panics and popular fears about 'dangerous' Muslim masculinity. The 'Salman Rushdie Affair' proved to be a pivotal point in terms of British social and race relations. Publication of the book *The Satanic Verses* (1988) by British/Indian author Salman Rushdie was accompanied by public displays of outrage and anger by some Muslims in Britain and abroad. Copies of the book were ceremonially burnt in public and Ayatollah Khomeini declared a *fatwah*, or death penalty, against Rushdie. The issue brought to the fore differences between the Asian communities in Britain (Modood 1992); previously dualisms of black/white and Asian/black had been dominant, but these were now superseded by a new Muslim/non-Muslim binary:

> In Britain, Muslim-led protests against Rushdie's work shattered the analytically useful but ultimately untenable coherence of British 'blackness'. The hetereogeneity of non-white experiences and values in Britain – and worldwide – was made blazingly clear
> (Baker *et al*. 1996: 8)

Within this new Muslim/non-Muslim social binary, it has been suggested that the term 'Asian' has become synonymous with 'Muslim', which in turn has been connected to a range of negative images and stereotypes (Alexander 2000). Thus the *Satanic Verses* controversy heralded a major shift in British debates around the politics of 'race' and 'nation', challenging and redefining who and what could be included or excluded from 'black', 'Asian' and 'British' identities. It also provoked debate over whether 'Britishness' and 'Muslim' identity were compatible (Modood 1992; Solomos 1993) and it has been suggested that this period marked the emergence of a new, specific 'British Muslim' identity (Samad 1996).

Samad (1992) has also suggested that outraged reception of the publication of *The Satanic Verses* in Bradford was not just a religious expression, but had its roots in the social exclusion and discrimination experienced more generally by Asian youth in Britain. For example, Samad details differences in reactions between the largely Mirpuri Pakistani community in Bradford (who headed the international anti-Rushdie campaign) and the Sylheti Bangladeshi population of Tower Hamlets, who were much more muted in their responses. These differentiations were 'divided along doctrinal lines' and 'cultural identity was informed by locality of origin, village–kin networks and social stratification' (Samad 1992: 91). Contrasting generational structures within the two regional communities (namely the dominance of the first generation in Bradford and the second in London), were also key factors that explain variations in reactions to the book. In addition according to Samad, the media played a pivotal role in the production and provocation of defiance and reaction among British Muslim communities.

Within popular opinion, however, negative views of Muslim communities have continued to grow into a discourse of 'Islamaphobia'.[2] Throughout the 1990s, critics drew attention to a steady and discernible increase in public concerns over fundamentalist Islam (Anthias and Yuval-Davis 1992; Burman 1994; Lewis 1994; Shaw 1994), particularly within the media:

> The media have become fascinated by something called 'fundamentalist Islam' so much so that this phenomenon, whose nature and

meaning are assumed to be as self-evident as its implications are sinister – has become a routine component of the journalistic lexicon
(Lewis 1994: 58)

These views were further fuelled by concerns about social unrest among British Asian and Muslim groups following media reporting of the street 'riots' in the northern city of Bradford in 1995, and more recently in both Oldham and Bradford in July 2001. These disturbances entailed clashes between white and Asian (predominantly Muslim) young men and were portrayed as evidence of a crisis between the two communities. Such events were not restricted to the north of England, but were also evident in the capital (for example, 'Asian teenage gangs terrorising London', *Evening Standard*, 13 November 1996, cited in Alexander 2000: 3). As Alexander (2000) also notes, these occurrences have been accompanied by increased public concerns about whether integration/assimilation is possible or achievable. Indeed, the association of Muslim (male) youth with images of disturbance and concerns about poverty, crime and disaffection has led to their representation as 'a demographic time-bomb of Pakistani and Bangladeshi youths' (Alexander 2000: 7).

Against the backdrop of these social events, Alexander (2000) suggests that Muslim young men have emerged as the 'new folk devils' of popular and media imagination, being represented as the embodiment of fundamentalism. Thus, as the Muslim peer, Lord Ahmed, has signalled, Islamaphobia is still on the rise in Britain (*Guardian* 1999). The full strength of these panics about fundamentalism and terrorism reached a nadir in the wake of the terrorist attacks of 11 September 2001 and the subsequent US/ UK 'War on Iraq' that commenced in March 2003. The public demonization of Muslim groups continues to gain force despite the public and media appearances of numerous Muslim groups, community organizations and individuals denouncing the events of 11 September and arguing that neither Islam, nor Muslim identity, should be equated with fundamentalism.

The strength of Islamaphobic discourses is, however, manifold. Muslim boys and men have not only been conceptualized as 'dangerous individuals' with a capacity for violence and/or terrorism, but also as 'culturally dangerous', threatening the 'British way of life/civilization'. For example, media attention has been drawn to an apparent increase in the numbers of people practising Islam and a decrease in the numbers of church-going members of the public in Britain. Indeed, in May 1993 the Conservative Party MP, Winston Churchill, expressed his fears that within the next 50 years the 'British way of life' would be destroyed and 'the muezzin will be calling Allah's faithful to the High Street mosque' (cited in Burman 1994: 172). Such fears follow in the rhetorical footsteps of right-wing Conservatives such as Enoch Powell, Margaret Thatcher and Norman Tebbit, who – at various points in time – have all decried the 'invasion' and 'swamping' of Britain by foreign communities who they perceive as a threat to 'Englishness'. Thus, media reports continue to identify the 'outsiders within' and particular attention has been given to un/covering suspected fundamentalists and extremists (such as Sheikh Abu Hamza, who is associated with the Finsbury Park mosque in London and who has alleged links with terrorist organizations).[3]

In one sense the movement of Muslim identities into the social spotlight and the popular gaze might be read as a positive shift away from the previous widespread 'invisibility' and marginalization of Muslim identities within social and educational discourses. However, as Alexander (2000) points out, these changes have occurred under particular social conditions in which increased social visibility does not necessarily equate with increased social power. Drawing on the work of Cornel West, she argues how it is somewhat ironic that intense public scrutiny and attention can actually render Muslim young men 'less visible'. This situation arises when they are subjected to this glare of popular attention but lack the cultural and political power to manipulate or influence the ways in which their lives are interpreted and represented. In particular, they lack the power to present themselves as complex, agentic human beings and thus cannot contest 'the bombardment of negative, degrading stereotypes' (West 1993: 210). This is because 'The creation of a folk devil demands simplicity at the expense of any recognition of humanity, with all the complexity, contradiction and uncertainty that this entails' (Alexander 2000: 21).

Muslim pupils and schooling

Unsurprisingly, the social and political events of the last decade, described earlier, have impacted upon representations and stereotypes of Asian pupils. Stereotypes of Asian pupils as passive 'behavers and achievers' have been replaced by a new differentiation between higher-achieving Indian 'achievers' (who are predominantly Hindu and Sikh) and lower-achieving Pakistani/Bangladeshi 'believers', who are mostly Muslim (Modood 1992: 43). Concerns have been raised that Pakistani and Bangladeshi groups experience lower levels of academic achievement and high rates of exclusion from school (West and Lyon 1995; Watkins 1998). Muslim boys (who constitute the vast majority of those from Pakistani and Bangladeshi backgrounds) have thus been differentiated and singled out as educational 'problems' who form part of an 'underclass', as identified in the *Panorama* documentary, 'Purdah in the underclass' (transmission date 29 March 1993).

Muslim pupils have thus been singled out as 'more problematic' than other Asian groups in relation to issues of school uniform and lack of participation in extra-curricular activities, and popular attention has identified *religious*, rather than 'cultural', values as the source of these differences. Attention has been drawn to teachers' negative views of Muslim families as repressive and authoritarian (Ballard 1994; Verma *et al.* 1994) and, set against these assumptions, it has been noted that Muslim boys report suffering the highest rates of racism at school (Verma *et al.* 1994).

The rise of discourses of 'Islamaphobia' has been a widespread, global phenomenon that has impacted on the schooling of Muslim pupils not only in Britain but also abroad. For example, in France fierce debates have raged about whether Muslim girls should be excluded for wearing the veil (*hijab*) to school. The *Planet Islam* documentary (transmission date 2 August 1997) reported how the act of wearing the head scarf to school was viewed by some white French citizens and school staff as indicative of 'militancy', 'extremism' and 'fanaticism', and a 'refusal to integrate' among Muslim groups. As discussed elsewhere (Archer 1998), such arguments can be interpreted as examples of 'modern racism', whereby liberal discourses of 'equality' and 'cohesion' are drawn upon to argue for the maintenance of unequal power relations (Billig *et al.* 1988; Wetherell and Potter 1992). Similar themes of 'tolerance', 'harmony' and 'one nation' discourses have been critically examined within the talk of Pakeha (white) New Zealanders by Wetherell and Potter (1992), who demonstrated how these themes assumed, and imposed, a unity of interests (those of the dominant group) upon others in society.

In contrast to racist discourses – that seek to represent Islam as homogenous and static – feminist researchers such as Shain (2003) have emphasized the relational nature of Muslim women's Islamic identifications. El-Solh and Mabro (1992) have also drawn attention to the great diversity among and between Muslim women with regard to their enactment and performance of religious identities and their engagement in practices such as wearing *hijab*. This is not to say, however, that all such practices and identifications occur at merely an individual level, or that there are no strategic and political alliances made beneath the banner of Muslim community and identity. As demonstrated by Shaw (1994), Muslim geographical communities may unite for specific purposes (such as to protest against school closures) but this does not mean there is a permanent, wider unity. Local political unities may still mask deeper theological divisions and disputes between and within different traditions (such as the Deobandi and Barelevi traditions). Indeed, as argued in the previous chapter, Muslim identity must be contested, negotiated and constantly remade, like any other ethnic, racial or religious identification.

A critical, feminist approach to researching Muslim masculinities in schools

For teachers and researchers who wish to engage with, and/or conduct, research around Muslim masculinities, the endeavour can appear to be fraught with difficulties. The intention may be to produce careful, sensitive analyses that can do justice to the young men's understandings and experiences, but the practice of achieving these aims is far from straightforward or guaranteed. Ethical concerns are also paramount when working with young people in schools, and although professional associations produce valuable guidelines that should be adhered to, additional issues such as securing truly *informed* consent, may require considerable time and effort to achieve. The theoretical and methodological task itself – of attempting to disrupt dominant, negative and oppressive knowledges and discourses in order to make space for alternative, more emancipatory readings, identities and experiences – is also a considerable undertaking. These issues, and the ways in which I have attempted to tackle them within my research on Muslim masculinity, are considered below.

The book draws on data that were collected as part of a larger study exploring identity construction among Muslim boys and girls.[4] This study took place in four schools in Mill Town, a medium-sized town (population around 90,000) in the north-west of England. Economically, unemployment rates within the town are higher than the national average, and levels of deprivation have continued to increase among the town's primarily working class communities since the decline of the (cotton, wool and silk) textile industries. The town has a majority white population, but also a sizeable 'Asian' population, which predominantly comprises families from Pakistani and Bangladeshi backgrounds. Within Mill Town, Asian families tend to be clustered into particular housing areas and districts near the centre of the town. In comparison, settlement patterns among white families tend to be divided along class lines, with middle class families residing in the more affluent leafy suburbs and working class families living in the poorer, run down council estates that were created at the fringes of the town after the slum clearance programmes. At the time of the research there were over 5000 bilingual pupils recorded within Mill Town schools (2000 at secondary level). Of these bilingual pupils, the town's Language Assistance Programme recorded 85 percent as being of Pakistani and 13 percent Bangladeshi heritage. There were very few other ethnic groups represented within the town at the time of the research.

Pupils were drawn from one of four schools within Mill Town, which have been given the pseudonyms Lowtown, Hightown, Eastfield and Westfield schools. The schools were all mixed sex, county comprehensives with approximately 860 pupils in each, apart from Hightown School which had a sixth form and hence had a larger population of around 1560 pupils.

Of the schools, Lowtown had the highest proportion of minority ethnic pupils (80–90 percent), the vast majority of whom were from Bangladeshi backgrounds. Hightown School had the lowest proportion of Asian pupils on the school role (approximately 20 percent), most of whom were from Pakistani families. Eastfield recorded around 33 percent minority ethnic pupils and Westfield about 42 percent, most of whom were from Pakistani backgrounds. At the time of the research, only Hightown School had above average GCSE attainment, with 49 percent of pupils gaining five or more A–C grades at GCSE. The other schools all recorded between 23 and 25 percent of pupils achieving five or more passes at grades A–C (as compared to a national average of 44 percent).

Overall 31 Muslim boys, aged 14–15 years, took part in discussion groups with one of three interviewers. All pupil respondents were in national curriculum Year 10 at the time of the research. All the boys who took part had been initially identified via their teachers for participation in the research. All came from what could be broadly called 'working class' backgrounds. Nineteen of the young men identified as being of Pakistani origin, eight identified as Bengali and four identified as Pakistani/Kenyan. All the young men identified themselves as Muslim.

Half of all groups were conducted by myself (denoted as LA in transcript extracts), a white, British middle class woman researcher from the southeast of England. The other half of the interviews which took place in Hightown, Lowtown and Eastfield schools were all conducted by Tamar Dutt (denoted as TD in transcript extracts), an Asian Pakistani British woman (and a non-academic researcher). In Westfield School, two discussion groups were conducted by Nessa Sarwar (denoted as NS), who is also an Asian Pakistani British woman (and a non-academic researcher). Both Tamar and Nessa helped to structure the content of the discussion schedules, and discussed their ideas and interpretations of the data during periods of analysis and writing. However, because they were not paid to work on the study they did not formally engage with analysing the data. This is acknowledged as a highly problematic aspect of the research.

A discursive approach to Muslim masculinity

All the discussion groups were single sex in composition, and all discussions were tape recorded and were later transcribed by the author. Two discussion groups were conducted in each school: one of which was led by the white, female author and the other was led by one of the two Asian female interviewers (the role of the interviewer/researcher is considered in greater depth below). All discussions were conducted primarily in English.

Each discussion group lasted between one hour and one and a half hours. Discussions were semi-structured, based on an interview schedule that covered topics such as 'home', 'school', 'race and ethnic identity', 'racism' and 'gender identities'. These topic guides were intended to be flexible, as 'finding the right question is [often] more difficult than answering it' (Merton 1959, in Hammersley and Atkinson 1987: 34). Discussion groups were utilized as they provide a means for eliciting jointly constructed discourses and for examining interactions between respondents and interviewers in the construction of these discourses. As Morgan (1997, 1998) suggests, it is often through the process of interacting within a group that a range of possible views may be put forward. Group discussions can enable an individual to more fully articulate their own implicit views, because 'interaction in the group may present the need to explain or defend one's perspective to someone who thinks about the world differently' (Morgan 1997: 46). As Barbour and Kitzinger (1999) also write, discussion groups can facilitate an exploration of participants' own concepts and terms of reference, allowing the researcher to consider how particular accounts and points of view might be generated, expressed, censured, opposed or changed through social interaction. However, analytic attention must also be given to the ways in which both the local group context *and* broader social, cultural and institutional relations may encourage, or suppress, the expression of certain points of view.

An additional, small photographic diaries exercise was also undertaken, in which pupils at Lowtown School were invited to take photographs, and to create a folder, representing 'A day in my life' (see Archer 1998 for full details). Only two Muslim boys took part in the activity, and aspects of their diaries are referred to in Chapter 5.

Analysing Muslim masculinities

There are many different ways to analyse data discursively (Burman and Parker 1993), and the approach taken will relate to the philosophical framework adopted by the particular researcher in question. However, there are some broad factors that tend to be held in common across different discursive approaches, which Burman and Parker note as being 'a social account of subjectivity ... [and] attending to the linguistic resources by which the socio-political realm is produced and reproduced' (Burman and Parker 1993: 3). In other words, a discursive approach examines how language actively creates, constructs (resists and re-creates) particular social and psychological phenomena (such as identities and attitudes). Thus language does not reflect an objective, external reality, but rather it is a constitutive medium, through which identities are negotiated, contested, asserted and defended. Thus analysis may focus on exploring discourses (shared patterns of meaning) within boys' talk, and it may seek to identify the resources drawn on by the boys in their constructions of masculine identities.

This book examines the ways in which Muslim boys constructed and negotiated masculine identities within the discussion groups (and to a lesser extent, through their photographic diaries). A theoretical position is adopted in which identity is understood as being in process, or 'becoming' (Hall 1992, 1996). Or, to put it another way, identity is conceptualized as a verb, not a noun (Bauman 1996). From this perspective, the language that boys use becomes a central consideration within an analysis of Muslim masculine identity because, as Wetherell and Edley (1998) argue, 'talking like a man' is central to the production of masculinity.

Understanding the contextual, interactive production of masculine identities

A central tenet within any reflexive, feminist analysis is the recognition that talk is produced within interactions between individuals and groups. Accordingly, within this book analytic attention is paid to the role of the researcher/interviewer within the boys' production and negotiation of masculine identities. Particular care is also given to the racialized and gendered interactive context of the discussions. In this respect, critical/ feminist research differs from more positivistic research, in which the social identity of the researcher is rarely given much consideration. Indeed, social cognition research has been critiqued for its assumption that 'when the experimenter is white, the 'race' of the *experimenter* is held to be unrelated to his or her cognition, whereas the 'race' of the *subject* is held to possibly affect his or her cognitions' (Morawski 1997: 15). 'Objective' approaches to research have thus been strongly critiqued for producing oppressive knowledges, for alienating the researcher from the researched and for failing to address unequal power relations between interviewer and respondents (for example, Harding 1987; Lather 1988; Edwards 1990; Stanley and Wise 1990).

As discussed elsewhere (Archer 2002a), feminists have debated the merits and limits of same sex interviewing, predominantly within the context of conducting research with women. On the one hand, it has been suggested that same sex identification and 'matching' between interviewer and respondent is important because it can provide a means for addressing unequal power relations and for drawing on shared experiential knowledge within analyses (Oakley 1981; Finch 1993; Mies 1993; Hurtado and Stewart 1997). On the other hand, attention has been drawn to the power differences that exist between women, both within and outside 'feminist' research, for example, in terms of 'race' and social class (for example, Yuval-Davis 1994). These differences mean that same sex interviewing will not necessarily lead to more emancipatory or liberatory research.

Irrespective of the gender of interviewers and respondents, white researchers have been criticized for dominating research with minority ethnic groups (Wilson 1984; Blair 1995). Critics have argued that white researchers may have no shared understandings regarding experiences of racism (Adelman 1985), which may work to silence certain aspects of respondents' views (Essed 1990). White researchers' use of black interviewers may also marginalize minority ethnic groups further within the academic hierarchy (Rhodes 1994). Thus the 'race' of the researcher, interviewers and respondents constitutes an additional important consideration within any research project.

The notion of 'matching' respondents and interviewers through their social characteristics (gender, 'race'/ethnicity and class) has actually been shown to be of limited use. This is because the ideal of 'matching' is based upon realist, essentialist conceptualizations of identity and is thus grounded within the tradition of identity politics (Oliver 1992; Yuval-Davis 1994). There is also the potential within 'matched' relations that the researcher may 'over' identify and conflate her or his own experiences with those of the respondents. For example, in relation to interviewing white, working class mothers, Diane Reay has written how her 'fear of distorting the often similar experiences of the women whom I interviewed generated a constant sense of insecurity which in turn served to underline my power as an interpreter' (Reay 1996b: 62).

In this book, it is argued that ' "race" and gender positions, and hence the power relations they entail, enter into the interview situation but ... they do not do so in any unitary or essential way' (Phoenix 1994: 49). It is recognized that interpersonal and inter-/intra-group dynamics and interactions will combine within the production of identities and discourses within each discussion group, but that these interactions will not occur in any predictable or consistent ways (Buckingham 1993; Phoenix 1994). In other words, both the immediate and local context, and the wider social relations within which an interview occurs will play a role in the production of the research. Respondents' views, actions and experiences 'cannot be separated from their audience – from the relationships that sustain and support them, or from the patriarchal lens through which they are filtered' (Brown 1998: 91–2). Thus, both the context and a speaker's perception of their audience will influence what is said (Michael 1996).

A useful approach for the teacher/researcher approaching the study of Muslim masculinities is therefore to recognize the interdependence of interviewer/respondent subjectivities within their work through the employment of *reflexivity* (Henwood and Pidgeon 1995). Reay describes this as a processes of working towards 'uncovering/recognising the difference your differences make' (Reay 1996a: 443). This process may involve, first, examining the ways in which different discourses and knowledges are produced within particular contexts; second, exploring the implications of one's analyses for different groups; and, third, examining the effects of research upon both researcher and participants (Maynard and Purvis

1994). The researcher thus needs to critically examine her or his own role within the research, locating herself or himself clearly within the work (Stanley and Wise 1993), making explicit the values (Gill 1995) and procedures (Edwards 1990) employed within the research. The researcher can also usefully examine her or his own social positioning in order to interrogate social relations within the research process (Bhavnani 1988).

This technique has been employed within feminist research on whiteness and masculinity (see Fine *et al.*, 1997) and in research on black and Asian masculinity (Alexander 1996, 2000), and a form of 'comparative analysis' (Archer 2002a) is used within the study reported in this book. This form of analysis involves reading across the transcripts produced by different interviewers and producing analyses in light of these differences. However, it is important to remember that one account is not treated as necessarily 'more true' or 'more valid' than the other: neither in terms of the white researcher's so-called 'expertise', nor the Asian interviewers' shared cultural 'insider' knowledge. Rather, the book's aim is to unpick interactions of 'race', class and gender (as they are differentially produced through interactions within the groups) by reading across the different transcripts produced with different interviewers and respondents.

Summary

This chapter has traced the growth of the Asian diaspora in Britain, detailing changing dominant perceptions and stereotypes of Asian and Muslim groups and pupils. It was suggested that prior to the 'Salman Rushdie Affair' and the furore surrounding the publication of the *Satanic Verses*, Asian pupils tended to be represented as 'behavers and achievers'. Since then, there has been a marked increase in 'Islamaphobia', intensified by reporting of the regional 'riots' in Britain and recent world events, sparking global western fears over Islamic fundamentalism, extremism and terrorism. These changes have been reflected in increased concerns over Muslim boys and young men and their identities. The chapter concluded by outlining the critical, feminist approach that is used within this book for researching Muslim masculinities within schools.

Notes

1 Overall, minority ethnic populations comprise 7.9 percent of the total UK population: 1.8 percent Indian, 1.3 percent Pakistani and 0.5 percent Bangladeshi. In terms of religion, the census records that Muslims comprise the second largest percentage (2.7 percent) of the population after Christianity.

2 Halliday (1999) questions the use of the term 'Islamaphobia' and suggests that it

should be replaced with 'anti-Muslimism' because he argues that it is not the faith, but people of it, who are seen as the threat. He argues that 'Islamaphobia' implies a singular Islam and also denies possibility for critically engaging with the object of the term. While I recognize these criticisms, I have continued to use 'Islamaphobia' for reasons of clarity and comprehension due to the more common recognition and usage of the term.

3 He has been linked with eight British Muslim men found guilty of terrorism in Yemen (*Guardian*, 1999) and is increasingly suspected of having links with wider terrorist networks (*Guardian* 2002).

4 These data are part of a PhD study (Archer 1998) conducted between 1994 and 1998.

Part II

Identities

chapter three

'Race', religion and masculinity in school

Introduction

This chapter considers the various ways in which Muslim boys might construct ethnic, racial, religious and cultural identities. Drawing on data from my own study, it will show that in contrast to dominant popular conceptualizations of 'Muslim' identities (which tend to be negative and homogenous), boys' own identity constructions appear to be far more complex, shifting and contradictory. This is not to say, however, that their discourses of masculinity were random or without purpose. As the chapter will argue, the boys' talk can be read as highly strategic and political, produced in relation to a range of other social discourses and themes, such as patriarchy and racism. The chapter considers in turn the boys' constructions of 'Muslim', 'black' and 'gangsta' masculinities.

Muslim masculinities

TD: Do you think it's important to you [being Pakistani]? ... Why
          do you think it's important?
Shabid: Well it's not just like Pakistani ... like it's the religion mostly,
          like I'm Muslim ... you don't care if you're Pakistani or –
Javid: It's the religion

(Eastfield School, TD)

Deepak: We all think of our religion, man, so it's a big part of our life
Fazaan: It just makes sense and that, it keeps you close to, out of trouble
          and makes sense, everything's brilliant

(Hightown School, TD)

As illustrated by the above extracts, all boys in the study primarily identified themselves in terms of their Muslim identities. This happened across
the discussion groups, in all schools and with each of the interviewers. The
boys' strong religious identifications appear to confound social psychological and social cognition theories of ethnic identity and acculturation,
which assume that adherence to minority ethnic cultural beliefs, practices
such as language and religion, declines with each new generation (for
example, Constantinou and Harvey 1985; Phinney 1990). However, my
findings echo those of a number of other research studies, in which second
generation Asians/Muslims have also been found increasingly to define
themselves through their religion rather than their parental country of
origin or nationality (for example, Shaw 1994). Similarly, Modood (1997)
has noted that young British Muslims report holding stronger religious
beliefs than their white counterparts. Alexander (2000) also found in her
research that young Bengali Muslim men constructed distinctly 'un-hybrid',
'new' Muslim masculinities, in which they defined themselves primarily in
terms of their religion and Bengali roots, rather than their legal British
nationality. In this respect, she suggested that the young men in her study
might be viewed as distinctly 'un-British' Muslims. Indeed, none of the boys
in my study referred to themselves as 'British', and in this respect they
differed sharply from the Muslim girls (who took part in the wider study),
who described themselves as 'British Muslim' and 'English Muslim' in the
discussion groups (see Archer 1998).

Gardner and Shukur (1994) suggested that the increasingly 'strident
commitment' to Islamic beliefs and values among many British Bengalis is
actually a response to racism that provides a way to 'fight back' against
inequalities and negative stereotypes:

> Islam provides both a positive identity, in which solidarity can be
> found, together with an escape from the oppressive tedium of being
> constantly identified in negative terms. Even more important, Islamic
> rhetoric not only condones fighting for one's rights and acting in col-
> lective defence of a Muslim brotherhood, but explicitly encourages it
> (Gardner and Shukur 1994: 163)

However, I would argue that this type of explanation can be criticized for
its inability to explain gendered differences in identification. It also repro-
duces a homogenizing view of Islamic identification, both in terms of the
ways in which identities may be variously reconstructed and negotiated,
and through the underlying assumption that Muslim identities are merely
reactive responses to contemporary social conditions and racism.

The following section discusses an alternative potential reading of young
men's attachment to Muslim masculinities. Attention is drawn to the distinctly gendered dimension of the identity construction that was voiced by
boys in this study. It is proposed that the boys' Muslim masculine identities

can be read as organized around two central themes concerning *brother-hood* and the *authenticity of male voices*.

Brotherhood

As shown in the interview extracts below, brotherhood and *umma* (the global community of Muslims) were integral concepts within the boys' constructions of Muslim identities:

LA: Are you more proud of being Pakistani, Bangladeshi or being Muslim?
Gufter: Muslim
Imran: Muslim
Gufter: It's like a *religion* . . . it's . . . like *strong* and it's like
Jamil: Cos like if we all Muslims like you're all *one* . . . like they don't [say we're] Bangladeshi or we're not Pakistani
Gufter: Yeah, plus ethnicity is just where you're *born* er . . . whereas this is religion and its *important*

(Lowtown School, LA)

Muslim identity was talked about as a unifying force, one that superseded other, possibly conflicting, national identifications and loyalties, such as potential Bangladeshi–Pakistani differences. Another boy, Rahan, also suggested that the ideal of Muslim brotherhood and *umma* created strength and support through a global network of identifications, saying 'You got Muslim brothers all over the world so wherever you go a Muslim brother will help you'.

It is this notion of global networks that western popular imagination increasingly associates with terror and fundamentalism, particularly since the attacks of 11 September 2001. The discussion cited above predated these world events, but the boys' primary identification as 'Muslim', and their silence in relation to using a 'British' descriptor, invites further debate about religious and national identities and notions of 'belonging'. Without a critical counterreading, there is a danger that the boys' constructions might be read in light of racist discourses, such as Norman Tebbit's infamous 'cricket test', which was proposed as a means to ascertain the national 'loyalty' of 'immigrant groups' (for example, see the *Observer*, 22 April 1990). This notion, which used a seemingly trivial question (asking which national cricket team would British Asian young people support), constructed 'minority' and 'majority' identifications through an exclusionary binary. From such a perspective it is possible that the boys' assertions of global and local Muslim identities might be interpreted as a sign of that they do not feel a strong sense of national belonging and/or that their loyalty perhaps cannot be counted upon.

I would, of course, strongly argue against such a reading. I suggest instead that the boys' constructions of a 'strong' Muslim brotherhood might more usefully be read in terms of the intertwining of racial and patriarchal themes, through which the boys resist popular stereotypes of 'weak' and 'passive' Asian masculinity. The boys' identifications could be seen as straightforwardly challenging this stereotype, replacing it with an alternative association of Muslim masculinity with strength. The boys' associations between Muslim identity, unity and strength challenge contemporary western ideals of individualistic white masculinity, and elsewhere the boys differentiated between 'strong' collective Muslim families and unstable, highly individualistic western/white family structures. These themes have also been noted by Yip (2002) and are discussed further in Chapter 5, which details how the boys constructed ethnic differences using themes of 'family' and 'community'.

An interesting feature within the preceding extract is that Gufter separates ethnicity (which he relates to his country of birth) from religion (which is privileged as 'true' identity). He appears to be speaking within the context of overcoming conflicts between Pakistani–Bangladeshi national identities but, as I shall argue below, given that most of the boys in the study were born in Britain, Gufter's construction might also be read as exemplifying the construction of hybridized and diasporic identities. Within such constructions, identity is dislocated from nationality, national boundaries and 'country of origin' discourses. Indeed, similarly to Asian respondents cited in Frosh *et al.* (2002), boys in this study talked about feeling that they are 'outsiders' and 'English' when they visit families and relatives in Pakistan and Bangladesh. For example, boys described how they might be laughed at on account of their English accents and many talked about how their families 'back home' assumed that their relatives in Britain must all be extremely wealthy. However, as detailed in Chapter 6 boys also felt 'Othered' within Britain due to their experiences of racism. The effect of these experiences was that boys talked about feeling that they did not necessarily 'belong' in Pakistan, Bangladesh or England. These constructions contain implications for multicultural ideals of assimilation as they complicate and confuse simplistic notions of nationality and belonging.

It is also useful to consider who might, or might not, be included within the boys' constructions of Muslim brotherhood. It is unclear whether these notions of brotherhood extend beyond the racialized boundaries of 'Asian' identity, for example, to encompass white male Muslims, and across gender, to encompass Muslim women. As will be explored further in Chapter 4, the gender dimension of racialized identity was ever present within the boys' accounts. Patriarchal themes were interwoven with racialized discourses, as the boys tried to define themselves as powerful males in relation to Muslim girls/women (by controlling the boundaries of Muslim femininity), while also, simultaneously, resisting white society/men.

The close relationship between discourses of religious identity and patriarchal masculinity could also be detected through comparisons of the boys' data with transcripts from the Muslim girls' discussion groups. As mentioned above, girls constructed 'British Muslim' identities, which they used as points of solidarity and unity (Archer 1998). Thus, whereas the young women appeared to 'shrug off' a singular racial identity (Wetherell and Potter 1992: 122), the young men were more likely to actively take up issues of 'race' through a discourse of racialized religious identity. This gender difference may be grounded within the boys' defence of local male powers and privileges, in other words, men may be more defensive because they generally have more power than women, and thus have potentially more to lose (see also Archer *et al.* 2001b; Archer and Yamashita 2003b).

I would suggest that racialized patriarchal identities can never be isolated from wider social and political relations and discourses. The discussion groups took place in the wake of the Rushdie affair, and some of the boys drew on the prevalent social notoriety of Muslim identification that the affair aroused, as demonstrated in the following extract.

TD: What do you think about umm the umm Salman Rushdie thing?
            [all talking over each other]
Abdul: Man need to be killed, innit!
Gulfraz: – I'm gonna kill him –
Fazaan: I – I'll kill him!
TD: You'd kill him?
Abdul: I – I'll kill 'im ... if I see him now –
Fazaan: I'll kill 'im as well
TD: What about you ... what d'you reckon?
Abdul: He – he he he did that, but ... but like ... behind that it – he
            could – he did it for publicity, that's what he did it for, I – to get
            people ... well known and that – that's what he did it for – to
            make a bit of money and that ... but I tell ya, I not gonna give a
            fuck if I get to uh ... jail and get killed, whatever, I not really
            give a fuck, but – if I see that guy, man ... [F. starts to interrupt]
            N-nno! No! hhh I aint finished! Anyway, right, But when I see
            that guy, if I ever see him and that, and you n-n-know that guy,
            that umm Prime Minister – y- y-you got – he beg the world for
            him and that and ... err big money for you know if anyone kills
            him and that – people ummm dead –
Fazaan: Like if-if I see that man –
Gulfraz: – see [inaudible] why don't we bash the libraries?
Abdul: I don't really give a fuck, man
Gulfraz: – Why – why ... in Mill Town ... [if] all the blacks are around
            the building, they wouldn't let him go! ... It's like the –
Abdul: -he-he was hiding! I thought he was big – I thought he was big!

	You know what I mean! I really didn't – I thought he was big! How come he's hiding now?! ... Why's he hiding?!
TD:	Why do you think it's so bad, what he did?
Abdul:	Because –
Gulfraz:	– because –
Abdul:	Because he's offended our religion!
//	
Abdul:	– know what I mean? – he uhh he took – he took mick out of our religion
TD:	– but uh but uhh yeah, but obviously I wouldn't kill him because it doesn't affect me –
Abdul:	– of our religion ... all the white people must have been laff-laughing and that – [at] all the Bengali's [F: yeah, the Sikhs –] yeah – uh ... uhh I tell you, when I see that guy ... he's gettin' chopped up!

(Hightown School, TD)

It is important to note first of all that the above extract was unique to this particular discussion group, and was not representative of any of the other groups. In this respect, the context of the group is also an interesting issue for consideration. It was in Hightown School that we recorded the most, and strongest, complaints of racism (as experienced in the town, school and local area). It was also the only school in which we, as interviewers, had felt any degree of racial tension as we went about the research. Tamar reported feeling particularly uncomfortable during interpersonal interactions with some of the school staff. For example, when we were jointly introduced to a particular member of staff, only my hand was shaken, and all talk and eye contact was directed to me (the white researcher) rather than to Tamar (the Asian interviewer). Whatever the cause of this behaviour (whether accidental, imagined or due to racial prejudices) the effect was that the Asian interviewer felt racially uncomfortable within the school.

The preceding extract can be read at a number of different levels. On the surface, the boys appear to express strong views – which could be labelled as extreme or fundamentalist – when they talk about supporting (and potentially being willing to get involved in) the killing of Salman Rushdie. In other words, the extract *could* be taken as evidence to support popular views about the increase in more militant identities among young Muslim men in Britain.

Alternatively, the extract can be read as illustrating the discursive production of masculine identities through interconnecting discourses of 'race', religion and gender. The aftermath of the Rushdie affair made available new forms of 'hard' British Muslim masculinity, which stood in stark contrast to prior stereotypes of 'soft' and 'effeminate' Asian masculinity. The discursive production of popular, powerful masculinities can involve participants engaging in verbal tests of toughness and jockeying for position (Brown 1998; Archer 2001). Whether or not the boys would have ever fulfilled any aspects of these fantasies/imagined scenarios is highly debatable, but the discursive strength of the boys' views is not dependent upon 'real' actions. Myths can perform important roles and functions within the production of identities, and I would suggest that the strategic purpose of such stories and constructions relates both to the negotiation of masculine *and* racialized identities (see also Kahani-Hopkins and Hopkins 2002: 290).

'Strict' religious identifications can also provide a source of pride, solidarity and status among Muslim boys. Frosh *et al.* found that girls from various ethnic backgrounds reported admiring Asian boys for their 'strict' religious commitments, viewing them as 'responsible, mature, not dirty and rude to girls' (Frosh *et al.* 2002: 128).[1] The discursive 'talking up' of violence, action and 'hardness' through religious idealism and martyrdom (for example, Abdul says he would not care if he died or went to jail for exacting retribution) evokes a particularly potent, powerful form of masculinity. The boys' assertions can be read as directed both at Muslim women in general and at the Asian female interviewer in particular. In this way, the boys are able to assert gender dominance through their claims to racial authenticity, which is enacted by their positioning of themselves as defending the honour of their religion.

The boys' talk also engages with the construction, and defence, of intergroup ethnic boundaries through the invocation of collective Muslim resistance to protect against potential criticism from other ethnic and religious groups. *The Satanic Verses* is used as a symbol around which the imagined community of a collective Muslim identity, conceptualized as both an ethnic and religious identity, can be mobilized. The theme of territoriality (both symbolic and geographical) can also be read into the boys' claim that it would be their responsibility to tackle Rushdie in the event of his arrival in their town. Thus it is their duty to defend the symbolic territory of the Muslim community (to protect the community from Rushdie's 'insult' and from being 'laughed at' by other groups), which is translated via a geographical responsibility for performing these duties only within the local area.

Despite the apparent clarity of these boys' positioning of themselves within a particular construction of Muslim identity and community, these were not fixed identifications that endured across the entire interview, or across different groups. The Hightown boys' negotiations of ethnic, racial and religious boundaries needs to be read in conjunction with passages from other points in the discussion and indeed from other discussion groups, in which boys engaged in debates about the definition of a *'proper'* Muslim. The boundaries of Muslim identity were constantly negotiated and contested within the discussion groups (see also Chapter 4) and the boys asserted, resisted and justified various positionings of themselves within or outside particular boundaries. In particular, while the boys claimed authentic Muslim identities through a notion of strength of feeling, or belief, they also acknowledged their more peripheral location in relation to ideals of Muslim identity as enacted through religious practices. For example, almost all the boys said that they did not take part in key practices such as fasting throughout Ramadan, regular reading of daily prayers (*namaaz*), or abstinence from alcohol and smoking. In some cases, the boys' participation in particular religious practices was positioned as conflicting with the demands of popular masculinity and 'westernized' British youth identities and schooling.

Rahan: But we can't be called proper Muslims
LA: Why not?
Rahan: Because you don't do – we don't we don't follow the – like pray five times a day … and er go to Mosque every Friday cos we in school
Wajit: Like I've seen loads of umm … Asians – and like – is like beginning to go like into pubs

(Westfield School, LA)

TD: I mean – do you think being western – being western's *good*?
Naseem: dunno –
Sham: well I've only been western – so I don't know what it's like to be … like uh –
TD: Well, like comparing yourself to your parents?
Sham: Well, yeah! Cos we seem to have more fun! hhh!
Jagdip: A lot!
Sham: well yeah – I mean … its *good*, but then from what I believe, I'm gonna rot in hell! So I shouldn't be doing it! so – hh!

(Lowtown School, TD)

As will be detailed in the next chapter, the boys also justified their 'authentic' Muslim identities through gendered discourses and their positioning of Muslim girls as 'inauthentic' and 'less religious', requiring moral guidance and policing from boys/men.

Black masculinities

Across all the discussion groups, boys talked about differences between 'black' and 'white' people, predominantly when discussing issues of racism. However, it was only in discussion groups with an Asian interviewer that boys explicitly and consistently described *themselves* as black boys/men. As

I will discuss further below, the boys' assertions of black identities were linked with issues of power, particularly the notion of 'being strong'. Black identities were primarily used as political identities from which to discuss racism and to provide a point of resistance. But black identities also proved to be contentious and ambivalent identities, because the boys' authenticity (their claims to being 'black') could be challenged.

The centrality of themes of power and resistance is apparent within the following extract. Here Yasser makes links between racism and the boys' local struggles for dominance within school, suggesting that racism increases as 'black' pupils 'take over more and more' from the 'whites'/ 'British'.

TD: Why do you think you can't change [racism]?

Yasser: Cos you look down at the Year Sevens now ... and the other years ... it's not that you know I think that its gonna carry on like that ... I'm not saying that 'oh, we're the hardest' or anything [Tamar: uh huh] but it's like have you noticed [that it's] the blacks mostly that are taking over more and more ... and racism is just gonna carry on and carry on ... there's never been *whites* since I joined the school that have taken over, has it? ... I think the British listen to quite a lot of us now [Tamar: they do?] I think they got used to it, you get the odd few who don't like ... who give you cheek

(Eastfield School, TD)

When discussing issues of racism and power between racialized groups, the vast majority of boys (and girls) in this study used the language of 'black' and 'white' identities. These identity positions can be understood as rooted within popular dominant discourses of cultural racism that position blackness and Englishness as mutually exclusive identities (see Gilroy 1987). Thus the young men here draw on, and invert, this binary identity position in order to define themselves relationally (and oppositionally) to white masculinity. This collective black identity thus provides a point for resistance and a source of strength through coalition between all 'non-white' groups.

The boys' association between black identities and local power within the school (the power to have a voice, be listened to and to 'take over') may also be read as drawing on wider, popular discourses of racialized hegemonic masculinity, in which blackness is associated with 'hardness' and power. For example, young men in Alexander's (1996) study also talked about how 'the black guys run the school' (1996: 54). The association of popular black identities with hegemonic ideals of masculinity, such as status, 'coolness' and strength, are further explored later in this chapter in relation to the boys' constructions of 'gangsta' masculinities.

Although boys frequently aligned themselves with black identities, these identifications were unstable and required boys to become involved in various processes of negotiation and justification. In other words, the boys' identifications as black could be ambiguous and potentially open to challenge within certain contexts. As Modood (1994) has written, the use of 'black' identity as a political position may entail particular problems for Asian groups. As illustrated within the extract below, the political power of the boys' constructions of black identities was tempered by these issues of ambiguity and authenticity.

TD: Has anyone been punished for saying anything [racist]?
Deepak: The blacks have
Tamar: The black?
Deepak: We, I mean we have
TD: You have?
Deepak: All the Asians

(Hightown School, TD)

The negotiation of black identity in the above extract arises because Tamar does not identify herself as black and so she subsequently questions the meanings implied in Deepak's use of the term. Alexander (1996) found that among young Asian and African/Caribbean men, black identities were used as common places from which to challenge racism, although definitions of who was included or excluded within such constructions varied across time and context. She noted that '[a]t their widest extent, the boundaries of "the black community" were expanded to include all non-white minorities ... the stress was on shared experience in the face of a common enemy' (Alexander 1996: 54). However, the Asian young man in her study was precariously positioned by aiming for acceptance within the black African/Caribbean group. He 'insisted in defining himself as part of a black group – with mixed success' (Alexander 1996: 19) because Asians were regarded by the other young men as 'occupying a space between the black and white extremes, and their loyalty could therefore not be guaranteed' (1996: 55). There were very few African or Caribbean groups in Mill Town to challenge the boys' use of black identity positions, but they still needed to re-negotiate the boundaries of black identities within and between themselves and with other Asians (as exemplified by the misunderstanding between Tamar and Deepak).

Modood (1994) has challenged the discourse of political blackness (the notion that all minority ethnic groups can occupy a black identity), arguing that it disadvantages Asians in two key ways. On the one hand, not all Asians may identify as black and, on the other, he suggests that Asian groups tend to be marginalized within discourses of blackness (for example, not being 'black enough'). These points are illustrated above, where

Deepak's claim to blackness is questioned by Tamar. As detailed in earlier chapters, the hegemony of 'black' identities within political forms of resistance to racism has been challenged (Hall 1992; Modood 1994) and attention has shifted to constructions of cultural identities. Following the Rushdie affair, black identities have become even more contested, as the 'debate about religious absolutism within minority communities challenged the political category "black" in the changed social and political environment of the 1990s' (Back 1996: 3). Political blackness has thus become an unstable identification, and alignment with a black identity may be particularly tenuous for non-African/Caribbean groups, particularly those who cannot draw on additional authenticating discourses of 'racial' blackness (for example, biological discourses relating to pigmentation and skin colour).

Interestingly, the boys engaged with potential challenges to the authenticity of their black identities by drawing on discourses of religion, 'pigmentocracy' and racism, as illustrated below.

TD: How do you feel about black people uh like Afro-Caribbeans –

Abdul: Very stupid for mixing in with the white, very stupid because behind the black they're saying ... 'you nigger' this that, 'you negro' and

Fazaan: That's what they call them, but they're black, so are we

//

Abdul: It's like I'm not saying they're dumb but by mixing in with the white you know what I mean? They always be racist and that, saying 'black bastard' this that, and they shouldn't be ... they – God created their heart, know what I mean, um, that I'm black

Fazaan: They should realize cos they more blacker than us! You know, like really black instead of brown [TD: yeah] they shouldn't be like that

(Hightown School, TD)

This extract can be read as revealing the conflation of 'race' and masculinity within the boys' engagement in discursive struggles over the ownership, definition and control of particular symbols of 'race' (Gilroy 1993). The young men identify and contest alternative, competing versions of black identity and they attempt to justify and legitimate their own constructions by mobilizing religious and biological discourses.

> The criteria for the achievement of blackness are dictated by those who set themselves up to prescribe what constitutes blackness, but the policing of that 'authentic' achievement is on the basis of the ascription of 'blackness' through biological difference
>
> (Phoenix 1998: 863)

As discussed in Archer (2001), in the above extract Fazaan and Abdul can be seen to negotiate between competing discourses around 'skin colour' and 'political blackness'. The continued dominance of competing, biologically based discourses of 'race' means that their own skin colour, being *'brown'*, potentially invalidates their claims to black identity. The boys challenge and resist this potential inauthenticity by accusing African/Caribbean groups of *'mixing in'* with whites. In other words, they argue that by 'mixing in with whites', African/Caribbeans are equally liable to 'dilute' their own claims to blackness. The construction draws upon a powerful discourse of 'culture as therapy' (Wetherell and Potter 1992: 131). In other words, the boys suggest that blacks who mix in with whites are 'going against their nature', and therefore require cultural enlightenment from more enlightened, 'truly' black (and therefore more authentic, powerful) Muslim boys.

This element of 'true', 'internal' blackness is inferred through the notion of a racialized *'heart'*. Abdul constructs an alternative conceptualization of blackness as being an internal, 'natural', biological quality, and, by dis-associating skin colour from blackness, he effectively protects his own black identity from potential challenges. His construction of black identity interweaves discourses of 'race' and religion, as he suggests that race is divinely ascribed ('God creates your heart black or white'). The boys thus also locate themselves within blackness and position themselves as authentic by their attempts to claim, define and police the boundaries between black and white identities.

It has been argued that one of the problems with these types of nego-tiation over black identity is that the political and representative power of such identities may be compromised. Modood has argued in particular that 'willy nilly, it gives a leadership role to those Asians who, whatever their standing in or commitment to the various Asian communities, can identify with and internalize the politics of anti-colour discrimination' (Modood 1994: 92).

The boys' talk also revealed a close, but restrictive, link between their identification with black identity and 'gangsta' masculinities, which, as will now be considered, were grounded within particular stereotypical con-structions of popular black (American/Caribbean) manhood.

'Gangsta' masculinities

Imran: It's like they go looking for fights
Gufter: Yeah he's the nigger type your brother
Jamil: He's a *proper* gangster! ha ha! [Gufter: mmm Snoop Doggy Dogg] his brother drives a Merc and they go around in gangs!
                                             (Lowtown School, LA)

The boys drew on popular racialized styles of masculinity within the discussion groups, and it was their constructions of 'gangsta' masculinities that elicited the most animated responses and discussions. 'Gangsta' masculinities were associated with black, urban American rap music, typified by self-styled gangsta rappers such as Snoop (Doggy) Dogg. As Jamil outlines, the performance of gangsta masculinity draws upon the myth of the 'rude' masculinity, exemplified by the display of 'flashy' symbols of success, such as driving expensive cars and experiencing violence/danger through gang membership.

It has been noted that these popular, phallocentric masculinities are also characterized by an emphasis upon 'individual performance and skill, sexual prowess and anti-establishment sentiments' (Noble 2000: 153), hyper-heterosexuality and public hyper-visibility (Archer and Yamashita 2003b) and other aspects of a style which has been termed 'cool pose' (Majors and Billson 1992). Cool pose entails 'expressive and conspicuous styles of demeanor, speech, gesture, clothing, hairstyle, walk, stance and handshake' (Majors 1990, in Frosh *et al.* 2002: 69). As has been the case with other youth styles and fashions, mainstream popular cultural discourses have seized on these stylized displays and performances, representing them in negative terms as sub-cultural symbols of moral decline and problematic minority ethnic youth. For example, research has drawn attention to the ways in which teachers may negatively interpret manifestations of cool pose among black pupils (Mac an Ghaill 1988, 1994; Sewell 1997). Within the popular imagination these styles have been collapsed into symbols of crime, social decay and anti-education attitudes, which are doubly feared because they may be taken up and enacted by ethnically diverse, dispossessed and/or alienated youth. The combination of public fear, desire and loathing evoked within popular constructions of 'rude' black masculinity is revealed within Sasha Baron Cohen's popular comedic TV character, 'Ali G': Ali's hyper-heterosexuality is both desired and ridiculed, he is 'street-wise' and amusing, yet also represented as incredibly stupid, ill-educated and ridiculous. In particular, though, it is his pretence to this form of masculinity, and the frequent revealing of his inauthenticity in this pretence that provides the audience with the means for relieving their fears of the potency of this form of masculinity. For example, Ali lives in the 'harmless' home counties' suburbia of Staines and the actor who plays him is Jewish and hence not 'really' black.

In contrast to the abundance of moral panics concerning black masculinity, attempts have been made to produce more considered, complex theorizations of black cultural styles. Noble (2000), for example, locates 'rude' masculinities within a discourse of 'slackness'. She draws upon the work of Cooper (1993) to argue that slackness is embedded within heterosexuality and centres around tightrope negotiations between 'reputation' and 'respectability'. Slackness is an inherently gendered discourse that is also culturally orientated, being organized around resistance to Euro-centric ideals of respectability. It thus represents ' "backward", "rude" folk/ghetto culture, vying for recognition and value within official Jamaican national identity' (Noble 2000: 151). It is also 'a politics of subversion ... a metaphorical revolt against law and order' and is 'the antithesis of Culture' (Cooper 1993, cited in Noble 2000: 154). Noble's nuanced con-ceptualization of slackness (as a politics of subversion) are, however, lost within popular British constructions of 'rude' masculinities.

For the boys in this study, as is the case within wider popular discourses, gang membership was identified as a defining aspect of 'bad' or 'rude' mas-culinity. Most of the boys claimed to be members of gangs, although the boundary between friendship 'group' and 'gang' was often completely blurred.

LA: Are any of you lot in gangs?
Imran: [quietly] yeah [LA: yeah?] we all are
                                               (Lowtown School, LA)

As found elsewhere (Sewell 1997), popular 'gang' masculinities are expressed and embodied through speech and clothing and through cultural styles, such as particular ways of walking, or 'bopping'. These identities echoed elements of 'rough' working class masculinities (Walkerdine *et al.* 2001) and hegemonic masculinity, focusing on violence and 'hardness':

LA: Do do people know like who's in a gang just by looking – can you tell just by looking at someone?
Imran: Yeah
Gufter: Like if anybody swears at you or anything like that, diss you or something and they get cheeky with you and thing then you say you know stop messing saying things like that or we'll get our back-up and get yer head kicked in! hh!
LA: ... Right how would I know ... like who's – ... how would I be able to pick someone out and go – oh no! I won't mess with him cos he's in a gang?
Imran: The walk
Gufter: The walk!
LA: The walk?
Gufter: The gangsters! hh!
LA: [laughs] Is that it? The way you walk? [Imran: yeah!] Is the way you dress and that or not?
Gufter: Yeah p'raps, sometimes
Imran: Sometimes
Lou: What sort of dress?
Imran: About ... Prakash and me – Prakash he's um ... baggy pants and–

Gufter:	And walk with a broken leg!
Imran:	Yeah! ... and the walking ... as if they ... drunk or something! hh!
LA:	So do you get on with people from other schools ... or [inaudible]
Gufter:	Well it depends how they are cos like some-sometimes they come like looking for fights and you just have to ... you know get involved ... but ... they don't all the time

(Lowtown School, LA)

As Alexander (2000) explains in her excellent book, *The Asian Gang*, membership and allegiances within these 'gangs' are highly complex phenomena that constantly shift and evolve, encompassing often contradictory generational, familial, cultural, personal and geographical loyalties and identifications. But despite the tenuous and fragile composition of such 'gangs', popular/media concern has been increasingly directed towards the 'Asian gang', reifying and demonizing such groups as dangerous forces within deprived inner city areas.

The close association between 'gangs', masculinity and locality/territoriality has been noted in various other contexts. For example, territoriality has been found to be a key aspect within the construction of white working class masculinities in Northern Ireland, where the defence of territory through strength is admired within constructions of popular masculinity (Connolly and Neill 2001). Similar findings are also apparent among diverse inner city boys (Archer and Yamashita 2003b), particularly in relation to black, urban masculinities, which may be closely associated with notions of place/locality, safety and danger (Westwood 1990). Several boys emphasized that gangs provided an important source of safety for boys, and it was suggested that membership could be a means for avoiding violence because the knowledge that a boy has 'backup' can act as a deterrent to potential aggressors. As Wajit said to me, 'Miss, it's like you're afraid to like hit him, afraid to touch him because you know that he's got backup'. Rahan provided a more elaborate picture of the role of the gang within peer conflict and relations:

> I beat him up, he won't beat me up because he know he can't beat me up. He'll go and tell the other gang group, the gang – and then the gang, the leader, he won't come by himself ... he'll get his gang with him and I won't have a gang so ... I just get beaten up
>
> (Rahan, Westfield School, LA)

As also noted elsewhere, these cultural styles can be understood as not merely public displays, but integral parts of the process of 'doing masculinity' within male peer groups (Archer and Yamashita 2003b).

The boys did not only enact popular Muslim masculinities through particular styles and behaviours – they also performed and asserted such masculinities by 'talking tough'. Gangs were associated with crime and violence, although the boys also thought that Mill Town was 'safer than other towns' (Imran, Lowtown, LA) because *they don't have bombs and things'* (Gufter, Lowtown, LA). Concerns were expressed however that 'there's a bit of drugs going down' and 'too much robbery and that – its pretty rough' (Abdul, Lowtown, LA). The nearby city was regarded as particularly dangerous because 'there's all fights and guns and things'. In comparison, the boys' experiences of violence in Mill Town were mainly described in terms of gang fights, which they suggested 'everywhere all over Mill Town' (Sarfraz). Connolly and Neill (2000) found that young people in Northern Ireland could derive increased status from particular local relations and associations with violence. They found that boys in particular gained status and capital by knowing, and talking about, particular violent incidents and notorious local (violent) men. Thus, engaging in 'tough' talking can generate power and credibility.

The prestige and power (the local hegemony) of these discourses of masculinity also derives from their specific cultural and racialized context, and attention has been drawn to the ways in which white boys may be attracted to black male styles (Back 1996; Cohen 1997). As these extracts and other research (Archer and Yamashita 2003b) also suggest, boys from a variety of ethnic backgrounds may draw upon aspects of these popular 'gangsta' or 'bad/rude boy' identities and styles. Black 'gangsta' forms of masculinity may be particularly valued forms of popular masculinity, and the ability to successfully perform these types of masculinity can increase a boy's popularity and status among his peers. This is because, as Frosh *et al.* (2002) and Sewell (1997) have noted, African/Caribbean boys are most likely to be viewed as 'super-masculine' within schools:

> They are seen as possessing the attributes that are constructed by young men as indicative of the most popular forms of masculinity – toughness and authentically male style in talk and dress. Paradoxically, while they are feared and discriminated against because of those features, they are also respected, admired and gain power through taking on characteristics which militate against good classroom performance (Mac an Ghaill 1988; Back 1996)
>
> (Frosh *et al.* 2002: 150)

Thus 'acting black' can form part of the racialized 'jockeying for position' among boys (Edley and Wetherell 1997).

However, as demonstrated within this chapter, Muslim boys did not reconstruct these masculine identities in simple or straightforward ways. They creatively fused 'rude' and 'gangsta' discourses with religious and racialized identifications. As such, their identifications can be read as 'culturally entangled' and diasporic (yet locally grounded).

As previously suggested, the Muslim boys did not simply or homogenously take up these popular 'gangsta' masculine identities. Rather they negotiated the boundaries of their identifications and constructed limits to the extent of their engagement. These limits were described primarily in terms of engaging in 'bad' (in other words, un-Islamic behaviours, 'stuff like drugs'), and being seen to ape American 'fashion':

Gufter: You get these *Asian* people who they not really religious they're not Islam you know . . . they into bad stuff like drugs and all that and they think they're niggers – you know like . . . you get these nigger type people from America . . . they hear about it and they think its fashion – [Jamil: yeah they dress like them] yeah I'm a gangster and–
Imran: too much films innit?

(Lowtown School, LA)

As illustrated by the following extract, while most boys reported identifying to a greater or lesser extent with 'black' and 'gangsta' styles and identities, they also distanced themselves from 'total' identification and resisted notions of a black underclass.

Gufter: Whereas you know in America its like they do it as a way of survival cos like the black people don't get treated well . . . they were treated as low class people [LA: mm] so they just bought – its like survival they just – to do it – they got into drugs and like that . . . and like you know make their way of life . . . its like over here they see it and they think alright I like that, that's fashion
Jamil: like oh I really like that style its *fashion* but they *had* to do it –
Gufter: – here it's fashion over here
Jamil: yeah they *brought* that –
Imran: Black people over *there*? They've got no education or *nothing!* and they just . . . release a song and it goes into the charts and they make their money!

(Lowtown School, LA)

The boys seem to express similar views to the sub-group of 'Arab multiculturalists' identified by Nagel in her (2002) study. She found broad differences between Arabs in Britain who either identified, or distanced, themselves from other minority ethnic groups and the notion of black identity or black underclass. For example, Nagel defined 'Arab multiculturalists' as those who distanced themselves from other minority, especially 'black', groups. In comparison affluent 'young cosmospolitans' reported embracing hybridized identities. One potential reason for these differences might relate to social class, as the taking up of hybridized identities may depend to some extent upon having the resources and social capital to pass across boundaries. As Nagel suggests, the Arab Muslims who strove to maintain cultural distinctiveness tended to come from lower socio-economic positions and thus lacked resources to leave disparaged or disadvantaged identity positions.

The next chapter, which focuses on issues of gender, will consider the boys' constructions of *Asian* masculinities. Boys identified themselves as Asian primarily in the context of gendered relations, specifically in relation to themes of 'culture', 'tradition' and 'sexism'. In particular, Asian identities were drawn upon in relation to issues of 'change' within 'western' society, often to argue against social and moral changes and to defend particular 'sexist' behaviours and attitudes as tradition or culture.

Summary/discussion

This chapter has detailed some common themes within the boys' constructions of racialized and religious masculine identities. Negotiations around power and struggles for authenticity have been key features within the boys' constructions of 'Muslim' and 'black' identities and imagined communities. The young men's discourses can be read as part of a process of 'imagined' identity construction in which traditional notions of essentialized cultural or racial entities are constantly being reinvented and challenged (Alexander 1996). Black, Asian and Muslim masculine identities were conceptualized and mobilized in differing ways and in relation to different ends.

A tension was evident within and between the boys' different constructions of Muslim and black masculinities, as these identities were made, reworked, contested and justified within the discussion groups. Identities were not simply or homogenously asserted and accepted, for example, boys both identified with, and distanced themselves from, 'black' identities. Black identities were primarily drawn upon 'as a shared site of solidarity against racism, as a resistance to whiteness but also as a means of drawing divisions between black groups and as an assertion of masculine power' (Archer 2001: 98). As Back (1996) suggests, new ethnicities are created out of the tension between global and local influences, where the meanings of 'Muslim', 'black' and 'British' identities are called into question. Thus the boys' negotiations between Muslim, black and 'gangsta' masculinities may be read as points of resistance, as attempts to redefine and distance themselves from unpopular versions of Asian masculinity.

Note

1 Although, conversely, the same girls also described Asian boys as 'odd' and thought that they were restricted by their families.

chapter four

Boys, girls and gendered identities

Introduction

This chapter examines the ways in which boys in the study produced gendered (masculine and feminine) identities. I argue that the boys' masculinities are inherently relational identities – that is, they are formed in relation to feminine identities – and I consider some of the ways in which boys construct these gender differences. Consideration is also given to the boys' 'performance' of 'laddish' identities and to their constructions of specific Asian 'sexist'/patriarchal identities. Attention is drawn to the varied ways through which boys 'do' (enact and perform) patriarchy in their talk about gender relations, through their identification as 'Asian' boys and through the actual research situation itself. The contradictions and implications found within these identities are drawn out and discussed.

Masculinities in the classroom: 'lads' and 'boffins'

As discussed in Chapters 1 and 2, Muslim boys have occupied a contradictory position within various popular educational discourses about gender and achievement. As *boys*, they fall within the scope of widespread concerns with the male 'under-achievement', although as *Asian* pupils they have been assumed to be 'good pupils' and 'achievers'. As *minority ethnic* pupils they have been lumped together with others as educational 'problems', and more recently, as *Muslims*, they have been positioned as problematic, under-achieving pupils with low rates of post-compulsory participation. The boys within this study could also be classified as *working class*, and thus are also subsumed within long-standing concerns over working class educational exclusion and alienation and corresponding low levels of achievement.

The boys' talk can be seen to contain traces of these various, contradictory discourses. They were aware of the 'boys' under-achievement' discourse and they talked about their teachers' higher expectations for girls.

Abdul: Yeah they [teachers] all say, they all say is 'look at the latest charts, the girls are doing miles better than the boys in exams and that'
TD: How does that make you feel?
Abdul: I'm not really bothered [TD: you're not bothered?] nah, I couldn't give a damn, it's all about marks, innit? As long as I, as long as I get my GCSEs as well I'm not really arsed what they get, as long as I get eight [GCSEs], I don't give a fuck if they get A stars or A moons!

(Hightown School, TD)

Abdul's extract can be read in various ways: at face value he seems to be suggesting that he is unaffected by girls' success in examinations and is only concerned with his own performance, which he feels will be satisfactory as long as he achieves eight passes in his GCSEs. However, he made his point very strongly and throughout the discussions there were numerous instances when boys complained about teachers unfairly 'favouring' girls. In this respect, the example of Abdul, above, could be read as illustrative both of boys' wider feelings of resentment and of their attempts to re-assert themselves in relation to girls' 'over-achievement'. The example of Abdul also indicates that – rather than trying to raise their own attainment to match girls, for example, by doubling their efforts or seeking additional assistance – boys commonly reacted by distancing themselves from girls' achievement and positioning themselves as 'not really bothered'. In educational policy terms, such attitudes could be read as representative of low aspirations. They could also be placed within a wider discourse of 'laddishness', in which being seen to do, and care about, schoolwork is derided and resisted.

As discussed in the introductory chapters, the performance of 'laddish' identities within the classroom is characterized by 'anti-schoolwork' attitudes and cheeky or 'naughty' behaviours. The boys interviewed by Jackson (2002b) suggested that there are different sorts of 'lad behaviours' that are differentiated by lifestyle codes (characterized, for example, by trends in dress and behaviour). However, Jackson also notes that, despite local variations in the enactment of such identities, certain common features are present in all constructions of laddishness. These key themes include being popular, 'hanging out' with mates, being good at sport, having the 'right sort' of clothes and not being seen to work too hard at school. Similar traits have been noted by other researchers (for example, Francis 1999; Haywood and Mac an Ghaill 2001; Frosh *et al.* 2002), and the boys in this study were no exception.

Among the Muslim boys, 'messing about' was constructed as a typical feature of masculinity, as Rakim (Hightown School, LA) said, 'boys mess about'. These behaviours included not paying attention and/or talking to friends during class, 'playing up' and talking back to teachers. In the discussion groups, most boys were keen to emphasize that they messed about in class, for example, Mehmet and Javed both said that their school reports criticized them for talking too much and joking around in class, and Assim admitted (with some pride) 'I mess about too much'. 'Messing about' was also characterized by 'being stupid' and getting into fights with other boys. But rather than being constructed in derogatory terms, as would be the case within educational discourses, boys positively associated 'being stupid' with 'having a laugh', 'fighting' and popular masculinity. 'Being stupid' was also positioned in opposition to 'serious' femininity. Most boys were happy to suggest that both their male friends and girls would describe them as 'stupid'.

Mushtak: We mess about too much and do silly things
Ali: Yeah an' boys get into fights so the girls think that's bad
LA: So you lot think its bad?
Rakim: Yeah cos we er get into fights for stupid little things like er that
         was it er like Paul saying that 'I'm the hardest' or something like
         that

(Hightown School, LA)

The role of humour and 'having a laff' within the production of working class masculinities has been noted across numerous studies with both black and white boys (for example, Willis 1977; Corrigan 1979; Mac an Ghaill 1994; Sewell 1997; Skelton 2001). As Skelton (2001) details, heterosexual masculinities can be regulated through humour (Kehily and Nayak 1997) and practices such as 'fun fighting' can provide a way for boys of varying ages to develop collective identifications and to establish bonds with one another.

Boys gave two main reasons to explain why they engaged in laddish behaviours: first, the role of teachers in creating differing pupil behaviours; and, second, innate, biological gender difference that predisposed boys to mucking about. These themes were inter-related and were often mentioned concurrently. Boys blamed particular teachers and/or teaching styles for encouraging the performance of laddishness, for example, they suggested that boys are more likely to play up to teachers who are unable to control boys and in classes where teachers are perceived to favour girls. This latter reason was also located within a discourse of 'natural' biological gender differences. Boys suggested that teachers may treat girls 'better' (in other words, they do not shout at them as much, or punish them as harshly or in such a physical manner) because girls are delicate, soft and require protection. As one boy put it, 'they [teachers] treat them [girls] like, like *eggs* or something!' (Majid, Westfield School, NS). In comparison, boys suggested that males are tougher and harder and, as a result, are treated more harshly by teachers: 'the teacher might be a bit harder on the boys' (Rahan, Westfield, LA).

Rakim: I reckon girls get treated a bit better because they [teachers] perceive them to be maturer than boys
LA: In what ways do they treat them better?
Ali: Just, er they don't get chucked out of class
Rakim: Yes, they don't get in as much trouble as boys ... probably because they don't mess about, just get on with their work
                                                (Hightown School, LA)

As illustrated by the above excerpt, boys stereotypically associated femininity with 'maturity', which they suggested was displayed through girls' conformist pupil behaviours and their willingness to 'get on with their work'. Their other suggestion, that particular teaching styles are in some way implicated within the production of masculinities, is reiterated within the wider research in the field. Various studies have drawn attention to the ways in which 'classroom practices are active in the construction of and sustenance of particular forms of gender identity' (Raphael Reed 1999: 105). The organizational practices of schools create 'symbolic gender cultures' (Francis 1998: 47) that produce and reproduce hierarchical gendered identities. School practices such as pupils' access to, and use of, physical spaces, can be highly gendered (for example, Skelton 2000, 2001) and racialized (Archer 1998). The gendered nature of curriculum and class materials can also shape the dominant modes of acceptable masculinity and femininity (Davies 1989). Styles of discipline and teaching can also play a key role in producing and legitimating different types of masculinity. For example, it has been widely noted that the more violent and 'hard' masculinized teaching styles adopted within certain school sports and subjects (particularly within traditionally 'male' subjects) are closely linked to the production and valorization of 'macho' masculinities in secondary schools (Willis 1977; Corrigan 1979; Mac an Ghaill 1994).

In addition to the role played by teaching practices, boys from across the discussion groups drew upon biological discourses of masculinity to argue that laddishness at school is an inevitable product of 'natural' gender differences. In particular, boys suggested that they possessed an innate short temper, aggressiveness and hot-headedness. These traits were described as conflicting with school culture and authority, and several boys said that they would prefer to change their attitude and 'cool it down with the teachers and that [... because] I get cheeky and that with the teachers' (Abdul, Hightown, TD). Thus some of the boys suggested that popular, macho masculinities were 'naturally' at odds with dominant stereotypes of the idealized passive, well behaved pupil, but they displaced their own responsibility or agency for these behaviours onto external or biological factors.

Muslim boys also defended their comparatively lower levels of academic achievement as being due to a conscious lack of effort and 'slacking', rather than being the result of lower ability or intelligence. In this respect, boys reproduced a familiar public discourse that assumes that males have superior intelligence, but hide their abilities through a lack of application (see also Epstein *et al.* 1998). The boys explained that a typical statement on one of their school reports might say that 'if we worked a bit harder we would be able to do well on our GCSEs yeah and we could achieve our goals but we're slackin'!' (Rakim, Hightown School, LA). The boys suggested that they 'slacked' because they did not want to be seen by their peers as displaying 'too much' effort at school and because they get 'bored' by schoolwork. Several of the respondents also seemed to engage in delicate discursive balancing acts within the groups, tentatively testing the water with regard to how much, or how little, homework they were prepared to admit that they 'really' did. Occasionally boys challenged one another directly, implying that particular behaviours could be interpreted as 'looking like a boff'. For example, Deepak accused Abdul of staying at home in his bedroom, doing his homework, rather than coming out regularly to play football with the other boys. This accusation was backed up with an implied insult to Abdul's sexuality, as Deepak suggested that Abdul was not interested in girls either. Abdul attempted to justify his non-hegemonic behaviour by saying 'boffs have the best laugh at the end' (Hightown, TD), but this was not necessarily accepted by the others. As Frosh *et al.* (2002) suggest, this hiding of effort was primarily geared towards resisting being labelled a 'boff' or 'boffin' by their peers.

The issue of laddishness constitutes an ongoing concern within schools. This concern is evident within educational literature and popular/media reports and within everyday discussions in schools among teachers. Certainly, I find that the issue is regularly raised when I am conducting fieldwork in schools. As detailed in the introductory chapters, laddishness has been blamed for contributing to boys' 'under-achievement' within schools due to its antithetical stance to schoolwork (Frosh *et al.* 2002). But is this the whole story?

Jackson (2002a, b) proposes that boys may enact laddish behaviours as a means of distancing themselves from both academic failure and 'the feminine'. She discusses this in relation to the specific rejection of academic work, suggesting that laddish behaviours enable boys to act in ways consistent with hegemonic masculinities within their schools, and they provide an excuse for failure and a means for augmenting success. Public performances of 'laddishness' can thus be read as part of a self-worth protection strategy aimed at avoiding failure (and the implications of failure) by hiding effort. Indeed, research indicates that many boys admit to doing their schoolwork 'undercover' (Frosh *et al.* 2002). The performance of laddishness can also lessen the potential effects of educational 'failure' because, first, failure is seen to be due to a lack of effort, rather than to a lack of intelligence and, second, the increased peer status that laddish identities entail may compensate for boys' loss of power in the face of girls' potential higher achievements. In other words, associations between hegemonic masculinity and 'winning' can be maintained and defended by redefining the parameters of (what counts as) success and by providing a means for 'opting out' of situations that may not be easily 'won'.

In common with boys in a variety of studies, the Muslim boys unanimously claimed to engage to a greater or lesser extent in some laddish behaviours, and all but one boy emphasized that they were 'not boffs'. Yet their constructions of laddish masculine identities did stand out from boys in other studies in a number of ways. For example, the Muslim boys widely suggested that their behaviours were part of an 'act' or a performance of popular masculinity, which they felt was often misunderstood by girls and teachers.

LA:	What do you think the girls in your class – or your *year* your school ... say about you? As in you know, what are the boys here like?
Gufter:	They probably say something like they're bigheaded and ... they be *dumb* they don't understand anything!
LA:	Why do they all think you're big-headed?
Gufter:	It's just the way we act innit?!
LA:	*Are* you bigheaded?
Gufter:	No! hhh!

(Lowtown School, LA)

Several boys were also keen to stress that even though they messed about in class, this did not necessarily mean that they were academically failing. All the boys who were interviewed said that they valued education (see Chapter 7), and all intended to achieve some qualifications. Most of the boys reported that they were doing 'OK' at school in terms of their levels of achievement. For example, Mehmet and Javed (Eastfield School) suggested that, apart from messing about and talking too much in class, they worked hard and achieved quite well. Wajit, from Westfield School, also thought that teachers would 'probably say good things' about him and his friends. Boys at Lowtown School made similar suggestions:

LA: [Laughs] What sorts of things do you lot get on your reports?
Imran: I–I actually get *good* reports
Gufter: Yeah most of us do
Imran: Yeah ... everyone that's in this room I think
Gufter: Yeah just sometimes you get people with satisfactory and must
           improve, cause for concern, but most of us are alright
                                                    (Lowtown School, LA)

The boys' claims might be explained to some extent by the fact that some of
them (like Gufter) were in the higher sets/streams (although boys are generally more likely to be in lower sets, see Arnot *et al.* 1999). Some of the
other schools, such as Westfield School, taught in mixed ability classes and
did not group pupils into ability bands. The study was also conducted prior
to the introduction of widespread SAT testing, which has been identified as
highly damaging for working class pupils who tend to achieve lower results
and who thus come, from an early age, to regard themselves as educational
'nothings' (Reay and Wiliam 1999). Many of the boys who took part in the
study may have largely managed to avoid such forms of divisive practice
which reinforce and ingrain 'failed' learner identities among working class
male pupils.
    The performance of 'laddish' behaviours by Muslim boys can also be
read as a means of resisting racism in that it allows boys to challenge
dominant constructions of themselves (such as the stereotype of Asian
masculinity as 'effeminate', 'good' and 'well behaved'). It was notable,
however, that across the discussion groups boys claimed that 'normal'
laddish behaviour was consistent with gaining educational qualifications.
For example, Sham was described as both 'hard working' and 'violent' by
his friends in the group. Forms of laddishness were linked with, but were
also distanced from, 'gangster' behaviour, the desirability of which was
contested between the boys. Kabir said, for example, 'I'm just put off by
these people ... these gangsters [in school]'. As Chapter 7 discusses, the
boys' taking up of laddish identities appeared to be mediated by a universal
belief in the importance of education.
    The following section will now consider the ways in which the boys'
performances of 'laddishness' and masculinity are embedded within their
wider constructions of sexualized/gender identities. As I will suggest below,
these conceptualizations centre around issues of power, status, patriarchy
and the control of women.

Masculinity and 'hardness'

As other research in the field has consistently found, the boys in this study
constructed masculine identities that were characterized by power and

'hardness', antithetical to 'soft' and 'emotional' feminine identities. For instance, when asked to describe the ways in which they felt masculine, boys said things like men are 'meant to be the boss' (Naseem) and 'sort of like [have] power over women' (Jagdip) (both Lowtown School, TD). Boys often appeared to be dismissive of girls, saying that they would not associate, or 'hang around', with them because girls are 'stupid' and inferior. As Mushtak put it: 'nah it's just boys, jus- just boys basically ... they're not worthy of being with boys'. It was suggested that girls would describe their male peers as loud and 'nasty', mainly because boys often make fun of girls at school.

Male power was linked to 'hardness', which, as detailed in Chapter 3, was asserted through constant references to fighting and violence. In comparison, femininity was constructed as characterized by emotions and more passive behaviours; the boys suggested that girls do not like to be made fun of, and consequently get in 'moods', cry and retaliate against their tormenters by giving 'dirty looks'. Feminist literature has examined how dominant constructions of femininity revolve around notions of intimacy, care and friendship. These qualities are defined in opposition to 'hard' masculinity, which is exemplified through independence, hardness and assertiveness. Thus, boys described how male peer relationships are internally regulated in such a way that prohibits intimacy and the display of 'soft' emotions or feelings – for fear of public derision and shame. For example, Sham suggested that whereas girls talk about personal, 'intimate' things, 'lads don't, they just laff at yer' because crying and talking intimately to friends is 'not manly'. Instead, the boys suggested that within their friendship groups any discussion of personal or sensitive subjects (such as heterosexual attraction) would be dealt with through hyper-heterosexuality and the use of humour. As one boy put it, 'if a boy likes a girl it's all phwoarggh!' Boys also engaged in teasing one another about liking, or expressing interest in, girls. For example, Fazaan attempted to embarrass and ridicule two of the other boys in the group by saying 'him and him talk about birds'.

An active/passive dichotomy underlay many of the boys' constructions of gender differences. Male 'action' was typified through the boys' accounts of the vast quantities of time they spent playing, and talking about, football. Most boys said that they spent their break times playing football, and this pastime was reflected in the photographic diaries that pupils (both boys and girls) produced for the wider study.[1] The boys also said that girls tend to spectate, rather than participate in, football ('they watch us'). Girls were usually constructed as unsporty and moody, getting easily 'offended' during games lessons. The boys' constructions drew on notions of female bodies as unruly, sexualized, soft and non-athletic. Thus, Sham suggested, 'you can't play football with girls cos of what you might touch!' (Sham, Lowtown School, TD). Even when the boys did identify a (white) girl who was very good at football, they suggested that they could not tackle her because of sexual taboos.

This construction, of an 'active – male' and 'passive/sexual – female' gender division, was also evident in boys' assertions that girls talk about 'make-up' whereas boys talk about what they're 'gonna do' (Eastfield School, TD). Girls' interests and pastimes were predominantly constructed as frivolous, revolving around 'shopping, shoes and feelings', 'screaming too much' and forever talking to their friends, which rendered them, in the eyes of many boys, 'boring' and 'stupid'.

Gender differences were largely understood as being 'natural' and evident from infancy. For example, Yasser suggested that while he might ideally treat his future children 'equally', there would be inevitable differences because 'actually like when you get them ... girl wants a doll you know, you get your son wants, you get your son like an action man ... so its treat them differently all the way innit?' (Yasser, Eastfield, TD). Such views persisted even in the face of possible conflicting evidence from the boys' own experiences (for example, some talked about a boy they knew who played with dolls).

While it was generally agreed across the groups that girls were 'inferior', boys from Lowtown and Hightown schools also indicated racialized distinctions between the attitudes of white or Asian girls towards them. Boys at Lowtown School suggested that while Asian girls 'look up' to them, the white girls were not interested. Similarly, boys at Hightown suggested that although they would like to go out with white girls, 'they won't go out with a Asian guy' (Fazaan) because they are 'stuck up' (Abdul).[2] I would suggest that Fazaan's and Abdul's association between racism (white girls' refusal to go out with Asian boys) and social class (calling these attitudes 'stuck up') reveals how discourses of 'race', racism and class can interact with patriarchal identities to circumscribe the boundaries of 'local' hegemonic masculinities. However, boys also used 'race' as a site of counter-resistance – boys at Lowtown School, for example, claimed to resist white girls through language. As Imran said, 'when they really annoy us, right ... we just talk in our language ... and that annoys them they go stop talking your language and we go this is *boys'* talk!' (Lowtown School, LA).

Constructing gender identities through 'culture' and 'tradition'

Boys identified themselves as 'Asian' within the context of gender relations, and specifically in relation to themes of tradition and sexism. Asian identities were mobilized when discussing changes within gender and social relations. Boys utilized Asian identities to argue for the maintenance of 'tradition' in the light of what they perceived to be negative changes in gender relations brought about by exposure to western society.

Across the discussion groups, boys constructed British Asian Muslim masculine identities through themes of 'duty' and 'responsibility'. In particular, they suggested that one of the defining features of Muslim masculinity was a duty to 'patrol' their female peers. This patrolling involved maintaining a close surveillance of the acceptability and respectability of Muslim girls'/women's clothing, appearance and sexuality. It also entailed defence of the belief in a gendered division between 'home' and 'work'. The remainder of the chapter will demonstrate ways in which the boys attempted to construct powerful masculine identities by controlling the 'boundaries' of ethnic identity, defining what is/is not 'appropriate' cultural behaviour for 'their' women. Examples illustrate how the young men used notions of 'culture' to defend their views against charges of sexism. However, I will also suggest that – in spite of their strong emotional investments in such discourses – the boys' views did not necessarily reflect 'real' gender relations between themselves and Muslim girls. In particular, boys seemed perplexed by their observations of how Muslim girls 'actually' behave, which they described as the girls being 'out of control'.

Home, work and gendered responsibilities

Across the discussion groups, boys perpetuated the (dominant) stereotypical assumption that home is a place of freedom and autonomy for males and a site of restriction and subservience for females. A typical remark was that at home 'you [boys] get to do a lot of things that they [girls] don't' (Yasser, Eastfield, TD). This view (which was largely resisted by Muslim girls, see Archer 1998, 2002b), is examined here for its role in the boys' assertions of racialized, patriarchal masculinities.

The boys drew on a traditional gender dichotomy in which men earn/ work, providing for the home, and women have domestic responsibilities. They justified the gendered division of domestic labour, and the restriction (out of school) of Muslim girls to the home, as part of religious and cultural 'tradition'. This situation was widely acknowledged to be to their benefit by the boys. For example, the close association between Muslim femininity and domesticity was reiterated in relation to the boys' everyday home lives, as illustrated in the following discussion on whether or not boys do housework:

LA: What about you two – do you have to do it as well?
Sarfraz: I have to but ... I'm too *lazy*! My mum will tell us to clean my room up – I go OK and just go out! And that'll be it!
LA: Do your sisters go out as well?
Gufter: Every now and then yeah ... but most of the time they just like stay at home – list-watching videos ... listening music or – its mainly the boys that go out

LA:	Is that because they want to stay at home or cos – ?
Gufter:	No its mainly cos it's the Asian, Asian tradition
Imran:	Muslims, Muslims right, girls have to stay home don't they?
Gufter:	Yeah . . . I – yeah yeah . . . Islam . . . cos yeah they're *supposed* to be hidden from men [LA: mmm] after – before they get married
LA:	What do you lot think about –
Imran:	It is in a way cos . . . girls don't get freedom don't they?
LA:	So do you think it's . . . that it's fair do you think it's –
Gufter:	It's not really fair but . . . we just got to do it

(Lowtown School, LA)

This construction, of 'it's not fair, but we['ve] just got to do it' was common across discussion groups as a way of both asserting, and justifying, Muslim male privilege. And, as evident in the extract below, girls were seen as requiring supervision and control for their own good, so that they do not 'mess about'.

TD:	Do you think you should do any of that stuff [housework]?
Fazaan:	Never!
Abdul:	Nah
TD:	No, you don't? Do you think it's fair?
Abdul:	Yeah hh!
Fazaan:	It is fair, yeah
TD:	You, why d'you think it's fair?
Abdul:	Cos, because if they don't do that –
Fazaan:	Muslim go inside [inaudible]
Gulfraz:	Cos they the girls and they go out and mess around [inaudible]

(Hightown School, TD)

Boys also argued in favour of the 'traditional' restriction of girls to the home on account of the dangers of the local area. As detailed in Chapters 3 and 6, boys constructed the streets of Mill Town as home to gangs and gangsters, and prone to regular incidents of racism ('after seven [in the evening], after around that you got *gangs* walking around' (Rahan, West-field School, LA)). In contrast, home was constructed as 'safe'. The restriction of Muslim girls and women to the home was thus justified as a practical protection strategy, although this view can also be read as bolstering the boys' assertions of dominant masculinities, through the positioning of themselves as more powerful, able to care for and protect their weaker female peers.

Boys acknowledged that this situation might not be 'fair' in some ways (for example, in terms of western liberal ideals of gender equality), but justified their views through discourses of 'culture' and tradition. Gufter also invoked a traditional/modern dichotomy to argue that some girls 'understand' and know that the situation is 'right', whereas it is only more 'modernized' girls who do not accept the situation and complain.

Gufter: At home yeah its like ... s'more of a downside for the girl cos they have to stay in ... it's just like *Islam* [LA: mmm] that's it

LA: What do you think they'd say about it? ... what do they think about it?

Gufter: Mmm ... depends how they are cos like ... the one's who think they're you know *modernized* and ... they say something like, you know, 'it's not fair, I wanna go *out* see that'. ... But others will *understand* ... they'll say something like yeah it's right you know I don't mind cos ... they know it's right

(Lowtown School, LA)

There were some debates regarding the acceptability of wives undertaking paid employment, although it was universally agreed that this would not be at the expense of the woman's responsibility for housework and domestic tasks. Thus, Yasser's view was: 'I'd say you can do what you want ... as long as the house jobs are done, everything's fine, kids are safe and all that' (Yasser, Eastfield School, TD).

The association of girls with domesticity was also linked to a reciprocal construction of men as breadwinners and wage earners, 'cos women aren't the men who work in jobs' (Yasser, Eastfield, TD).

LA: Do you think it's fair that girls do the housework?

Assim: Yeah, 'cos it's the men ... make the money they, they shouldn't have to

(Westfield School, LA)

Muslim masculinities were often defined using a 'breadwinner' discourse, in which there is a responsibility to provide economically, not only for the immediate, nuclear family, but also for extended family and kin 'back home' (for example, in Bangladesh). These constructions have similarly been found in the talk of other Muslim Bangladeshi young men (see Archer *et al.* 2001b).

I just want to get a good job so I, cos I wanna feed my family like, you know, in Bangladesh, they're poor and so they need money and like I – my brother has to send money now and again. I, I just want to get a good job so I can send money

(Sham, Lowtown School, TD)

There were, however, a number of inconsistencies in the boys' accounts, particularly between their constructions of hypothetical and everyday gender relations. For example, some of the boys described how they actually had to do the majority of the housework at home, which was incompatible with the versions of masculinity that they attempted to assert. For example, Yasser and Abdul both complained that, as the youngest son of the family, 'my mum treats me like a daughter, makes me do all the housework' (Yasser). Abdul similarly complained 'my mum ... and she treats me like a girl as well, do all the housework'. Although these realities may have compromised the boys' claims to hegemonic masculinities, they did have other benefits, such as the increased social capital generated by the boys' subsequent 'good boy' reputation with other family members, especially aunts.

There were also hints of tensions between competing discourses of masculinity, such as contradicting demands of 'laddishness' and the ideals of 'responsible' Muslim manhood:

LA: So err what's your ideal wife sort of gonna – what would she be like?
Imran: Don't wanna get married!
LA: You don't wanna get married?! Why not?
Gufter: We can't take the responsibility!
LA: No? ... How do you have to be responsible if you get married? What do you have to do?
Gufter: Cos once you're married ... that's it you haven't got no life anymore – you gotta look after your wife and just go work – look after your kids and that's it!

                                                      (Lowtown School, LA)

It was also evident that the boys themselves were not quite as 'free' to go out as their gendered constructions might suggest. For example, boys at Lowtown School recounted an incident in which their fathers had found out that they had gone to a nightclub, culminating in one boy being dragged out and taken home. The patrolling of masculine identities by fathers is developed further in Chapter 5.

Appearance and dress

The construction of gender boundaries through the themes of 'culture' and 'tradition' was also discussed in relation to girls' appearance and dress. The boys drew on specifically 'Asian' identities to engage in the discursive regulation of femininity through notions of what constitutes 'appropriate' clothing.

Boys across all the discussion groups constructed gender boundaries between Asian males and females in relation to the wearing of 'traditional' dress. It was argued that Asian femininity is characterized by the wearing of traditional clothing (for example, *shalwar kameez*) at home but that Asian masculinity is not. The boys explained this disparity as due to cultural values being 'stricter' for Asian women, although their constructions can also be read as reproducing particular racialized discourses of femininity. As illustrated in the following extract, Gufter draws on a notion of 'exotic' Asian femininity:

Imran: Only sisters and that wear –
Gufter: *They* wear traditional Asian clothes
LA: Why don't you lot wear traditional Asian clothes?
Gufter: Just don't like 'em! [laughs]
LA: Do the girls like 'em then?
Gufter: Yeah ... they like it because –
Imran: – Cos they're used to it now aren't they?
Gufter: Its like ... its like *exotic* you know ... all these different colours and ... shiny things on them ... and they like it ... whereas there're not really an Asian clothes –
Jamil: It's Asian style, innit?

(Lowtown School, LA)

Boys at other schools also suggested that girls wore traditional Asian clothes because 'they're nice design and nice colours' (Mushtak) and because girls are 'into clothes more than boys, aren't they?' (Rakim) (both Hightown School, LA). Social psychological models of ethnic minority identity have focused upon the wearing of cultural dress and clothing as a marker for the 'strength' of an individual's ethnic identity (for example, Stopes-Roe and Cochrane 1990). In other words, such theories have taken the wearing of traditional clothes as an indication of a more 'traditional' (less assimilated or 'westernized') minority ethnic identity. However, all the boys in this study separated cultural identity (as defined by girls' wearing of Asian dress) from Muslim identity, and some argued that although girls were more likely to wear 'traditional' dress, they are actually less religious in their attitudes and behaviours than the boys.

For example, Wajit (Westfield School, LA) complained that girls displayed a frivolous and un-Muslim attitude by wearing 'technicolour' clothes and by failing to observe Islamic demands of covering the body (only showing their wrists and face in public). The reason for this, according to Wajit, was that 'most of these girls, Miss, they just can't, Asian girls can't be bothered!' He went on to say that 'if you go around all the country I bet you won't see one person, one Asian woman with the head-scarf'.

Within discussions about what might constitute 'appropriate' clothing for Muslim women, boys positioned themselves as guardians and regulators of ethnic boundaries through their sanctioning or disapproval of women's appearances. In addition to the issue of wearing *hijab*/covering up, boys argued that the wearing of 'western' clothes, such as jeans and 'bodies',[3] was a symbol of girls' moral and cultural decline/decay, which signalled that they had become 'uncontrolled'.

Imran: Cos like you know you see all these girls wearing *jeans* you know ... they they're the ones who are ... uncontrolled and everything
Jamil: Not *all* of them
Imran: Have you seen anyone wearing jeans?
LA: Are most girls here quite ... traditional then and *few* are ... like more –
Gufter: Actually more of them are *turning* into like ... the modernized type ... cos they – these you see them wearing these kind of *dresses* and ... you know ... it's just *different* ... it's not how it used to be [speaker unclear: They wear dresses outside –]
Gufter: Outside yeah ... they really give it ... they don't really *care*
Jamil: In our area they've started wearing ... uh ... *bodies* outside [LA: yeah?] yeah ... showing their uh ... stomach
Imran: Yeah – do you *like* that?! [laughs] hhh!

(Lowtown School, LA)

Boys also suggested that they would 'kill' their sisters if they wore skirts (unless these skirts were very long and reached the floor). Jeans, bodies and skirts were seen by the boys as inappropriately sexual, and were identified as symbolizing Muslim women's resistance to Muslim patriarchal norms and regulation. The research context itself also provided instances of ways in which young men attempted to 'do' patriarchy. For example, the appearance of Tamar, a Pakistani woman who was wearing (modest) western clothing, was met with some disapproval:

TD: Uh huh ... Right – do you think – cos – Pakistani women – cos I'm a Pakistani – do you think the *way I am* does that – bother you? ... or like – do you think I'm different to the Pakistani women *you* know
Naseem: You are –
Sham: You – you wouldn't get Pakistani women dressing like *that* round our area

(Lowtown School, TD)

As will be further detailed below, the boys' attempted regulation of women's clothing, appearance and sexuality can be interpreted as a process relating to the 'protection of femininity' (Wetherell 1993). The boys claimed the authority, and justified their privilege, to direct and constrain girls' behaviours through the notion of protecting honour, culture and tradition. As indicated in the extract featuring Gufter and Imran above, the boys also drew on notions of change and tradition to argue for the need to maintain (and increase) their powers of surveillance because girls are getting worse and turning into the 'modernized type'. These concerns were further heightened in relation to issues of sexuality.

Sexuality

Issues of clothing and dress were closely linked to the regulation of girls' (hetero)sexuality. In particular, boys indicated that they engaged in a careful patrolling and surveillance of their female peers' (potential) relationships with boys. Across the groups, there were various accounts detailing the retribution and violence that would be doled out to any of their sisters should they ever be found to have boyfriends or to have run off with a man. For example, boys talked about how, if one of their sisters were ever found to have a boyfriend, they would be prepared to beat up this man, particularly if he was white, in which case a few boys suggested they would 'break his legs'. The prospect of a sister marrying a white man proved more problematic, since the man would then be a relative (and it was generally agreed that the religious conversion of the man to Islam should, theoretically, make the situation 'OK'). But within the scenario of a sister running away with a white man, boys suggested they would 'go and find him and chop him up'. This imagining became progressively more elaborate and fantastical, as boys drew on popular mafia images of retribution to compete with one another for verbal one-upmanship ('I'll get a butcher's knife and chop him up into little pieces and that ... and I'll send every piece to his relatives and that', Abdul).

Masculinity was thus defined through the protection of femininity, and through the operation of moral 'double standards', in which what is forbidden for women is acceptable for men, a situation described as 'it's good for us, innit? We're lads'. Several boys admitted to having white girlfriends themselves, which they justified as also part of the protection of Muslim femininity:

LA: How would you feel if you your sisters were going out with ... going out with boys?
Jamil: Beat 'em up!
Gufter: We'd beat them up!
LA: Beat up the boy?
Jamil: The boy!
Gufter: The boy!
LA: The boy ... what if your sister *wanted* to go out with him?

Gufter:	Hhh, she ain't got no choice
LA:	Is that, would that be like –
Imran:	But I ain't going out with an Asian though!
LA:	You aren't? You going out with a white girl? [Imran: nods] Do lots of Asian boys go out with white girls?
Gufter:	Yeah
Imran:	Yeah
LA:	What do you think about that?
Gufter:	Well I – I … its better than going out with … uh *Asian* girl – they they *know* that they're not supposed to do that. Whereas uh *whites* … its like they believe their own religion … whereas the Asians they know that their religion is Islam and they know they're not supposed to do it … so it's … it's better than going out with Asians
	(Lowtown School, LA)

These gendered double standards were justified through the discourse of 'reputation', with the argument being made that girls' behaviours reflect upon family reputations, whereas boys' do not. Thus the boys claimed that by going out with white girls, they were actually respecting the reputations of Muslim girls and their families.

LA:	Do people talk about … girls and boys doing things like that differently? … like if your parents knew that you were…
Gufter:	It's actually *worse* for a girl … cos that's what they say … if a girl … does summit like that it puts a bad reputation on your family
Sarfraz:	They are *engaged* straight away don't they?!
Imran:	Send 'em back home!
Gufter:	Half of them run away … half of them run away from home … whereas if it's just a boy … they just beat up the boy and that's it and say you know … don't do that
	(Lowtown School, LA)

Thus it was suggested that Asian and Muslim women who attempted to pursue pre-marital relationships with men would be labelled 'slappers', and would bring shame on their families. In particular, as suggested by Sham in the extract below, boys' concerns over their sisters' behaviours were intricately bound up with their own personal reputations among male peers.

TD:	Now – they've got used to it … they can't – they can't really do anything about it – but yeah – I live with … a group of girls – there're four of us who live in – who share a house [Sham: yeah] in London … but it *was* a … big deal! [Sham: yeah] I'm the only

one that has ... out of my community [Sham: oh right] like – yeah – I don't know ... would that bother you? If-if your sisters did that [lived away from home] if they were like me? [pause] Would – would you have less respect for them?

Sham: I don't want to be offending, but yeah! [TD: yeah?] Yeah!

TD: I mean does that change the way you view me?

Sham: No! No – cos – you're not my *sister* – so! hhhh! You know – you know ... I'm not bothered what you do! [TD: yeah] so ... but ... I don't know with my sister – like ... *you* do this – I won't get caught for it! People will say oh! Look at her! Its *your* fault – but if my *sister* did it – people would say – oh! you didn't realize – [N: yeah] you this and that! ... really ... its like ... we *say* we understand now – like you're doing all this, but ... even if like say – *his* sister ... ran off – we'd still call him. Even though we know what it's like nowadays – we'd still say – your sister's this – your sister's that – even though we know that ... it's ... I don't know – *unfair* for girls not to be ... I don't know – it's just the way we've been brought up.

(Lowtown School, TD)

Sham acknowledges that this relationship is not grounded upon logic, or 'fairness', nor is it mediated by close personal understandings and friendships ('even if like say – *his* sister ... ran off – we'd still call him. Even though we know what it's like nowadays'). Rather, his explanation evades personal responsibility for the reproduction of gender inequalities, and reifies differential gender relations within 'culture' and 'tradition' ('it's just the way we've been brought up'). Consequently, while Sham acknowledged that their double standards might not be 'fair', he used a two-handed rhetorical technique ('it's not fair, *but* ...') (Van Dijk 1984; Billig *et al.* 1988) to claim this as a defining feature of traditional Asian masculinity ('It's like all the lads do it, all the Asian lads do it all the time so ... nobody says anything'). These can be read as part of what Reynolds (1997) has termed boys' symbolic sexual performances.

'Girls are out of control'

The boys' attempts to tightly define and control their female peers' behaviours did not necessarily reflect their everyday interactions and experiences with Muslim girls. Rather, despite their assertions of male privilege and power in relation to girls, the boys also bemoaned a common concern that girls are 'out of control', exemplified by girls answering back and resisting the boys. 'But these days girls are getting out of control, aren't they? Swearing back at us and everything. And we can't say nowt, they're *girls*! We can't hit 'em or nothing, can we? But then you wish that they were boys so you can punch them' (Yasser, Eastfield School, TD). Thus the boys constructed locally hegemonic masculine identities which they set in opposition to an idealized notion of passive, quiet, subservient Muslim femininity. However, they then faced the difficulty of reconciling these identities with their actual everyday experiences of loud, boisterous Muslim girls, who spent school break times 'screaming' and making noise. These experiences were perplexing to the boys, because they were not open to the methods of control and assertion of dominance (in other words, fighting) that they commonly used in relation to other boys. Boys at Hightown School attempted to account for this situation by positioning these 'loud' Muslim girls outside the boundaries of normal femininity, describing them as 'mental' and 'un-Islamic'.

TD: Mmm – do you think umm . . . do you think they'll all go to Uni – do you think they'll all be educated?

Fazaan: I've no –

Abdul: No- no- they're mental! [speaker unidentified: No]

TD: They're mental? hh!

Deepak: All these Asian girls – what they do –

Abdul: They just go after boys!

Deepak: Go after boy, and they laugh so loud, yeah [Abdul: Yeah] you can hear them all down corridor!

Abdul: They just piss you off, man –

Fazaan: They follow you all the time!

Abdul: Yeah – they don't follow the Islamic path – they they follow –

TD: They're foll- what they following?

Abdul: The wrong path

TD: OK . . . Umm –

Fazaan: They gonna be struck down

Abdul: They used to be straight, all the Indian girls and that – but they get messed up now

TD: How – how are they messed up?

Abdul: Just

Gulfraz: From going out with boys and that

TD: You don't think that's right?

Abdul: Just – Islam say –

Deepak: Boys coming in our school – taking them in their car, taking them – 'oh yeah, cool yeah' and that

TD: Why do you think that's –

Abdul: [inaudible] they get [inaudible] whatever else could happen to them, yeah, and . . . pregnant some of them, then they go home and [inaudible] and our parents are like – [all talk over each other] girl from Sri Lanka and that [other boys interject] pregnant or summit, then they're just gonna go home and that . . .

and they won't be able to tell their parents and that, and they'll
be too scared of losing them, and that'll all that'll happen –
though, th- that's what the lads want and that's it

TD: Do you want that?

Fazaan: Th – the girls want it – I

Abdul: I-I got some respect, man – if I had err

TD: If you had one? hhh What about the rest of you? ... Cos you all
say, that that's what other boys want ... but you're all boys – ?

Abdul: Uh-if-if the girl respects – you know, respects you, you respect
her back – if she doesn't ... then don't respect her back.

(Hightown School, TD)

The boys explained this 'mental', 'uncontrolled' behaviour as caused by
girls going out with (other) boys. They therefore suggested that 'other' boys
are to blame for the malaise afflicting 'their' Muslim girls, and this notion
of masculine territoriality and propriety of Muslim femininity is illustrated
by Deepak's outrage against the boys who 'com[e] in our school, taking
them in their car'. The boys' talk contained hints that the source of the
'problem' is the girls' interest in 'other' boys (namely those with more status
and social capital, such as older boys with cars). This situation threatens
these boys' status/power because it denies them the opportunity to exercise
the protection of femininity.

In comparison to their images of 'mental' British Muslim girls, the boys
constructed an idealized notion of 'traditional' women from Bangladesh
who, it was assumed, had not been influenced by western liberal values and
would not resist or challenge the boys' authority:

Imran: They say that girls from Bangladesh right ... are or from
another country ... they got a better personality ... they [take]
care of you and everything but ... girls from this country –

Gufter: They've got a higher status, that's why ... cos like if you say
something wrong to them they say something like 'we've got
rights *as well!*' [Imran: yeah] And we're *divorcing* you, like that
... so you just gonna get married to someone ... another
country

(Lowtown School, LA)

Summary

This chapter has looked at the ways in which boys' constructions of
racialized identities are integral to their production of patriarchal identities.
I have suggested that young men's constructions of masculinity are cross-
cut by themes of power and are underpinned by discourses of 'natural'

biological gender differences. The boys constructed 'locally' hegemonic masculine identities by associating Muslim masculinity with power, privilege, 'being the boss', hardness and hyper-heterosexuality. They also drew on specific racialized/religious discourses through which they constructed themselves as active free agents who were responsible for controlling Muslim girls. Masculinity was associated with the world of work and paid employment, with the boys suggesting that Muslim masculinity was defined by the duty of guarding and protecting Muslim women, a practice which they justified using discourses of 'culture' and tradition. These qualities of masculinity were positioned in opposition to an idealized notion of femininity, which was portrayed as passive, of lower status, emotional, and restricted to the domestic sphere. However, these constructions were located within the realm of fiction and fantasy, and were not born out by the boys' everyday experiences of Muslim femininity.

Notes

1 In addition to the two participating boys' photographs, some of the Muslim girls also included photographs of boys playing football in the playground within their diaries.
2 Although not all white girls refused to date Asian boys, indeed as detailed later in the chapter, a couple of the other boys in the study talked about their white girlfriends.
3 A leotard-style top, popular in the early–mid-1990s

chapter five

Identities out of school: home, leisure and family

Overview

A main tenet of the theoretical rationale underpinning this chapter is that issues of masculinity and schooling do not exist in a vacuum, that is to say, they can never be isolated from the wider social world. So, in order to understand boys' constructions of Muslim masculine identities within school, it is useful to consider the wider social and familial context in which these identities are grounded. There is also a more practical reason for the inclusion of this chapter: during the course of my research a number of teachers said to me that they were very interested in finding out more about the out of school lives of their Muslim pupils. As one teacher put it, 'I'd just love to know what they *do* at home'. Of course, this chapter does not set out to directly address this request by providing an objective window onto, or depiction of, the out of school lives of Muslim pupils, not least because, as proposed earlier, there can be no singular truth or unitary experience to uncover. Instead, the chapter draws on data from discussion groups and photographic diaries to examine the complex ways in which young Muslim men drew on themes of leisure (music, film, going out), culture and family within their constructions of identities outside of school. The aim of this approach is thus to provide teachers and researchers with holistic, egalitarian/feminist insights and ways of understanding pupils in the classroom.

Within the discussion groups, we asked the boys questions about their home lives and what they did after school hours. These broad topic areas included various prompts to elicit their views and experiences of family and sibling relations, leisure activities and religious and cultural practices. Issues of home, leisure, friends and family life were not, however, neatly sectioned off or discussed in isolation; they were also raised by the boys in relation to other discussion topics, such as 'racism', 'gender' and 'ethnicity'.

The broader PhD study, on which this book draws, included a photographic diaries exercise, in which pupils were invited to document 'A day in my life'. As detailed elsewhere, nine Muslim girls and two Muslim boys (Samad and Youssef) took part in this strand of the research. It was interesting to note that the majority of the girls' diaries focused on the school day (Archer 1998, 2000) whereas the two Muslim boys' photographic diaries, and in Samad's case overwhelmingly, focused on the boys' after school experiences. Descriptions of the content of these boys' photographic diaries are used to illustrate some of the themes within this chapter.[1]

As will be demonstrated, the young men's discursive and visual data can be read as opposing and resisting popular assumptions that Asian/Muslim pupils experience (culture/identity) conflict between the worlds of home and school. The chapter explores how British Asian Muslim young men *themselves* experience and portray these different worlds, focusing on the interplay between themes of gender, 'culture' and masculinity. The chapter begins by setting out the ways in which boys constructed the after school activities that they engaged in away from the home and family (namely friends and leisure activities). This is followed by a consideration of boys' constructions of 'home' identities (those revolving around family and siblings).

'Hanging out' after school

There was a reasonable level of consistency between most boys' accounts of their after school lives and activities. They talked about hanging around with their friends, playing football, going shopping, watching TV and listening to music. Some boys also talked about their engagement in religious activities, such as praying/reading *namaaz* and going to mosque after school. A typical description of a boy's after school activities might include coming home (maybe via the shops in town), getting changed, watching TV, eating, then going out (possibly to the Mosque first) and meeting friends to play sports and/or 'just hang around or play football, something like that' (Naseem). Only Ali mentioned working, but he also talked about just hanging around 'nowhere in particular'.

LA: What do you do, like in the evenings, afternoon, umm, like after school and at weekends?
Ali: Uhh, work.
LA: Work? What about you?
Mushtak: Go out! Hhh!
Rakim: Go out!
LA: Where do you go?

```
Mushtak:   Relatives
LA:        Sorry?
Mushtak:   To see my – to see our relatives
Ali:       Or uh go out for a doss!
LA:        Do you hang around, or err, go anywhere in particular? Or?
Ali:       No. Nowhere in particular, just around.
```
(Hightown School, LA)

Typical weekends were described as combining a trip to town with seeing family:

```
LA:        So um ... what sorts of things do you do? Here in Mill Town?
           Like after school and that?
Imran:     Mainly sports stuff, innit? ... Cos most of us go footie ... and
           like boxing ... that's it ... we just hang out
Jamil:     Most of people [inaudible] we play snooker [inaudible]
Imran:     Hang round with mates
LA:        Hang around? ... What do you do at weekends? Do you do
           sports as well then or?
Gufter:    yeah
LA:        What ... do you go out?
Sarfraz:   At the weekend on Saturday we go into town ... and then come
           back ... you know?
Jamil:     We have a good time and sometimes go to my friend's house and
           on Sundays we go to our gran
```
(Lowtown School, LA)

Similar themes were evident within Samad and Youssef's photographic diaries. For example, Samad included photographs of himself going shopping in town (which he captioned 'Going in to shop' and 'went to Granadas') and Youssef took photographs of his friends walking back from school ('my friends woking home' [sic]) and of himself 'hanging about' in a street near his home ('me standing outside my hous neare a shop' [sic]). Samad also included images of himself and his friends smoking together in small groups round the back of the school (captioned, 'Smokeing' [sic] and 'having a fag with my mates outside school').

Throughout their accounts, Muslim boys represented their out of school identities as characterized by being active and 'outdoors', spending time in public spaces (local streets, parks and the town centre). The boys framed these identities within a broader 'gender binary' (Davies 1989) in which they constructed Muslim femininity as passive and located (outside of school) within the domestic sphere. As detailed in Chapter 4, for example, the boys made numerous assertions that Muslim girls characteristically stay indoors and must do all the housework. This is not to say that the boys spent all of their after school time outside the home. Indeed, as suggested by the photographic diaries and discussion group extracts later in this chapter, home was an important site within boys' identity constructions. However, boys drew on established patriarchal discourses to construct popular masculinity as a highly visible, public and active identity. For example, descriptions of their lifestyles were characterized by playing football, spending time with (male) friends, 'hanging around' and (but only for some boys) smoking.

It has been noted by other writers that Asian boys' public visibility (and their presence on the street) is linked with a negative construction of them within the public imagination. For example, Alexander (2000) writes about how public fears of young Muslim masculinity are fused with 'the physical presence of young men on the imaginary landscape of the city' (2000: 229). The boys in my study were similarly visible on the streets (albeit in particular areas) of the town, and their 'hanging about' in groups of male friends would no doubt be similarly negatively interpreted by some of the white Mill Town residents.

Within the popular British imagination, links have been made between the visible street presence of minority ethnic youths and fear of gangs, crime and riots (for example, reporting of the riots in the northern towns of Oldham, Burnley and Bradford in the summer of 2001). The increased 'hyper-visibility' of young Muslim men in the mass media reflects the intensifying of new moral panics and fears about the 'underclass', 'fundamentalists' and the (Asian) 'gang' (Alexander 2000: 229). Certainly some of the boys in this study did promote an image of the 'dangerous', 'gangster-ridden' streets of Mill Town (as detailed in Chapter 3), but these notions of danger were not raised when they talked about their everyday after school lives.

In contrast to popular public fears, the young men's discussion group accounts and the two boys' photographs of their everyday, out of school lives were remarkably mundane. This comment is not meant to be read negatively, because the 'mundane', the everyday and the popular are important theoretical sites for accessing the lived realities of marginalized young people. In other words, an analysis of people's subjective experiences and everyday realities can provide alternative forms of knowledge that might represent the Other as the subject, rather than the object, of knowledge. However, sensationalized fears about Muslim young men (in which they are positioned as social and educational problems) have to date hidden the (small amount of) research that has been done on the 'mundane', everyday identities and experiences of Muslim boys.

The highly visible public presence of young Muslim men on the streets of Mill Town should also be understood within the context of social class. The boys all lived in the overwhelmingly Asian, working class areas of the town. These areas contained tightly packed streets of Victorian terraced housing with few gardens or open green spaces. Almost every boy talked about having a number of siblings with whom they shared a bedroom. These descriptions were reinforced within the boys' (and girls') photographic diaries, with many images suggesting that pupils shared beds, as well as rooms, with siblings. Boys were thus more likely to meet their friends in streets and public places, which enabled them to have space and privacy. Issues of 'race' and gender also structured the boys' experiences (and constructions) of public spaces. For example, they described their local areas as poor, crowded but also friendly and safe, in contrast to the centre of town and the white residential areas, which were described as 'racist'. The boys also described home as a primarily female space and 'outdoors' as a male area, which I would suggest may also be interpreted as part of their attempts to claim separate gendered spaces. Indeed, themes of territoriality, space and 'belonging' are often key features within the construction of masculine identities (see Westwood 1990; Connolly and Neill 2001; Archer and Yamshita 2003b) and will be considered further in the following chapter on racism.

In practice, however, the boys' inhabitation of public spaces was not exclusive and, of course, girls were not solely restricted to the home and domestic sphere. As the following extract illustrates, occupation of these spaces was not clear-cut and some of the boys worried that girls could challenge them and 'show them up' within public spaces. Nazir and his friends, for example, talked about being embarrassed by an Asian girl from his class at school who spoke to him in front of his family while they were out shopping on a Saturday.

Nazir: Hhh! one that I *really* hate is [when] every time you're in town with your parents or something she always comes at you [saying] '*HI*' *hhh*, Innit! ... urghh!
NS: Oh no! ... so, if you're with your mum and dad like, she just says ... [Nazir: yeah!] and you think 'oh! not in front of mum and dad, *please*'?
Nazir: And she's an *Asian* as well!
Majid: She should *understand*!! hhh!
NS: Yeah
Nazir: I was walking with my mum in town yesterday ... she come up to me and my mum goes 'is that *her*?' [Nessa: laughs] I go 'I dunno! I never seen her in my *life*!' She goes 'yeah yeah' ... But she's in our class so ... that really *bugs*!
(Westfield School, NS)

The above example thus illustrates how some girls might challenge, and transgress, the boys' imagined public–private sphere gender boundaries.

Identity, music and film

Within the discussion groups the boys talked about the types of music that they listened to in their leisure time. As I have written elsewhere (Archer and Yamashita 2003b), these musical preferences are often closely tied to young people's constructions of multi-ethnic, multi-racial gender identities:

> The use of popular music as a site for the examination of multicultural and cultural entanglements is not new (e.g. Hebdige 1996; Gilroy 1991). For example, Hebdige has pointed to the role of entangled black musical styles, such as reggae, in creating 'a diasporan identity among the black urban dispossessed' (Hebdige 1996: 138). Gilroy (1991) has also written of the importance of processes such as 'sampling', 'remixing' and 'constant repetition' (versioning) within black diasporan music and how they can operate as counter-hegemonic discourses
>
> (Archer and Yamashita 2003b)

As discussed in earlier chapters, the Muslim boys' masculine identities can be understood to be 'culturally entangled' (Hesse 2000) and these entangled identities can be read within the boys' taking up, and performance of, 'style'. In other words, identities and cultural styles are not distinct, homogenously bounded entities, rather they slip and transgress across and between ethnic, racial and cultural discourses. Identities and styles are fluid and complex phenomena that stretch across different social spheres. Educational identities are thus also intertwined with, and located within, broader cultural and popular discourses of masculinity, 'race', class, identity and style (see also Ball *et al.* 2000).

Various writers have drawn attention to the rise of 'new' and 'hybrid' second generation Asian ethnicities, which they regard as transgressing previous ethnic boundaries and blending together aspects of different cultures. It has been suggested that such identities are exemplified by recent musical forms which create new cultural spaces, spanning – and drawing influence from – diverse ethnic groups, styles and traditions. As Hebdige suggests, 'as rhythms, melodies, and harmonies are borrowed, worked with, quoted, and returned to the airwaves, new connections are made, new "communites" made possible both within and beyond the confines of race and nation' (Hebdige 1996: 138). These processes are illustrated within new waves of Bhangra music (and indeed in a range of other hybridized, eclectic combined musical forms) that sample traditional classical Asian beats, black US rap, Caribbean dub and reggae, and combine these influences with British regional accents and vocals (for example the band Asian Dub Foundation). Claire Alexander extensively cites the work of Bannerjea (2000) and Sharma *et al.* (1996), both of whom outline new 'hybridized' cultural forms of resistance among young British Asians. As these writers point out, these forms do not exist in isolation, and notions of the 'Asian underground' have filtered back into broader youth culture (for example, the recent popular craze for wearing *bindi*; Madonna's appropriation of Asian style in her *Frozen* video).

Within cultural studies, the popularity of Bhangra music has been linked with new formations of second generation ethnic identities. For example, Hebdige (1996) points towards a fusion of Indian and Pakistani folk forms with western popular music, which he terms 'Indi pop' (encapsulated by the commercial sounds of Apache Indian, and more recently the critically acclaimed band Cornershop). He suggests this represents how:

> a novel British-Asian (more accurately, British-South Asian) cultural identity has begun to form and find its voice – an identity uniquely adapted to local conditions, attuned to the diverse, often conflicting experiences of parents who emigrated ... and their children born and brought up in Britain.
>
> (Hebdige 1996: 139)

Hebdige suggests that the identities/new musical forms engage with intra-Asian differences, in addition to being formed relationally against western identities:

> Bangra and Indi pop, the vibrant trademarks of a growing number of second-generation British Asians, are played across the gaps and tensions, not just between the 'home' and the 'host culture' ... not just between two cultures ... but between many *different* South Asian cultures, between the multiple boundaries which for centuries have marked off different religions, castes, ethnic traditions within a 'community' which appears homogenous only when viewed from the outside.
>
> (Hebdige 1996: 139)

Interestingly, however, the boys in this study distanced themselves from Bhangra and related forms of Asian music: they did not value these forms of music as the 'new Asian cool'. It is possible that Hebdige was describing a scene more particular to the global city/metropolitan experience and a slightly older age group, but in the everyday lives of the boys in this study, 'Asian music' was resisted as 'uncool' and was widely described as being 'for girls'. Across all the schools, boys echoed Abdul's (Hightown School) sentiment that 'It's all crap, I've never listened to Indian music, I hate it':

TD: I mean, do you listen to Indian music?
Sham: I don't, no. People *call* you when you listen to it [N: yeah, yeah] cos like
Naseem: Like all the Asian girls, all the Asian girls like they have some

Indian songs and like are always talking like Indian films, the lot like, all that

(Lowtown School, TD)

LA: Do you like Indian music or just –
Kabir: No I don't like it
Rahan: No
Wajit: It's English music, English rap
Rahan: When my sister got it full blast, the girls, some, they, they listen to Hindi shit . . .

(Westfield School, LA)

LA: Do you like Bhangra and Indian music and that?
Gufter: No! ha ha ha! *You* do! ha ha!
LA: Why do you like it – what do you like about it?
Jamil: Dunno – We just put it on like . . . and listen to it most of the time – like listening to it it's good
LA: Why don't you lot like it?
Imran: I don't understand it! Its like errrrr errrr!! [mock wailing] [laughter]

(Lowtown School, LA)

Only a couple of boys said they liked 'Indian' music (used as generic term for music from across Asia) and one or two Asian popular musicians were identified as being 'good', in particular the artist Bally Sagoo (who creates 'cross-over' fusion, sampling Bhangra, Bollywood hits and western dance music). Overall though, boys still emphasized that they preferred black, US R&B and soul music, and constructed cool/popular masculinities through these musical styles. Asian and 'Indian' music was resisted by the boys as unmanly, it was presented as something that Asian girls liked. As Haywood and Mac an Ghaill (1996) demonstrate, heterosexuality can be foregrounded and normalized within performances of working class masculinities through particular 'fashions' (such as the consumption of popular styles of clothing, nightclubs, cars, pubs and so on). The boys' constructions can be understood as reproducing and drawing on racist discourses that position Asian culture as effeminate, against which the boys aligned themselves with 'harder', more masculinized forms of black reggae/soul and swing music in order to assert more powerfully hegemonic masculinities.

LA: Err what sort of music do you like? Do you buy?
Gufter: Soul swing reggae
Jamil: Swing
Imran: Reggae!
Gufter: We don't like we don't like *indies* like Oasis and all that . . . sad

man ... it's like The Doors and something ... it's not good ...
we just like the swing – R Kelly [LA: yeah] like that
(Lowtown School, LA)

This strident dislike of Asian music and privileging of black music was
interesting given that there were very few African/Caribbean families living
in Mill Town, although this may have enabled the boys to adopt black
identities more easily through a lack of competition.

The boys' aligning of their tastes with 'English music, English rap' is
interesting as it highlights contradictions across their identity constructions.
It could be argued that within the spheres of popular culture and young
masculinities, the boys constructed 'fusion' identities, combining Englishness and blackness, through which they resisted (feminized) Indian/Asian
identities. These constructions contrast sharply with their resistance of
British/English national identities within their discussions of nationality and
'race' (Chapter 3).

The key to explaining these contradicting, shifting identifications might
lie with issues of gender and the boys' positioning of their identities relationally to girls. As argued previously, the boys asserted specifically *Muslim*
masculinities (and their associated political and mythic prestige/power)
when they talked about issues of 'race', ethnicity and nationality. Yet
within the sphere of popular youth identities, Muslim masculinities may not
carry the same cultural capital or prestige. Instead, the boys drew on
popular black identities and distanced themselves from feminized Asian
popular culture and identities. The association of Muslim girls with Asian
culture and music within the boys' talk can also be read in light of Anthias
and Yuval-Davis's (1992) analysis of dominant discourses in which women
are positioned as the representatives and bearers of 'culture'. But it is
interesting to note that whereas the boys asserted powerful Muslim masculinities within the political sphere (Chapter 3), and patriarchal 'Asian'
identities in relation to issues of gender (Chapter 4), these were both
resisted (in favour of black identities) within the sphere of 'youth culture'
(and racism, as detailed in Chapter 3). Thus different masculine identities
commanded different degrees of cultural currency across different contexts.
Consequently, within discourses of style and popular culture, boys asserted
themselves as superior to their female peers in terms of their taste and
'coolness'. Within such constructions, Muslim girls were positioned as
'culture-bound' (not 'modern') and unfashionable.

In contrast to the literature outlined earlier, the Muslim boys in this
research did not appear to buy into the 'new urban cool' of contemporary
hybridized Asian music and style. For these boys, Asian styles did not
appear to provide a unifying point through which to assert resistant diasporic identities. Instead, the boys' constructions of masculinity and femininity appeared to play a key role in the boys' resistance to Asian music,

and they reproduced a stereotypical association between 'masculine' black cultural styles and feminized Asian cultural styles.

The boys' apparent dislike of Asian music was closely linked to their views about Indian 'Bollywood' films. These are widely popular musical films that produce much of the current commercial (Indian) chart music. While Muslim girls reported listening to this music and watching Bollywood films, the boys were rather scathing about the whole industry.

Within their photographic diaries (see Archer 1998), several girls included photographs of themselves watching Hindi films on video to represent their daily lives. A couple of the girls included photographs of themselves reading Bollywood film magazines. Girls in the discussion groups also talked about watching Hindi films. These themes were not reflected in the two boys' photographic diaries nor in the male discussion groups. Boys suggested instead that they disliked these films, and claimed that only their parents and their sisters watched such films. Several boys were rather embarrassed to admit that they themselves did sometimes watch these films:

Rahan: My dad watches Hindi films but I'll just go upstairs
Kabir: I don't like Hindi films
(Westfield School, LA)

TD: Do you watch Indian films or not?
Sham: I used to as a kid but I wouldn't admit that, so shh! Keep it to ourselves!
(Lowtown School, TD)

TD: Do you watch Indian films?
Abdul: Nah no way, no. My parents watch them sometime and that
//
Fazaan: I don't like, I hate them, they're crap Indian films
(Lowtown School, TD)

Wajit went into considerable detail of his dislikes, listing the excessive running time of the films (often around three hours), the repetitious and unoriginal story lines, 'rubbish songs' and 'boring, no good backgrounds'. The main charge made by the majority of boys against Hindi films was 'it's not realistic'. In particular boys were derogative of the 'fake' violence and unrealistic stunts and fight scenes in Hindi films, which made the films 'boring' according to Mehmet. Kabir also complained that 'the stunts and that are so unreal', and that they contained too much fantasy action at the expense of realism. For example, boys complained that characters 'get up after being shot fifty times' and have unrealistic, superhuman powers, such as being able to leap an entire building in a single bound. In other words, the boys seemed to dislike the rather fantastical representations of masculinity within these films. One particular Bollywood film was singled out for praise by some of the boys because it was regarded as more realistic. Some boys also suggested that they enjoyed watching Pakistani dramas and comedies from the 1980s that had 'good jokes'. But generally across all the discussion groups Bollywood films were widely derided and contrasted with more realistic, 'hard' American films, which, as suggested in Chapter 3, were held up by some of the boys as a source of fashion and insight into racialized ('black'/gangster) styles and identities.

Home discourses: constructions of masculinity through 'family'

The other key site that boys talked about in relation to out of school activities and identities was, of course, the home and family. Issues around masculinity, home life and family relations have occupied contradictory spaces within dominant discourses concerning minority ethnic communities. For example, discourses of 'masculinity in crisis' have tended to focus primarily on relationships within school, to the neglect of family relations, when discussing young men's identities. In contrast, policy discourses have tended to link boys' social and educational 'problems' to poor or weak family relations, particularly in the case of minority ethnic, but especially Asian, boys.

As discussed in the introductory chapters, mainstream social psychological and positivistic sociological theories of ethnic minority identities have placed an emphasis on home life as an important index of ethnic *minority*, but not majority, group identity. As previously indicated, such theories have tended to reify and homogenize minority ethnic 'culture' and identity. Quantitative measures of 'ethnic identity' have identified factors such as practising 'cultural traditions' and speaking other languages at home as indicating the strength of second/third generation ethnic identities (for example, Phinney 1990). Positivistic sociological approaches to ethnicity have focused closely on themes of 'family', 'culture' and 'community', particularly when focusing on Asian groups. As Alexander notes, Asian groups 'are still largely framed and made known through traditional anthropological concepts such as "culture", and "community", [which are] themselves imagined primarily as bounded and static ideals' (Alexander 2000: 230). As Rattansi (1992) has argued, popular discourses continue to represent the Asian family as problematic and a source of inequalities, and I would agree that there is an urgent need for critical, non-pathologizing accounts of the role of family relationships within young Muslim men's identity constructions.

'Respect' and 'responsibility': the family and Muslim masculinity

Across the discussion groups, boys described their family lives in over-whelmingly positive terms, associating home life with warmth, love and security. For example, Sham described his feelings about home as entailing 'security . . . you feel safe when you're in your house, don't yer?' (Lowtown School, TD).

The boys universally invoked a discourse of the (heterosexual, normative) Muslim family (within their constructions of Muslim masculinity). As I have noted elsewhere in other research with Asian Muslim young men (Archer *et al.* 2001b), boys identified specific family duties and responsibilities (notably being the family 'breadwinner') as key defining features of 'being a Muslim man'. Boys in this study constructed boundaries between ethnic groups and collectivities by drawing upon competing discourses of 'family' and 'morality'. In particular, they portrayed Muslim and Asian families as strong, enduring and reciprocal, whereas they suggested that these characteristics were reversed within white families, which they described as 'unstable' due to their privileging of individualistic, autonomous forms of white masculinity (and more liberal notions of female sexuality). As Yasser put it,

> You like get the white ones don't you who call their mum and dad and swear at them . . . you know hate them, you know [Abdul: yeah, yeah] you know like the whites, you get the families and they're married and then they're divorced and then they have boyfriends, its funny, innit?
> (Yasser, Eastfield School, TD)

These extracts echo findings from research with other Muslim groups in Britain. For example, Nagel (2002) examined constructions of identity among Arab immigrants living in London and found that, for many respondents, Arab identity was understood through 'a particular world-view marked by attachment to family and high regard for hospitality: traits which interviewees intend[ed] to pass on to their children and to "preserve" in Britain' (Nagel 2002: 271). Nagel argues that the 'reality' (or not) of these traits is not an issue in question, because '[w]hat is material is that interviewees understand these traits as constituting an Arab community, and that imagined sense of commonality provides a basis for collective and individual identity' (Nagel 2002: 271). Notably, Nagel found that respondents constructed Arab identities relationally to other identities – but especially in relation to (contemporary constructions of) 'English' identities. In particular, as with the boys within my study, differences were drawn in terms of family relations, in which English culture was constructed negatively due to high rates of single parenthood and divorce. Yasser's extract can be read as resisting popular western interpretations of family values. His passage employs notions of family/community, combined with themes of heterosexuality, morality and the social un/acceptability and un/desirability of divorce, to distinguish Muslim families from white families in Britain.

Boys also differentiated Muslim families from white British families through the theme of (close) family ties and responsibilities. Their constructions can be read as opposing western middle class white ideals in which maturity and male adulthood is achieved through a process of increasing autonomy, individualism and separation from parents. The young men constructed a counter discourse of 'responsible' adult (Muslim) masculinity that was characterized by caring for one's parents in their old age. As Nazir (Westfield School) put it, 'when they're old like, you just wanna let them just relax while you do everything for them'. This responsibility was positioned as more important than just fulfilling expectations and traditions, it was integral to the boys' drawing of ethnic boundaries:

LA: Uh ... do you think there's stuff that I don't know about you because I'm white? That I *can't* ... that I don't understand about ... what sorts of things ... would you think that I – I don't understand

Gufter: Uh ... Asian ... it's like once your parents are old its like your responsibility to look after them ... whereas –

Imran: It's like you would give them most of the cash and you keep what you need

Gufter: Yeah whereas whites ... it's like ... we get the uh picture that ... once you're old you lead your own life

Imran: That's why ... they tell Asians to you know study more and get good jobs where there's good pay ... cos you gotta pay a *wife* ... and er –

Jamil: *Kids* and then your parents

                                                          (Lowtown School, LA)

Majid (Westfield School, NS) explained that his duty of care to his parents would also constitute a form of recognition of the hardships that working class migrant parents had endured for their children. In other words, boys were fully aware of the struggles and difficulties that their families had gone through in order that their children might grow up with 'a better chance in life'.

This theme of 'responsibility' to one's family was not only performed through physical acts of caring and economic provision. It was also extended to encompass a form of discursive protection, specifically defending the honour of the family. Thus boys talked passionately about how they take strong offence, and retaliate, if their family members are (even indirectly) insulted in any way. The boys suggested that this mode of being distinguished them from their white peers to such an extent that they personally could not understand why white boys did not act and respond similarly. As Jagdip said, they all found it strange that 'White people like don't care if you call [insult] their parents'. In this way, the boys delineated the boundaries of ethnic groupings through the limits of 'habitus' (Bourdieu 1986), the boundaries at which 'our' understandings are shared or contested.

The centrality of 'respect for family' as a defining feature of Muslim (masculine) identity has been echoed elsewhere. For example, Alexander (2000) provides an excellent deconstruction/exploration of the re/construction, transformation and transgression of boundaries of 'community' and 'family' in relation to Muslim young men. She identifies 'respect' as a key discourse through which young Bangladeshi men (who often perceived themselves in other ways as at the margins of the 'community') may become more centrally positioned within discourses of community. As Alexander explains, young men:

> placed themselves at its [the community's] heart in terms of responsibilities to, and protection of, its members. Respect was thus due to, and legitimated by, a network of family ties rooted locally and spanning beyond this territorial base to a wider imagined community
> (2000: 178)

All the young men in Alexander's study thought it was important to show respect to older people in the community. For example, as Humzah is reported as saying 'in our culture you have to respect the elders, that's the rule – it's like a *big* thing. Even if they're wrong you have to' (Alexander 2000: 178, original emphasis).

Boys also described how the practice of 'respect' (at home and within the wider community) is stratified hierarchically by age between siblings, and like the boys in Alexander's study, is linked to notions of 'reputation' and 'face'/honour (*izzat*). For example, Sham talked about being 'rowdier' at school than at home because there he has two younger sisters to consider. The boys also talked about being quieter at home when their fathers are present.

Gufter: Yeah ... cos at home its like ... you don't really *care* about anything ... its like ... um ... about your *reputation* ... it's it's just do whatever you want whereas in school you don't get in trouble with the teachers and you're more *aware* 'bout ...
Sarfraz: At at home it's *better* you can be sensible at home
(Lowtown School, LA)

The theme of respect also links the boys' family lives with their highly visible public lives outside of school because, as Alexander explains: 'The issue of respect ... is then inseparable from the question of visibility ... the definition of respect pivots crucially on a disjunction between doing and seeing (or being seen), or between forms of knowing' (Alexander 2000: 195).

Respect thus operates through a discourse of 'saving face', or honour. This requires that the boys negotiate the degree to which particular actions and behaviours are made openly 'known' and/or are tokenistically 'hidden'/ concealed (rendered 'unknown') from particular audiences, to whom flaunting the activity would cause offence and a lack of respect. For example, shame and dishonour derive not so much from the performance of a particular activity or behaviour (such as having a girlfriend, smoking or going to a nightclub) but from boys' lack of discretion and/or their inability to hide these activities from becoming public knowledge. The discourse of 'face' demands that boys engage in careful negotiations to avoid causing offence and shame or showing a lack of respect for one's family within wider circles of kin and community. Thus by limiting their 'bad' habits or behaviours to the public sphere (away from their immediate family), boys suggested that they were able to maintain 'face' and respect for their families. The issue of smoking was, however, differently interpreted by boys in both Alexander's and this study. For example, it was a matter of heated debate as to whether smoking itself was an acceptable behaviour, and, as detailed by Alexander, boys may disagree as to when, and in front of whom, it might be considered a violation of respect and 'face'.

Fathers, mothers and brothers

Family relations were important to the boys' lives and identities. Youssef's photographic diary emphasized home and family relations, as illustrated by his inclusion of numerous photographs of himself with his older sister babysitting younger relatives.

The subject of fathers/fatherhood was also frequently raised within the discussion groups. It was striking how all the boys associated their fathers with power. Fathers were described as commanding the boys' awe, respect and sometimes fear. These constructions revealed the strong emotional attachments exerted by hegemonic forms of masculinity upon the boys, echoing the Freudian suggestion that a 'fear–desire' couplet underlies the reproduction of masculinities. Boys also drew on popular gender binaries in order to differentiate between mothers (who were represented as nurturing emotional workers within the family) and fathers (who were represented as strong, judgemental economic providers). Boys talked about how their fathers policed their sons' performances of masculinity by setting examples, and boundaries, in relation to the constitution of acceptable Muslim masculinity. In this respect fathers were variously described as 'strict', 'scary' and 'powerful'. For example, Majid (Westfield School, TD) said he felt 'safer' talking to his mother than his father because of the paternal policing role:

Sham: Yeah cos you have to respect the dad and your mum but uh like you're more frightened of your dad
TD: Are you, are you scared of your dad?
All: Yeah!
TD: Why? Why are you scared of –
Jagdip: I-I can say things to my mum that I can't say to my dad, like things [Sham: you can joke] like my dad might joke around yeah but my dad might take seriously that my mum might not
                                                                    (Lowtown School, TD)

The boys thus described gender stereotypical family roles, suggesting that mothers perform emotional and nurturing roles (mums 'look after you and everything') whereas fathers are economic providers (dads 'are more hardworking'). In other words, the boys reproduced an established binary between soft, caring and domestic/private femininity and hard, instrumental, public masculinity.

The majority of boys asserted that they looked forward to becoming fathers themselves one day, but the path to adult masculinity was viewed with some trepidation. For example, the boys knew that fatherhood is characterized by being 'strict', but some suggested they were unsure of the boundaries and had sought clarification from their parents. For example, Yasser said he had asked his dad 'how strict is strict and like safe at the same time?' (Eastfield School, TD). In Yasser's case, his fears seemed to be grounded within wider concerns around violence between himself and his brothers, although he described this violence ambivalently, as both excessive (in the case of his older brother) or normal (with respect to his younger brother). Yasser said of his baby brother 'for his age he's really clever – he punches me in the face for no reason sometimes', yet he also talked about the problematic and painful nature of his older brother's violence towards himself.

Marriage

Within their discussions about home and family life, the boys also debated the topic of marriage. All the boys in the study discussed their identities within a heterosexual normative context, and all suggested that they expected to get married in the future. There was an overall expectation that their families would be involved to some extent in finding them a potential wife, a situation which was generally (and happily) accepted. Debate arose, however, regarding the potential form that this family involvement might take, and the boys (and the girls, see Archer 1998) universally resisted the notion of 'forced' marriage (marriage that entails no 'choice' of partner). Interestingly, boys were more likely to frame their rejection of such marriages within a 'macho', misogynistic discourse (that focused on the 'quality' of woman they might marry), rather than, for example, in moral terms. Thus Nazir (Westfield, NS) expressed his worry that his future wife 'could be a witch or anything, you don't know!' Similarly, Nazir said he was primarily concerned that, without personally knowing or meeting his potential wife, he might not be able to judge whether she is 'good' or a 'tart' who would 'go out with anyone'. While Mushtak and Rakim (Hightown, LA) were concerned that they would not want to marry a 'spotty' girl, and they worried that a girl's bad skin could be easily hidden in the photographs that they, and their families, would use to help choose a potential wife ('if you see a picture of her and then like you, she might be spotty or summat!'). Boys at Westfield School also joked about how they wanted their future wives to be a 'cherry' (virgin) and 'someone who massages me every night', qualities that might not be easily verified within the usual procedures for arranging marriages.

The Hightown School boys who spoke with Tamar stood out from the others in terms of their views on arranged marriages. They argued that the system of arranging marriages was not an Islamic practice, but was simply an Asian 'tradition'. They complained that teachers in particular misunderstood this distinction, and they thought that this misconception contributed to negative public views about Islam. As Abdul said of arranged marriage:

> that's not Islamic that's just stupid tradition that – but all the teachers think it's Islamic and that, so they be funny and that. But it's not, it's just tradition know what I mean? Th- ju- all part of the people in your neighbourhood, I mean it's tradition.

While Abdul and his friends suggested that they were happy to go along with this tradition, they justified their priorities differently from the other boys, stating that they just wanted to marry 'a nice Muslim girl, that's it'.

Despite these concerns, the boys were generally supportive of the system of arranged marriages, which they considered to 'work out better than normal ones' (Rakim). In this sense, the boys suggested that they were unperturbed by the prospect of having their marriages arranged for them, saying 'we have a laff over it'. They suggested, however, that the practice may be experienced somewhat differently by girls. For example, Sham thought that arranged marriage is 'hard' for girls because 'the girl has to go to the boy's house to live'. Muslim girls, however, voiced rather different views, and emphasized that they felt they retained agency and choice within the tradition of arranged marriage (Archer 1998).

Summary

This chapter has examined the boys' constructions of masculine identities outside of school, within the context of home, family and leisure activities because, I would argue, pupils' identities do not stop at the school gate, nor do they finish at the end of the school day. Attention was drawn to the gendered aspects of the boys' performances of identity within the 'out of school' contexts of home and leisure. Stuart Hall argues in favour of analysing 'the popular' as a relational sphere, as 'those forms and practices which are excluded from, and opposed to, the "valued", the canon, through the operation of symbolic practices of exclusion and closure' (Hall 1993b: 294). Accordingly, analysis within this chapter highlighted the ways in which the boys' constructions of their home and leisure identities challenge dominant assumptions about Muslim boys in a number of ways. I also attempted to demonstrate the ways in which 'popular' masculine identities and activities were contested and negotiated across different contexts, particularly in terms of the differential valency of 'Muslim', 'Asian' and 'black' masculinities within the 'popular' youth spheres of music and film. I have attempted in particular to show how the boys' descriptions of their lives outside of school ('hanging out' with friends, the music and films they watch, and refuse to watch), and their experiences of family relations (particularly constructions of fatherhood and marriage), are all vital aspects of their everyday, gendered, classed and racialized masculine identities.

Note

1 I have not reproduced the boys' actual photographs within this book in order to protect the anonymity of respondents, their families, school and friends, and because of the complex ethics and practicalities associated with securing the informed consent of all those who are represented within the photographs.

Part III

Linking identities and inequalities

chapter / **six**

Muslim boys and racism(s)

Overview

This chapter reviews the ways in which British Asian Muslim boys in this study talked about their experiences of racism and examines their views regarding the causes of – and solutions to – racism. I argue that the young men's accounts reflect a variety of 'racisms', differing in structure, content and lived experience. The chapter addresses both the boys' views on the causes of racism, their experiences of racism, and the implications for tackling racisms within schools. It is suggested that the boys understood racism as a predominantly masculinized phenomenon and their proposed 'solutions' to racism reflected different discourses of masculinity. The implications of the boys' answers to racism, namely retaliation with violence or 'ignoring it', are discussed in relation to the school and wider social context. The boys' views are located in the context of academic theorizations of racism and implications are raised with respect to potential educational initiatives aimed at tackling racism within schools.

Racism emerged as a major topic of concern across the discussion groups. In all but one of the groups, boys themselves raised the issue of racism before the interviewer had asked any direct questions about it. It was only in the discussion group that I conducted at Eastfield School that this did not happen (and it was notable that the boys in this group were generally quieter and less forthcoming). As the chapter will detail, on the whole, boys across the discussion groups described a variety of experiences of racism, which they perceived as occurring both within the local area and, more specifically, within the school context.

Racism and the local area

Boys across the groups described Mill Town as racially segregated into *'black'* and *'white'* residential areas. The majority of the boys lived in the predominantly Asian, 'black' areas of Mill Town, which they described as 'friendly' (Imtaz, Westfield School, NS) and comparatively safer than other areas of town because 'there's no racism cos it's all black ... and the odd white, there's no racism' (Javed). White areas of town were associated with racism and antagonism. All of their schools were located in white areas of the town and the boys all recounted experiences of everyday racism on their ways to and from school. This was reported irrespective of the social class of the white neighbourhood in question. For example, Hightown and Westfield schools were located on opposite sides of the town – Hightown School in one of the town's more affluent, middle class white suburbs and Westfield School in one of the poorer, working class white estates, yet boys at both schools encountered similar problems:

Abdul: An' town's pretty racist and that, but you'll meet er racists [someone interrupts] [saying] 'Paki bastard' and that
Gulfraz: This area where you're in now –
Abdul: This area –
Deepak: This area, at home-time you, you can't walk through the short-cut. Go around there and you gonna get K.O.'d, man
Abdul: Cos it's pretty racist round here, it's a pretty racist area
                                                       (Hightown School, TD)
LA: So have you lot experienced racism in Mill Town?
Rahan: Loads
LA: Loads? Like what sorts of things
Rahan: It's like everyday life
LA: Everyday?
Wajit: You get racism everywhere in Westfield
LA: Like when you walk down the street?
Wajit: It happens everywhere really
//
Rahan: School is mixed so its OK [inaudible] but outside school you get –
Wajit: Fights
Rahan: Fights everywhere
                                                       (Westfield School, LA)

Many boys talked about living in the 'friendly' and 'safe' Asian areas of town, but they also described their ongoing tensions with local white people. Some of the boys talked about how the areas in which they currently live had previously been predominantly 'white' areas, prior to the

growth and expansion of the Asian community. They recounted the difficulties that their families had experienced during these periods of transition,
although as Wajit suggested, these areas had 'settled down' since becoming
more 'mixed'. Majid and his family had also experienced hostility and
violence from white people in their local area:

NS: Do you like where you live?
Imtaz: Me? Yeah
Majid: I don't really like it
NS: You don't really like it? Why don't you like it?
Majid: Cos er I live where the ... white people are [NS: yeah] and
         they're really uhh ... you know they're racist [NS: yeah? they're
         racist to yer?] yeah that's why I don't like to bother
NS: How are they racist to you? What do they do?
Majid: Uh they do loads of things ... throwing eggs at our windows ...
         throwing rubbish in our garden
NS: Throwing what in your garden?
Majid: Rubbish
NS: Rubbish? [tuts]
Majid: And er my little children ... my little err ... [NS: yeah I know]
         brothers and little sister they always go out to play in the eve-
         nings and they got beat up – they start beating them
NS: Beating them? [Majid: yeah] *Really?*
Majid: Yeah ... they come home *crying* and ... and uh they – when the
         neighbours – the neighbours were good to us and told us don't
         worry about this it's going to be alright ... [NS: mmm] after-
         after a time it becomes alright ... but when you're new they-
         they become racist to you

                                                    (Westfield School, NS)

In the extract above, Majid re/produces a conceptualization of racism as
arising from white people's responses to newness, change and the arrival of
'unknown' Others in 'their' neighbourhoods. He suggests that racism
subsides and diminishes over time, as white families become used to their
new neighbours. This construction echoes social psychological theories of
prejudice and inter-group relations such as contact hypothesis (for example, Pettigrew 1971). These theories posit that negative views of other
groups are natural features of inter-group relations, and that these prejudices can be alleviated through contact between members and through
increased familiarity (albeit under particular conditions, see Brown (1995)
for a comprehensive overview of social psychological theories of prejudice).
The application of such theories in the context of racism has, however,
been criticized by feminists and discourse analytic theorists. For example,
critics claim that such theories imply a white norm, and, moreover, the

conceptualization of prejudice as an inevitable result of individual human cognitive processes, normalizes and excuses it as a 'universal human failing' (Wetherell and Potter 1992). Such a conceptualization absolves individuals (and systems) of their responsibility for tackling racism and glosses over the powerful exclusionary material effects of racism. Similarly, the conceptualization of racism as a cognitive, inter-personal prejudice reduces it to an issue of individual psychology, rather than being related to wider social conditions and inequalities.

The boys' constructions of their experiences of 'local' racism(s) also point towards the importance of notions of 'territory' and 'belonging' within racist discourses. These themes were evident not only in relation to accounts of white families' resistance to the arrival of Asian neighbours (as indicated by Majid above), but also more generally in the boys' descriptions of living in Mill Town, as illustrated below:

TD: What, what about your parents and family? Have they had any racism?

Yasser: A lot

Shabid: A lot

Yasser: Like the NF spotted them –

TD: Was there, was there a National Front, National Front thing here?

Yasser: Yeah a lot have been beaten down

Shabid: Yeah quite a lot of people from uh like … once my uncle got chased … and my other uncles came out … for back-up

Yasser: And most of Barnton[1] must have come outside, they all used to come round outside my dad' s-when my dad all finished praying in the Mosque – and they used to come – they all used to go chasing … grab 'em

Abdul: Cos they know – … that there's a part where there's more Asians … there's, there's no white person or anyone yeah to hassle yer –

Yasser: But that's why they used to come *down* there! The Asians … they want to like take over [Abdul: take over] *now* they won't come because … all the um … all our big brothers they all grown up and they older and there's too much of us, innit? [TD: yeah] like our fathers … they're used to … if they being racist they'd pick a fight

(Eastfield School, TD)

As Yasser and Abdul indicate, National Front supporters would periodically target the predominantly Asian area of town ('Barnton') in violent attacks. Yasser felt that the impetus for such racist attitudes among National Front supporters was the Asians 'taking over' parts of the town (as exemplified in Enoch Powell's 1970 speech about 'immigrant invasion'). Within this discourse, inter-group hostilities are linked to notions of taking and defending local territories, which are grounded within exclusionary notions of 'Britishness', in which 'Asians' are positioned as Other and 'not belonging' (see Gilroy 1991). The boys mapped the town through 'geographies' of racism in similar ways to the black boys in Westwood's (1990) study, who divided their local area into 'safe' and 'unsafe' locales. Within these locales, 'neighbourhood nationalisms' (Cohen 1988) are enacted, with conflicts arising over the defending or claiming of particular neighbourhoods against racialized others.

There is a close link between discourses of hegemonic masculinity and 'race' within the boys' accounts of racism. They framed racism within a specifically male context and suggested that racism (as embodied by 'racists') can be resisted through fighting and physical dominance and strength and numbers. They also suggested that male Muslim generations united to resist and retaliate against racist attacks. On one level these explanations might be read as hopeful (because they can create 'racist-free' geographical spaces), but the liberatory potential of such discourses is also strongly limited by their narrow conceptual framing.

I would suggest that the boys' examples of 'local' racism(s) were also inter-linked with broader racialized discourses. Sociologists have argued that the state is implicated in the generation and reinforcement of new racisms, which are reinforced and enacted through the myriad of daily appeals to concepts of nationalism, sovereignty and unity (Rattansi and Westwood 1994; Billig 1995). In other words, the western obsession with nationhood, and the moral privileging of 'us' as a nation above other forms of allegiance, can be seen to heighten disputes over who can, or cannot, 'belong'. The racism reported by Majid and the other boys can therefore be interpreted as deeply entrenched within wider discourses of differentialism. For example, Majid's description (of rubbish being thrown into his family's garden) echoes the Far Right discourses espoused by Derek Beakon[2] of the British National Party whose 'rhetoric appeals to a nationalism of Britishness and a territorialization which invites racist mobilization to return Britain to the British and cleanse the streets of 'rubbish' – that is, the Asian communities' (Rattansi 1995: 56).

Boys drew on and reproduced a number of fairly 'traditional' liberal discourses in their constructions of the underlying causes of racism. As illustrated in the extract below, Asian 'agency', and the refusal to passively accept racism, was identified as one of the contributing factors to the continuance of white racist attitudes (although the boys also emphasized and justified their resistance:

TD: Do you think it'll ever change? Do you think you'll ever be able to stop racism?

All:	No
TD:	Why, why do you think it'll never change?
Deepak:	It'll never change because they, the people that –
Gulfraz:	Like all the white people –
Abdul:	Call like 'Pakis' and that, and you know we, we're not gonna say oh, we're not gonna say 'yeah, yeah' you know that's [Deepak starts talking over] but if you say it back, you know, 'you white hhh'! [TD: yeah] and err –
Fazaan:	[inaudible]
TD:	Uh huh
Abdul:	And their parents, you know what I mean, they – at the end of the day, it's not their fault, it's this country. Their parents are like that, but genuinely, if they're not racist, if they're not, nor are their kids
Deepak:	If they learn them while they're little, but – yeah, they go 'you Paki's, you Paki's' – what's the cause of that? It's only a little kid, it's dad['s fault] innit? His parents, obviously

(Hightown School, TD)

The discourse detailed in the above extract implies that racism will continue as long as Asian people keep resisting and 'talking back'. This notion is highly problematic because it shifts the locus of responsibility onto Asian groups (as opposed to the white initiators of racist behaviours). Within this logic there is little room for counter-manoeuvre, because the assumed inevitability and intractability of inter-group hostility closes off potential opportunities for intervention or action.

I would suggest that the boys' accounts were also (albeit subconsciously) underpinned by social learning theory, which they drew on to explain the reproduction of racism across generations of white family members. Thus Abdul and Deepak drew on this discourse to explain the cultural reproduction of racism, saying that children learn racist attitudes from their parents. This notion underpins various multiculturalist approaches to racism, built from the assumption that children learn racist attitudes from their parents and/or wider society. Consequently multiculturalist educational interventions might attempt to lessen, or counteract, these learned attitudes. However, I would suggest that this conceptual framework can be criticized on a number of levels. For example, it employs an assumption that racism is essentialized and embodied within the 'predjudiced/racist individual'; racism is also assumed to comprise a relatively coherent cognitive set of attitudes and beliefs which can be transmitted, learned (and potentially unlearned). However, as I will discuss within the next section, racisms may not always be rational or coherent, nor are they simply reducible to 'attitudes' and beliefs.

Racisms in school

Across the groups, boys talked about experiences and instances of racism at school. Racism was overwhelmingly discussed within the context of white and Asian groups (the focus of this chapter), although in Lowtown School the issue of intra-Asian 'racism' was also raised.[3] In two of the schools the boys linked racism to physical bullying, suggesting that when they were younger it had been a greater problem, whereas now they felt better able to resist as they grew older and stronger. Yasser and Shabid (below) extended the social contact discourse to explain changes in social relations between themselves and white pupils.

Yasser: No ... em [we get] just a little [racism] but not in Year *Ten* not any more. No, like when we were all Year Sevens, we'd get bullied, all of us. We were all bullied, from whites as well [Abdul: yeah] that's *why* we was bullied, I was bullied from whites, a lot, but now like the whites are like our friends. We bully them back. They start, we start back. Like we have a laff with them now

Shabid: Yeah like some of my mates got bullied, called 'black bastard' and that by whites, by them, innit?

(Eastfield School, TD)

Yasser and Shabid suggested that through retaliation they had overcome racisms within school to the point where they are now 'friends' with white pupils and can 'have a laff'. A feminist reading of this construction would argue, however, that this 'solution' is only tenable within a wider discourse of hegemonic masculinity, because success is dependent upon having the strength to 'bully them back'. The implication is that 'weaker' boys and girls may have to endure racist bullying, as resistance only appears to be possible through taking up hegemonic masculinity. Indeed, the extract can be read in terms of the boys using the enactment of hegemonic masculinities to resist racist constructions of Asian masculinity as weak/effeminate.

Inter-related themes of status, pride and masculinity can be read within the following extract, in which Hightown boys talk about how they are made to feel subordinated and 'like dirt'. This account suggested that the boys were subjected to dehumanizing and degrading racist discourses that impacted upon their sense of self-esteem.

Fazaan: You can't – unless you come to the school – [if] you come new to the school ... everyone's going to pick on you – [unidentified speaker: It's like the, the racists – they all gang up outside]

TD: All, all of them, yeah? I mean, d-do you get ... involved?

Abdul: Yeah

Fazaan: Yeah
Deepak: Yeah
Gulfraz: You, you – we, we, we get all our friends in, we just get [inaudible]
Abdul: Yeah
TD: I mean, what does it make you feel? How does it make you feel, when that happens?
Gulfraz: It makes you feel small, err it's like, uhh they don't – they're higher than you and we're lower [TD: uh huh] they're h-higher and we're lower
Abdul: Treating us like dirt

(Hightown School, TD)

The specifically colour based and masculine context of Yasser and his friends' constructions of racism are also evident below:

Yasser: Its mostly *whites* though that would kick off you [Abdul: yeah] [Shabid: yeah] it's not like Chinese or some other Jews or summat, it's mostly whites who –
Shabid: It's like what *colour*, like black, white
Yasser: Like, see white and see black, they wanna fight, we wanna fight. It's a lot of thing like that happen
TD: Have there been any-any stuff with girls at school and racism? ... I mean what are the white girls and the Asian girls – ?
Yasser: Not many of them ... not as much as boys

(Eastfield School, TD)

In this example, the boys drew on 'differentialist' discourses, asserting the 'natural' colour difference between whites and Asians as being a source of conflict, but Tamar's questioning also revealed a tension across gender. While the boys framed racism as a predominantly male issue, this was not correlated by the girls (who recounted their experiences of racism from both male and female protagonists). For many of the boys, incidents of racism within school were tied to fighting and conflicts within an all-male context, in which struggles for local male power (and the desire to be the 'cock of the school') were conducted along racialized boundaries:

Yasser: Yeah that bastard was cut there, but I was the one who had to put the report down, I was kicked in my ribs. They started it for no reason, they were in my brother's year, we were about Year Eight [Shabid: eight, yeah], we were Year Eights and Prakash, who kicked a stone –
Shabid: It just missed him, just went through his legs
Yasser: Just went through his legs or summat, and err there was Year

Elevens – all massive, you should have seen the size of them! [Shabid: Yeah!] come up to wack us, one of them, he goes – started starting a fight with him, and we all said in our language, innit, 'punch him! punch him!' and he turned around and punched him – they all grab back, I started beating them up, I bashed Duncan, and you just kicked them, innit? Kali jumped in and he was kicked in the ribs and his head and then...

(Eastfield School, TD)

I suggest that the recounting of such incidents can be read as part of the process of 'doing boy' within these friendship groups. For example, tales of fights and bullying, and discussions about particular incidents, provided points of bonding and recognition between the boys, enabling collective boundaries to be drawn to delineate 'us' (Muslim boys) from 'them' (white boys). Frosh *et al.* (2002) similarly found that discussions about racism generated strong feelings of mutual interest and support among Asian boy respondents.

However, racism was not only constructed in physical, rationalistic and attitudinal terms. As the following extract illustrates, boys at Lowtown School talked about some of the more subtle, irrational and contradictory permutations of racism.

TD:	Do you change when you come to school?
All:	No
Sham:	Don't think so ... s-some people
Jagdip:	Cos usually we all go round together at home –
Sham:	It depends, some people are! Like some people are here ... and err, they talk to us like ... summit, it depends like you know? Cos there's a bit of racism, like I said, but not in school ... you know, when you go outside. You see they wouldn't talk to you, wouldn't if they were with their mates ... Like I mean white guy[s].
Said:	Like when they're here they're really quiet but like when they're with their friends, parents, they talk and all that
Sham:	Yeah, yeah hhh!
TD:	What about you? Are you like, I mean would you talk to them outside of school if you see them?
Sham:	Yeah [All: Yeah] We did, but they ignore us! And then they come in school and you know, they try and hide it, [we say] 'how come you didn't say hi?', [they say] 'oh, I didn't see ya'. But we *know*. It's really –
TD:	How does that make you feel?
Sham:	Not bad, I gu- its just *life*, it's, everyone has t'put up with things

TD: Do you all feel like that? Are you all not bothered? Or – or does it – does it bother you?

Sham: Someone is – I know someone I've met, if they do that, uhh he's very – so, you know. If they do that the next day as well then I say 'why did you do that?'. He says 'Cos I didn't see ya'. I go 'NO, you're racist, aren't you?'. So, innit.

(Lowtown School, TD)

In the above example, the boys described how white boys would be friendly with them at school, but would ignore them in public when they were with their friends and families. Sham suggested that he and his friends had, on occasion, challenged these white boys about this behaviour, and had been given the excuse 'I didn't see ya'. The events within this scenario can be read as illustrative of 'modern' racism, a subtle and barely discernible form of racism. These permutations of 'modern' racism have been interpreted in different ways by academic commentators. From the more positivistic angle, it has been suggested that 'modern racism' is characterized by 'increased social distance' and 'mild aversion' (Brown 1995), rather than through the display of overt racist views and behaviours. These changes are assumed to have arisen due to the influence of liberal values within contemporary society, and through conformity with public social norms which dissuade overt displays of 'traditional' racist views. From this perspective, modern racism might be understood as representing a positive movement away from more 'traditional' forms of racism.

I would agree, however, with Wetherell and Potter's (1992) critique of modern racism, namely that such discourses are not necessarily preferable to traditional forms of racism because 'new' racist discourses protect the status quo (and maintain social inequalities). These discourses gain their power from the assumption that changes in the form of racism represent a 'step in the right direction'. This assumption hinders the implementation of anti-racist actions and criticisms because society is already seen to be engaging in a process of change. Furthermore, as will be discussed in relation to institutional racisms, when racism 'goes underground' and becomes less explicit, it becomes more difficult to name, target and address.

Narrow definitions of modern racism as 'social aversion' also fail to take account of some of the more emotive, subtle and contradictory experiences of racism that are hinted at within the preceding interview extract. The complexity of discourses of racism is highlighted by the research of Billig and Cochrane (1984), who recount an instance in which a white girl, who expressed highly racist attitudes about black groups in the research interview, was later seen arm-in-arm with an Asian girl friend as she was leaving school. Work by Cohen (1989) also illustrates the importance of social context upon the expression of racist discourses: he found that white working class young people expressed varying views on issues of 'race' and racism within interviews depending upon the specific discursive contexts and issues under discussion. Back (1996) also draws attention to the contradictory emotional forces that can underpin racist discourses and identifications. He found that white working class boys expressed not only respect for black boys and black male styles (and indeed, attempted to imitate these styles) but also contempt. In other words, white boys upheld contradictory values as they admired and envied particular aspects of black masculinity but would also express racist views against black groups within other contexts.

The issue of what constitutes racism is also complex. Racist discourses are not always clearly identifiable at face value, as Wetherell and Potter (1992) explain in their analysis of white Pakeha (New Zealander) discourses of racism. Wetherell and Potter's research demonstrates how racist views can be couched within discourses of 'culture', liberalism and actual denials of prejudice, which sociologists such as Gilroy (1987) have termed the 'new racism'. For example, individuals may draw upon a variety of discursive techniques to position themselves as 'not racist' while asserting a view that reinforces, or supports, racial inequalities (typified by the phrase 'I'm not prejudiced, but …'). As will be discussed later in this chapter, racism(s) may also take many forms and can be enacted at the level of the individual, group, institution and society. Racism(s) are thus plural, dynamic and ever changing, and can shift and change in form, 'assuming different shapes and articulating different political relations' (Gilroy 1987: 43).

These issues raise a number of problems for schools with respect to tackling racism(s). Javid's suggestion that 'well there ain't really a lot of racism, not in school' gives a cause for both hope and for concern. In one sense, the boys' extracts represent the 'success' of liberalism within their schools, as white pupils do not, on the whole, engage in overt racist behaviours. From another perspective, however, the data highlight the inadequacy of 'traditional' popular conceptualizations of racism for engaging with inequalities. The complexity of the issue (namely how to engage with the multiple forms, modes and mutations of racism) thus entails a range of difficulties for educators. We want to be able to target diverse forms of racism and we want to ensure that the success of such strategies persists outside, as well as inside, the school gates.

The shifting, complex nature of racism was particularly evident within boys' constructions of racist teachers. For example, I interpreted the accounts of boys at Hightown School as representing an experiential, embodied and subtle form of teacher racism. As suggested by Deepak in the extract below, the boys did not experience teacher racisms as overt displays of particular attitudes or behaviours. Rather, he suggested that such racisms were experienced as a more subtle 'feeling', a tacit knowledge that the boys can read 'in their [teachers'] eyes':

TD: Do, do you think the teachers – are – racist here?
Fazaan: Yeah, I do –
Deepak: There's not [inaudible] other teachers here
TD: No – Not at all?
Fazaan: I, I reckon teachers are racist
Deepak: Teachers are racist – you can see it in their eyes, man
Fazaan: Like Miss L – people say she's racist as well

(Hightown School, TD)

Boys at Eastfield School also talked about teacher racism(s) as subtle, characterized, for example, by 'ignoring' or 'talking over' the boys:

TD: Yeah ... What are the teachers like generally here? ... Are they alright?
Yasser: Some are racist
TD: Are they? Have they said things to you? Like or have they just ... just done things that have made you think they're racist?
Yasser: Yeah
Shabid: Yeah
TD: What kind of things?
Yasser: They ignore you
TD: They ignore you?
Yasser: Or just talk over us ...

(Eastfield School, TD)

Boys tended to identify particular teachers as racist individuals on the basis of their interactions with them. But they also drew upon a notion of institutional racism, arguing that Asian pupils were collectively disadvantaged by particular school rules and conventions. In particular it was argued that such inequalities were reproduced within typical institutional responses to incidents of violence between pupils.

LA: Is the school strict about it, do they –
Rakim: They don't do anything about it, they just like – they let them off for two days, that's all, then they're like back in, back in.
LA: Why – why don't the school do anything?
Rakim: They can't do anything, can they? Know what I mean?
Mushtak: Probably give the school a bad reputation, then they won't get many pupils ... or
LA: Do you think the teachers *should* do something about it?
Mushtak: Yeah! chuck them out [LA: chuck them out?] Yeah.

(Hightown School, LA)

The perception was voiced, particularly by boys at Hightown School, that the school was unwilling to tackle incidents of racism and would persistently favour white boys, due to its policy of non-intervention, and because issues of pupil violence were rarely treated as issues of racism. Thus the Muslim boys complained that *they* were unfairly punished by the school, rather than white boys, following incidents of 'fighting back' against racism from white pupils. In other words, some boys suggested that an institutional position of 'not getting involved' or 'neutrality' (for example, treating all incidences of fighting as the same irrespective of context) constituted a form of racism, because it resulted in white boys escaping punishment.

TD: D- do you think you can change it [racism]?
Abdul: Nah – can't do anything about it, if you do anything about it, say anything about it, stand up for yourself – they say you're out – get thrown out
TD: Get thrown out?
Abdul: – Stand up for yourself – you're out...

(Hightown School, TD)

The boys' strategy of 'dealing' with racism by 'fighting back' created a tension in relation to the school rules. Deepak described how teachers attempted to discourage fighting between black and white boys by appealing to the notion of upholding the school's 'reputation' ('Like, an' at lunchtime, if they [teachers] see, they say don't give our school a bad attitude! A bad thingy- whatever!'). From the boys' point of view, however, this situation rendered them helpless (or emasculated) victims of racism and brought them (unwillingly) into conflict with the school rules and institutional ethos. I suggest that the following extract illustrates some of these feelings of helplessness as Deepak suggests that the system is stacked in favour of 'the white guy' and against 'the black lad':

TD: Um, at school – I mean, do you get a lot of racism at school? [All: yeah, racism? – yeah, yeah]
Gulfraz: Yeah, too much
Deepak: You know we walk around, we walk around school
Gulfraz: And they call you names
Deepak: Last week, [in] the, the holidays, this lad, he called me and that, and he was with these two white girls, and they come in and go – sss! I'm afraid I can't swear – uhhh
TD: No, you can swear if you want, I don't care!
Deepak: Uhh they go 'What you doing?' and he turned to the girls and, and the-the lad was ... like knocking out totally, I mean – because he got too much racist. I don't wanna – I, if I'd wanna,

I'd have broke his nose and that, but he was with his mates. If – he got too much mates then that's why I didn't do nothing – [but] if I'd had wanna, I'd have killed him

Gulfraz: [inaudible] if they say anything, then you can just cane them

TD: Yeah

Deepak: But then again if you do do summit, and they get a beating, then you get the blame for it – even if they started it – nah – jus' can't beat the white guy – the white guy is straight, the black lad's messed up.

//

Deepak: There was this girl, and she – there was there was this white lad getting – really racist, just every time you walked past, he'd come up to your head, I was walking up and down the corridor, past – up [interruptions] and he battered Asian girls for nothing, pretty badly and err then, and everyone got him back and battered him and a few weeks, well – all the A' Levels – that did the exam – and they – they battered him these two – for these two Asian girls [F: that's what I'm on about] pretty severely, put 'em in hospital and that – and th- nothing happened about that I don't think –

TD: Nothing happened?

Deepak: I don't know – nothing

Abdul: Nothing

(Hightown School, TD)

I would suggest that the examples cited above and below illustrate the combined physical, psychic and symbolic violence that is engendered by racism(s). As Rattansi (1992: 21) writes, 'The sheer prevalence, intensity and normality of abuse, harassment and violence directed by white students against British Asian and Afro-Caribbean students as part of the informal, popular culture of schools is horrifying'.

TD: You know ... like ... trying to stop it, have they got any ... Yeah ... No-is- has anyone been punished for saying anything?

Deepak: The blacks have

TD: The black?

Deepak: We-I mean we have

TD: You have?

Deepak: All the Asians

TD: You've got punished? [A: yep] rather than the white people have?

Deepak: Yeah – we get suspended

TD: You've been suspended and they haven't? Really? hhhh – yeah, God!

Fazaan:	Didn't want to say nothing on that paper yesterday, because we thought it's not … we thought like the teachers would see – because like schools pretty rough –
Abdul:	It's a crap school, man
TD:	It's a crap school? What about other schools? Is it, is it as bad in other schools?
Abdul:	Everywhere, it's everywhere in Mill Town – everywhere's like the same
Fazaan:	Everywhere's the same

(Hightown School, TD)

Deepak's assertion that they 'the white guy is straight, the black lad's messed up' echoes bel hooks' (1992: 89) critical comment that black masculinity has been conceptualized within dominant discourses as psychologically 'fucked up'. But whereas social identity theories have positioned cultural identity crises as the source of this internal conflict, the boys identified institutional systems as the source of the problem for perpetuating the myth that the white guy is always 'OK' and the black lad is always to blame. The boys thus constructed racism(s) as accentuated and perpetuated by the school system. As Rattansi suggests, such accounts are not unusual within the British education system, and they can be read as forming part of the institutionalized processes through which racial inequalities are reproduced:

> A frequent complaint of black students is that their reports of racial abuse and violence are habitually ignored or their racialised elements denied by white teachers. This is only one form of teacher collusion with racialized processes. There are many others, again amply documented
>
> (Rattansi 1992: 21)

Some of the boys suggested that one of their responses to the tension that they experienced between adhering to school rules and retaliating to racist incidents was to respond outside of school. For example, Yasser suggested that 'we went to file a complaint and it didn't happen, did it? Cos they wouldn't do their exams, they'd left school to do their exams, so the next morning they all just got their heads kicked in from our people'. In many of the boys' accounts, school time incidents were described as originating when older white boys pick on younger Asian boys. These incidents subsequently escalated and were dealt with outside the school, where the boys had access to greater resources (namely their older male relatives) with which to retaliate. Issues of pride and 'belonging' were clearly central within these accounts, and boys explained how 'our people' were able to exact retribution for attacks on Muslim boys. As I will argue further below, however, a critical feminist reading of the boys' transcripts highlights the limitations of both 'violence' and 'impartiality' as 'solutions' to issues of racism.

Boys' responses: violence, counter-racism or 'just ignore it'?

Between themselves, the boys constructed contrasting possible 'solutions' to racism, advocating either 'fighting back' with violence or 'ignoring it'. These different constructions were produced in relation to different interviewers. As Ann Phoenix argues, this difference between interviewer–groups is interesting in itself:

> If different types of accounts about 'race' and racism are produced with black and white interviewers this is in itself important data and may be a good reason for using interviewers of both colours wherever possible since it illustrates the ways in which knowledges are 'situated'
> (Phoenix 1994: 66)

In this case, and as detailed in the following examples, 'radical' discourses (of violence and/or counter-racism) were more often produced in relation to the Asian interviewer, whereas the notion of 'just ignoring' racism was more often voiced in discussion groups with the white interviewer.

The use of *violence* to combat racism was advocated by boys at Hightown and Eastfield schools, and was proposed in particular by those boys who were interviewed by Tamar.

TD: How would you bring up your kids differently?
Abdul: I'm gonna say to them, you know what I mean – I'm gonna say to them ... when you're called 'you black bastard' – you deck them – dec- dec-deck them! Kill him!
Fazaan: Stick all –
Abdul: Stick to your – [F: Yeah, stick to yourself] – When someone call you, don't, don't st- stand in the corner and just ignore them and that – and don't let the – all – people who just say 'ignore them' and that – How can you ignore them when they're saying it to you?! ... You *can't* ignore it – when they say it – kill 'em! ... break – batter 'em.
TD: Do – do you really think ... violence is the answer? ... Do you think it's the only answer?
Fazaan: Yeah, definitely
Abdul: Not an answer, but....
Fazaan: Right, they – like ... we couldn't have got –
Abdul: It's not the answer, it's not an answer – just a good solution, though! hh! [laughs]
(Hightown School, TD)

TD: Do you think there's any other solution to it except violence?
Yasser: No
Shabid: No one's heard of talking it out
Yasser: You just want to let it all out on them, though ... you're psy-
          ched up inside – and you have a nice *chat* with them?! Its not
          right! Well, fighting isn't good either though, but you know, the
          only reason I like fighting is, you know, someone gets me mad or
          summat – wouldn't have a nice chat, yeah?! I wouldn't want to
          take it out on something else, so I take it out on them – that's
          what my big brother does, he beats me up for no reason! He
          kicks me in! Kicks me in, gets shouted at, you know for my
          mum, he comes home really late like at twelve or one o'clock
          and gets shouted at – comes upstairs and Bang Bang! – I'm
          asleep and he wakes me up again, that's what happens all the
          time.
TD: What do you think – I mean how does that make you feel?
Yasser: Well, I'm used to it.

                                                        (Eastfield School, TD)

The above extracts can be read as located within a discourse of hegemonic masculinity in which physical conflict is normalized as a 'natural' way for men to solve problems and engage in disputes. The boys draw on, and counter, notions of (Asian) passivity and invisibility, as they specifically argue against 'standing in the corner' and 'ignoring racism'. Their accounts reproduce traditional masculine ideals of action which work to polarize alternative nonconfrontational approaches, rendering them 'feminine'.

Despite their support for 'violent' responses to racism, the boys also acknowledged the limitations of this approach, agreeing that it is not the 'answer', and merely a 'good solution'. In one sense, the boys might be understood as adopting a pragmatic response to situations in which they feel they have few other resources to mobilize. Thus their macho, aggressive talk could be read as representing an attempt to re/assert power and autonomy by mobilizing discourses of hegemonic masculinity. Such constructions may also be read as classed discourses, in which 'rough', 'active' working class masculinities are valorized over potential counterclaims by more 'rational' middle class solutions.

Fighting is also constructed as a therapeutic activity by Yasser, who suggests that it can provide a means for venting the pent-up emotions experienced by boys as a result of racism. He draws on a popular construction that positions masculinity as unable to engage with sensitive or difficult feelings (in other words, masculinity is defined as the opposite to femininity, which is popularly characterized by emotionality, mutual confiding, talking and so on). Thus potential 'feminized' and/or 'middle class' reactions to racism (which, to some extent, the female interviewers may have represented), such as talking about the issues ('having a nice chat'), are resisted and dismissed as unnatural, abnormal and unrealistic. Yasser further justifies the responsibility of his assertions, suggesting that by fighting 'racists', he actually protects other people because it means that he does not need to find outlets closer to home on which to vent his frustrations.[4] The two preceding extracts thus convey the boys' strong emotional reactions to experiences of racism. As illustrated earlier in the chapter, the boys described their experiences of racism in mostly physical terms (for example, recounting fights and attacks and emphasizing the physical injuries sustained by those involved), but I have also attempted to indicate the psychic violence that is exerted by racist practices and discourses, which impacted equally strongly upon the boys.

As detailed below, the promotion of, or resistance to, violence as a solution was also linked to the taking up, or not, of 'gangsta' identities. In particular, boys from Lowtown School who were interviewed by myself, the white researcher, largely resisted the notion of violence as a solution, which they challenged as an inauthentic attempt to 'act black'.

LA: Do you think Black people and Asian people deal with racism and stuff and respond in a different way?
Gufter: Different ... but most Asian kids will go looking for fights you know they [try] to be like black ... you know they try talking black as well ... like 'I'm a nigger don't start with me!' ... But they're *not*! But ... they they just they just ... *weird*! Thick!
Imran: And the ...the only word that they use is innit '*man*!' ... *man*! hhh!
Gufter: [Laughs] Talk weird! [laughter] It's like the black people they do it because ... that's the way *they* [Jamil: been brought up] brought up ... whereas here they do it because they think ... right 'I'm a black'. It's fashion they *try* to do it like that
                                                        (Lowtown School, LA)

Gufter thus linked 'looking for fights' to the enactment of black 'gangsta' masculinities. The authenticity of this form of resistance was questioned by some boys, who suggested that these black identities may be taken up as 'fashion' by other Asian boys.

'Counter' racisms

TD: Do you think it affects the way you answer questions, the fact that I'm Asian as well? Do you think if I was white it would be different?
Yasser: It would yeah, it would actually
Shabid: I wouldn't be saying some things

Abdul: Racist things
Yasser: Cos we are saying racist things and that but uh … like what
            we're saying is racist like, with white we don't like white …
            that's us though, innit? We hate white, they hate us [Tamar: uh
            huh] they can't do nothing about it, we can though … we are
            saying racist things but we are racist, that's it
TD: How do y- … are you all saying that – you all say that you're
            racist?
Yasser: Yeah [All: yeah]
TD: I mean w-what do you think about … the fact you – you openly
            admit to it?
Yasser: We're not – we're not r-racist like you know to white you know,
            swearing this that, you know? [if] then *they* start somtimes …
            we might start it –
Shabid: Cos they get *cheeky* some of them
Yasser: Like, like if they give us cheek

(Eastfield School, TD)

In the above extract, I suggest that the boys can be read as drawing on, and
subverting, a popular discourse in which racial differences and antagonisms
between 'us' and 'whites' are represented as 'natural' phenomena. To some
extent, their talk once again contains echoes of the racist rhetoric of differentialism, which was encapsulated by Derek Beakon's public assertion: 'I
am happy to describe myself as a racist. I just want to live among my own
people' (*Sun* 18 September 1993: 7, cited in Rattansi 1995: 55–56). In this
sense, the boys share a common discursive position with white racists that
favours separatism between the two mutually exclusive and hostile 'communities'. Their accounts could therefore be accused of reproducing racist
discourses that 'homogenise and naturalise social categories and groups and
deny shifting boundaries as well as internal power differences and conflicts
of interest' (Yuval-Davis 1994: 179). However, the boys also made an
important distinction between their own 'racism' and white racism, portraying their own racism as a matter of 'choice' and/or a reaction and
response to white racism. In contrast, they positioned white racism(s) as
'proactive', instinctive and unprovoked. Yasser thus suggests that while
racism is a 'natural' feature of whiteness, it can also be actively taken up by
Asians as a means to challenge inequalities ('they can't do nothing about it,
we can though'). As such, his comments can be read as espousing resistance,
or 'fighting back', against discourses that position Asians as passive victims
of racism.

I would suggest that the boys' counter racism(s) also differed from
dominant white racist discourses in terms of the power relations underpinning the different discourses. As detailed in Gilroy (1987: 42), Omi and
Winant (1983) proposed that racism(s) can be conceptualized in terms of

three key elements: first, it entails a set of processes through which unstable beliefs/practices are articulated within an ideology based on race; second, racism ideology is reinforced by processes of racial subjugation at institutional and individual levels; and third, racist discourses are ongoing processes which involve constant redefinition and evolution. From this perspective, the differences between Muslim and white boys' appropriation and use of 'racist' discourses becomes apparent.

The strongest views on racism, and the solutions to racism, were voiced in discussion groups with Tamar (the Asian interviewer), and these boys admitted that they would not have expressed the same views with the white interviewer. On one level, this admission might be read as revealing the power of the interviewer's 'race' in silencing particular accounts within the discussion groups. It might also indicate, however, the differential production of masculine identities within particular discursive contexts. Brown (1998), for example, detailed how young working class women in discussion groups engaged in 'verbal tests of toughness', using misogynistic language to draw boundaries between themselves and other girls/women. The young men in these groups could thus be similarly interpreted as performing such actions through their 'tough' and 'racist' talk, that is, appropriating 'powerful' racist discourses to test one another and to create and maintain gender and racial boundaries.

'Ignore it'

Boys in Lowtown and Westfield schools, but particularly those who were interviewed by the white researcher, talked about a strategy of ignoring racism, rather than fighting back against it.

LA: Like when was the last time that someone was racist to you?
Rahan: [pause] I think racism is a bit hard to remember [LA: mm] where
Wajit: Cos you normally just ignore it, y'see
LA: Like is it, I dunno, is it like people coming up and threatening you or beating you up? Or is it just like shouting stuff out?
Rahan: No-no, it's become a bit stupid now and you just look at them, go 'what are you looking at?' You go like that and it's end of story! . . . Just leave

(Westfield School, LA)

As indicated by this extract, Rahan and Wajit suggested that racism is becoming less prevalent and less potent a force within society, to the extent that they described it as 'a bit stupid now'. They suggested that racism may be conveyed by a 'look' rather than through explicit words or actions and, in this sense, the boys proposed that instances of racism can be easily countered and challenged. For example, potential situations can be easily resolved by simply questioning the protagonist and asking 'what are you looking at?', which usually stops the racist behaviour ('You go like that and it's end of story'). Rahan also suggested that this form of racism can be so subtle that it is 'a bit hard to remember'. However, I would suggest that it is important to distinguish between the boys' experiences of – and their potential resources with which to counter – these 'looks' from white peers as opposed to the 'looks' from white teachers that were discussed earlier.

It is also important to consider the role of the interviewer within the production of these discourses. As already suggested, the white interviewer's 'race' may have discouraged the expression of more radical and challenging accounts and constructions of racism. For example, the boys' suggestion that racism is easily countered and/or 'a bit stupid now' may also be read as a form of resistance to my attempts to position the boys within a passive 'victim' role. Similarly, the boys may have 'played up' their more 'macho' responses with Tamar as part of the discursive construction and articulation of masculinities in relation to her relatively powerful position, as an Asian female researcher, within the discussion groups. In other words, I would like to argue that boys' accounts of racism should not be treated as simple reflections of an objective external social reality: they are inherently located within 'real' racialized relationships that occur within the research context.

Summary

This chapter has examined some of the different constructions of racism that were drawn upon and produced by the boys. In contrast to mainstream multicultural and anti-racist educational initiatives, I have argued in favour of engaging with complex theorizations of 'racism(s)' in order to address racial inequalities within schools. It has been suggested that racism(s), and responses to racism(s), are bound up with issues of identity and subjectivity and are also inextricably linked with gender identities and social class. Racism(s) are enacted through complex and continual processes of construction and production, they are constantly being made and remade. The emotional dimension of racism(s), and Muslim boys' responses to their experiences of racism(s), suggest that racist discourses are resistant to rational approaches and interventions. In other words, simplistic, rationalistic pedagogies and institutional responses will only ever be of limited effectiveness.

For example, simply providing white pupils with 'more' or 'better' knowledge, information and/or contact with Asian/Muslim pupils and their 'culture' will not necessarily impact on these identities, behaviours and racisms. Such strategies may help to create an ethos in which white pupils 'know' not to be openly racist at school (as suggested by the data from boys at Lowtown School), but there is little hope that this alone will extend its influence beyond the school gates. Institutional responses will therefore need to be holistic in approach, and will need to be able to engage with boys' emotional attachments to multiple identities which are grounded outside the school in local territorial masculinities and neighbourhood nationalisms.

The boys themselves seemed to suggest that perhaps little can be done about racism, but this may not constitute the only way of looking at the situation. The young men predominantly used 'common sense' notions of racism, conceptualizing it in terms of individual attitudes and cognitions. I would thus argue that there is plenty of potential scope for work to be undertaken with respect to addressing institutional racism(s), and indeed, critically interrogating the normalizing assumptions that underpin many everyday practices and behaviours within schools. Further implications for schools with respect to engaging with racisms – and the question of how to produce and use less oppressive conceptualizations and ways of imagining Muslim boys – are returned to in the final chapter.

Notes

1 Barnton is the pseudonym for the predominantly Asian ward in the town.
2 Beakon (standing for the right-wing, racist British National Party) was elected in the Millwall local council elections of September 1993.
3 The issue of intra-Asian pupil 'racism' is not discussed within this book. This is predominantly because the boys described Pakistani–Bangladeshi 'conflicts' as essentially good-humoured practices that involved boys teasing each other in relation to specific national stereotypes (which, to paraphrase one boy, consisted of Pakistani boys getting called 'chappati' and Bangladeshi boys being called 'fish'). These bouts of name-calling (and the occasional fights which ensued) were positioned in quite different ways to 'white racism'.
4 This point can be read in conjunction with Yasser's concerns about his older brother's violence towards him, as detailed in Chapter 5.

chapter / **seven**

Educational and occupational aspirations

Introduction

> Identity is socially and culturally 'located' in time and space and
> inflected by rejection, displacement and desire. Post-16 'choices' are
> bound up with the expression and suppression of identities
>
> (Ball *et al.* 2000: 24)

This chapter considers the ways in which British Asian Muslim boys view
education and their educational/occupational aspirations. I suggest that the
boys' responses provide an interesting angle to wider public concerns with
Muslim boys' 'under-achievement' and lack of progressing within post-16
education. The chapter also discusses the boys' constructions of Muslim
girls' educational 'choices', and I draw attention to interconnecting discourses of 'culture', gender and 'race' within these responses to argue that
'rational', individualistic models of post-16 choice are inappropriate. The
chapter illustrates instead how the boys' choices, preferences and aspirations are rooted within complex social relations and are cross-cut by themes
of culture and kinship and discourses of 'desirable/popular' Muslim
masculinity.

The boys' views of school and education

The most common view of education that was expressed among the boys
was that school is 'OK' but 'boring'. It was interesting to note that themes
of 'school', but particularly 'learning in class' or 'doing schoolwork', did
not feature as strongly in the two Muslim boys' photographic diaries, as
compared to the Muslim girls (see Archer 1998). However, across all the

groups, boys consistently expressed a strong belief in the value of education, and there was universal agreement to the question 'do you think
education is important?' The boys' views resonate with findings from other
research studies with male and female pupils. For example, Francis (1999)
found that 91 percent of 14–16-year-old boys and girls (drawn from middle
and top ability groups) thought that it is important to progress into further
education.

Among the Muslim boys in this study, the value of education was constructed primarily in instrumental terms, in other words, educational
qualifications were valued as a means for gaining paid employment and
entering the labour market. As the boys put it, education is important 'so
you end up with a good future' (Sham), so you can 'try and get a good
career' (Naseem), 'get a job' (Jahed, Wajit) and because 'you need to get
paid' (Kabir). Francis' (1999) respondents gave a slightly broader range of
reasons, but again, she found that the most popular responses focused upon
the importance of educational qualifications for getting a job, a 'good' job
and/or a 'better paid' job.

These boys' constructions of the instrumental value of education echo
findings from other research with working class respondents (Archer 2003),
particularly working class men from diverse ethnic backgrounds (Archer *et
al.* 2001b). Instrumental constructions of education appear to be gendered,
as girls are more likely to voice support for the intrinsic benefits of (further)
education, whereas boys are more likely to draw on instrumental, extrinsic
reasons (Francis 1999). Francis also found that fewer boys than girls talked
about the potential benefits that can accrue from increased learning, or the
importance of learning for its own sake. As shown by the following extract,
Muslim boys in this study framed the value of education in primarily
financial terms, as important for getting a 'good future' and a 'good career'.

TD: Do you all think it's – but why do you think it's important?
Naseem: [pause] Financial depends if you wanna work, innit?
Said: I don't want to – I don't want to learn –
Sham: So you end up with a good future
TD: So you –
Naseem: Yeah try and get a good career

(Lowtown School, TD)

Gaining educational qualifications was linked with notions of social
mobility and the possibility of getting 'better' jobs. Education was valued as
a means to access better-paid jobs, specifically jobs which pay more than
factory work (a common occupation in Mill Town). It was also regarded as
a resource to help the boys survive within an increasingly competitive job
market:

Yasser: If you got no education you can't get a job and if you don't get job, what you gonna do?

Abdul: It's hard to get jobs now

Shabid: It's hard to find a job now...

Yasser: Hard! Two, three pounds [an hour] that's it. Mostly factory jobs
(Eastfield School, TD)

A narrative in which education is valued primarily as an instrumental means to 'get ahead' has also been noted within working class adults' discussions about the utility of higher education for social mobility (see Archer and Hutchings 2000; Archer *et al.* 2003). With my colleagues I have previously found that working class men and women from a range of ethnic backgrounds view educational qualifications as important for 'getting a foot in the door' (Archer *et al.* 2003). Abdul and Shabid's observation that 'it's hard to get jobs now' also echoes a wider 'hard times' discourse (in which the job market is perceived to be becoming more competitive) which has been identified within the talk of 14–16-year-olds by Francis (1999). Within the new 'hard times' discourse, educational qualifications are regarded as increasingly necessary requirements for securing 'any' job. Like the boys and girls in Francis' (1999) study, Muslim boys in this research felt that there was a growing level of *competition* within the job market. This notion of competition is based on a pragmatic 'realism' and New Right economic arguments and proposals that the modern world is a competitive 'jungle', where one must 'battle to get ahead' (Francis 1999: 314).

However, some of the boys in Lowtown School suggested that not all Bangladeshi boys equally value education because the town's 'Indian' restaurant trade provided a reliable source of potential employment, without the need for qualifications

Gufter: Yeah cos like most people think school's a waste of time! They just come in cos they *have* to ... you know s'illegal that's it ... and they think – sometimes they leave school and they just get – go to a restaurant and get a job there [LA: yeah] cook or summit

Imran: Like in restaurant – there's no tax!
(Lowtown School, LA)

As Imran suggests above, working in the restaurant trade can be preferable to other low skill/low pay jobs because it enables young men to work 'cash in hand', avoiding tax. Thus for boys who thought that their futures would probably entail working in the town's restaurant trade, the instrumental value of qualifications, schooling and education in general, was lessened. Boys also talked about how family businesses, such as owning a shop, provided a safety net because this source of employment would always be available to them if other options failed. As Rahan (Westfield School, LA) said, 'basically I haven't got a problem because even if [I] doesn't get jobs then dad's got [a] shop so he'll take care of that'.

Boys at Hightown School were also of the opinion that, for minority ethnic groups, the value of education is compromised by racism in British society. Deepak, Abdul, Gulfraz and Fazaan all thought that it would be harder for them as 'black' men to do well and to get good jobs because teachers and employers will be biased in favour of their white peers.

TD: Do you think, umm, do you think it's worth sticking at school then? Do you think education's important for you?
Abdul: It is
Fazaan: It is important, but –
Deepak: It is – is important but you won't get no job's – an' ... it's less likely for the black
Fazaan: Nah, you try harder, though
Gulfraz: Yeah, but you'll get a job
Abdul: Yeah, you will
Fazaan: Yeah if you leave college and have the attitude you can't, then you won't get nowhere. I – you gonna have to try hard and that
Gulfraz: Yeah try hard
TD: Do you think it's more difficult for you?
Fazaan: Yeah, obviously more difficult ... for a black than –
Gulfraz: Yeah you have to work a lot
Fazaan: Yeah obviously more difficult for a black, but what I say is that, there's a black person and a white person, they got the same, err same ... qualifications and that, but the white person's got a more chance of getting a job because of his colour –
Gulfraz: The teachers help them as well

(Hightown School, TD)

In one sense the above extract can be read as critiquing dominant social and educational ideals, which assume that qualifications are straightforward, objective credentials that carry the same value and weight for all individuals, regardless of their social backgrounds. The boys argued that black groups have to try twice as hard as whites in order to succeed – a theme that is recognized by various other researchers (for example, Cheng and Health 1993; Parker-Jenkins *et al.* 1997). One possible strategy for minimizing this risk, as suggested by boys at Lowtown School, is to stick to the relative safety and security of the restaurant trade (working with 'our own people'). However, at Hightown School (the school with the highest average GCSE results in the LEA) boys advocated resisting inequalities in the job market by increasing their own levels of personal effort. Francis (1999: 305) argues that 'discourses of meritocracy underlying policy and debate on lifelong learning may give students a somewhat unrepresentative view of post-16 education as a direct route of access to desired jobs'. But I would suggest that the above interview extract illustrates that, to some extent, some boys have 'seen through' this myth of meritocracy. Their views echoed those of the black Caribbean and African girls in Mirza's (1992) study, who resisted racism by working extra hard to gain qualifications and achieved social mobility through strategic 'backdoor' routes. Unlike the girls in Mirza's study, however, the boys at Hightown School also expressed among the vaguest aspirations of all the boys in the study. As detailed below, both interviewers found that these boys aspired to 'get rich quick', and expressed somewhat far-fetched ambitions such as 'own my own airline' and becoming 'the richest man in the world':

Ali: I'm trying to become an entrepreneur – get rich quick! [laughter]
LA: [Laughs] Doing what? [laughs]
Ali: Don't know, I want my own airline!

(Hightown School, LA)

TD: I mean, have you all got ambitions, like things you really wanna do?
Abdul: I wouldn't mind, basically! The richest man in the world!

(Hightown School, TD)

Despite their predominantly instrumental attitudes to education, the young men in this study did not *only* value it in personal, individualistic terms. For example, Sham contextualized his instrumentalist constructions of education within a wider discourse of Bangladeshi masculinity. Bangladeshi masculinity was conceptualized through a 'breadwinner' identity, characterized by the responsibility to financially provide for wider family and kin, both locally and 'back home' in Bangladesh. This discourse has also been found among young Bangladeshi men in London (Archer *et al.* 2001b). Although Sham joked that 'I only do it [education] cos I know I'll get in trouble at home! [laughter]', as illustrated by the following extract, he constructed breadwinner masculinity not only as a duty but also as a source of pride and symbol of masculinity: 'I just want to get a good job, so I, c-cos I wanna feed my family, like, you know? In Bangladesh. They're *poor* and so they need money and like I – my brother has to send money now and again. I, I just want to get a good job so I can send money' (Sham, Lowtown School, TD).

The boys' instrumental construction of schooling (their equation of educational qualifications with gaining paid employment), was further reinforced by Rahan's counter-construction of what constitutes 'real', intrinsically valuable education. Rahan juxtaposed 'real' (in other words, religious) education with the instrumental gaining of qualifications and credentials, saying 'the money bit exists but the most important [thing] to me was sitting at home and reading the Qu'ran because you get education' (Rahan, Westfield School, LA). Other research has also pointed to a common working class discourse that resists the intrinsic value of formal learning and education. For example, in previous research I found that working class men and women widely regarded higher educational qualifications as merely 'paperwork' and of less intrinsic use or value than practical ('hands-on') experience and common sense (Archer *et al.* 2003). Fazaan and Abdul also suggested that their parents were not interested in the content (as opposed to the outcomes) of their schooling, as Fazaan put it 'my dad's not arsed about if I don't learn anything' and Abdul suggested that his parents 'should be more interested in education and that'. Thus, as suggested in Archer (2001b), these instrumental constructions of education can be read as part of boys' constructions of working class, racialized masculine identities.

The boys' favourite and least favourite school subjects

Research has found that the subject preferences of boys and girls in mixed sex schools (Francis 1996, 2000b, 2002), as well as girls in single sex schools (Francis *et al.*, forthcoming), have diversified over the past 20 years. The Muslim boys in this study also expressed a reasonably diverse range of subject preferences, although their dislikes were far more homogenous than has been the case in other studies.

Overall across discussion groups, the three most popular subjects among the Muslim boys were PE, English and Science. The boys also named a range of other subjects among their personal favourites, such as Art, CDT (craft, design and technology), Drama, History, Maths and Technology. These preferences broadly reflect findings from other studies that have been conducted with ethnically diverse groups of boys in co-educational schools. For example, Francis (2000b) found that the favoured subjects by boys in her study were English, Maths and Science. However, the Muslim boys' preferences in this study were slightly more vocationally orientated than Francis has found to be the case among boys in her research.

TD: Uh huh ... what are your favourite subjects? ... have you got any? Hh!
Naseem: Art hh!
Jagdip: Art and CDT
Sham: And PE I think
TD: What about you?
Said: M-maths and Eng-English, English

(Lowtown School, TD)

LA: What are your favourite subjects at school? ... Do you have
        any?! [laughing]
Ali: I don't know – anything that's easy!
Rakim: That's jus' you!
LA: What's easy?
Ali: Nothing at the moment ... sometimes it gets easy
LA: What sorts of subjects do you like?
Mo: PE
Ali: PE

(Hightown School, LA)

NS: What subjects do you all like at school?
Nazir: Physics, maths
NS: Yeah – you would like physics cos of civil engineering!
Nazir: Yeah, hh! French is alright – not that bad ... basically every-
        thing's alright – it's interesting you know there's not a subject
        that I don't really – dislike – I like 'em all!

(Westfield School, NS)

In terms of their reasons for liking these subjects, boys talked about
preferring practical and arts-related subjects, particularly those linked to
practical competencies which involved 'making' things.

TD: [Laughs] What about you two? What are your favourite sub-
        jects?
Abdul: Mine are ... technology and err ... English ... and science
TD: Why do you like them?
Abdul: Because ... technology uh we get to do like ... make some
        things out of wood or stuff and fabric and uh like doing that
        sometimes and uh ... maths ... uh th-that's alright cos ...
        dunno! ... it used to be too hard for me and I found that difficult
        ... lesson and uh if I don't get it – didn't get it then I get
        explanation off the teachers ... get them to explain a different
        way to get me used to it
TD: Yeah ... yeah and what about you?
Shabid: I like history and ... PE ... history is like ... *interesting* for me
        [TD: uh huh] I like doing history – *learning* about people [TD:
        yeah] and PE ... I like doing a lot of sports [TD: what kind of
        sports do you like?] umm cricket football rugby

(Hightown School, TD)

LA: Mm ... umm ... what are your favourite subjects at school at
        the moment?
Gufter: CDT!

Imran:	CDT!
Jamil:	CDT, yeah!
Gufter:	And PE! PE!
Jamil:	PE, CDT!
Imran:	PE
LA:	Why do you like CDT?
Jamil:	Cos of woodwork
Gufter:	Yeah!
Jamil:	You can just make things and *design* design
Gufter:	Cos at the moment- at the moment we're doing our own *design*! It-it's a major project. We start now and finish next year in GCSE and it's our own design and uh if the teacher approves of it, if you got like the measurements and that right, he'll let you do it!

(Lowtown School, LA)

I would suggest that the boys' subject preferences reflect their classed locations in the sense that they privilege practical competencies over more academic, text based subjects. However, their preferences were also linked to their views on particular teachers and teaching styles. Francis (2000b; Francis *et al.* forthcoming) found that girls in mixed and single sex schools preferred Art, Mathematics and English and the most common explanation for liking a subject was the quality of teaching, or the skill of the teacher. Muslim boys' subject preferences were similarly linked to their liking of particular teachers and/or teaching styles. For example, both Abdul and Majid reported enjoying Mathematics more since their teacher had explained it in a new way which had helped them to understand the subject better. As illustrated below, 'nice teachers' were also commonly cited as a reason for particular subject preferences.

LA:	What are *your* favourite subjects?
Mehmet:	PE and uhh science (.) maths a bit (.) English
LA:	What about you lot?
Jahed:	I like English (.) science
LA:	What do you like about those subjects
Ashav:	Teachers are really nice

(Eastfield School, LA)

It is interesting to note, however, that while '*good*' teachers seemed to encourage boys to like a particular subject, this did not necessarily mean that boys disliked subjects that were taught by unpopular or 'bad' teachers – science was particularly singled out in this respect:

LA:	Yeah ... what are your favourite subjects then?
Assim:	I like English

Kabir:	Science
Rahan:	Physics
Assim:	Yeah, physics
Rahan:	Chemistry hh! . . . *not* the teacher but!
LA:	Not the teacher?
Rahan:	The *class*

(Westfield School, LA)

I suggest that the boys' strong preference for science subjects related to wider gendered constructions of curriculum subjects. Francis (2002) discusses traditional perceptions of the sciences as higher status and 'masculine' (associated with rationality, objectivity) and the arts as lower status and 'feminine' (emotions, subjectivity) and notes that within this dichotomy, subjects are hierarchically arranged (Francis 2000a).

> The dichotomy is maintained by the hegemonic construction of the feminine (and traits ascribed feminine) as 'other' and substandard (see Walkerdine 1990). Hence 'the sciences' have traditionally been seen as more important, and more difficult than 'the arts' (Thomas 1990)
>
> (Francis 2002: 83)

Thus, boys' widespread preference for science subjects can be understood as an aspect of their gendered identity construction, although it should be noted that not all boys liked science subjects, and Science featured equally prevalently within the boys' least favourite subjects.

As detailed in Francis *et al.* (forthcoming), gender stereotypical subject preferences may also be racialized to some extent. The white, rural pupils in Warrington and Younger's (2000) study appeared to be far more gender stereotypical in their views of science than the ethnically diverse metropolitan pupils in Francis' research (Francis 2000a, b; 2002). Research also suggests that minority ethnic girls may be less gender stereotypical in their subject preferences than white girls (Mirza 1992; Lightbody and Durndell 1996). The preferences of the Muslim boys in this study, however, appeared to contain both gender stereotypical, and nonstereotypical, elements. For example, the boys' favourite subjects included traditionally 'male' subjects (such as Science and, 'masculine, working class' subjects, such as CDT/ woodwork and sports) as well as traditionally 'feminine' subjects (such as English, Art and History).

In comparison to their subject preferences, the boys' *least favourite* subjects were far more homogenized. Apart from one boy who said he disliked PSE (personal and social education), it was striking that across all the discussion groups only two subjects were identified as anyone's 'least favourite', namely Science and Mathematics. Francis' research revealed a greater diversity and range within girls' least favourite subjects, which included Science, Mathematics and modern Foreign Languages.

In terms of the reasons for boys' and girls' subject dislikes, Francis *et al.* (forthcoming) found that girls report disliking subjects that are hard, boring and badly taught. The Muslim boys in this study were also highly likely to give reasons associated with teachers and teaching styles to explain their least preferred subjects:

TD: Uh huh ... wh-what subjects do you hate?
Yasser: Maths and science!
TD: Maths and science! hhh! is that just-just just don't like them?
Yasser: I don't like the *teachers* [TD: mmm] like err the maths teacher Miss [name] she's *really* ... *not* good! [laughter] She's really nasty!

(Eastfield School, TD)

LA: What *don't* you like as subjects?
Ashav: *Maths*! hh!
LA: Why don't you like maths?
Ashav: Teacher [inaudible]
LA: The teacher? What don't you like about – ?
Ashav: Well she's always [saying] 'come here do this, come here do that'

(Eastfield School, LA)

LA: What about you two? What's your least favourite?
Imran: Maths and science
LA: Science? [laughs]
Imran: It's the teacher – she gives us too much to do! For science

(Lowtown School, LA)

However, another key theme underpinning the boys' subject dislikes was that of subject difficulty, as boys stated that they strongly disliked subjects which they found 'hard'.

LA: And what are your least favourite subjects?
Mushtak: Maths!
LA: Maths? Why maths?!
Mushtak: Its very hard...
Mo: Too hard
Rakim: Stressful!
//
LA: What are your least favourite subjects?
Rakim: Err, physics and maths – its quite difficult.

(Hightown School, LA)

LA: What are your least favourite subjects?
Gufter: Maths!
Jamil: Maths
LA: Why?
Gufter: Cos hh-
Jamil: Borin'!
Gufter: Not really, but it's actually ... it's too demanding mentally like
          in maths we're divided – there's a higher group and a lower
          group and that – especially being in the higher group it's ... it's
          alright actually but ... just ... different topics cos there's like
          Pythagorus, there's trig ... and it just depends if you're good at
          that part

                                                            (Lowtown School, LA)

TD: What don't you like at school? What subjects don't you like?
Naseem: Science
Sham: Maths!
Naseem: And maths [laughs]
Jagdip: I don't like science
TD: You don't like science – what about you?
Naseem: PSE, maths
TD: So none of you – except you like maths, don't you?
Said: Yeah
Naseem: S'hard though
TD: Hard?
Naseem: Yeah! [laughs]

                                                            (Lowtown School, TD)

A popular reason given by the boys for disliking mathematics was that it
was too 'hard', 'difficult' and 'stressful'. Conversely, one of the boys suggested that his favourite subject was 'anything easy'. It is possible to read
the boys' explanations for their preferences as part of the masculine/laddish
avoidance of failure (see Jackson 2002b), because they reported trying to
avoid subjects that are 'hard'/difficult.

The boys' widespread dislike of, and experiences of difficulty with,
Mathematics is interesting given that national statistics suggest that, overall, boys gain proportionally more of the higher grades in Mathematics
GCSE than girls (Boaler *et al.* 2000). Against this statistic, the Muslim boys'
propensity to name Mathematics as their least favourite subject indicates
some potential exceptions within broad-brush statistics relating to gender
and achievement. In other words, it leads us to question exactly *which* boys
may be included or excluded within these general figures. However, as
Gufter's extract also suggests, some of the boys who disliked Maths were

actually in the top set, and disliked the 'harder' level Maths that they were expected to learn.

The boys' constructions of Mathematics and Science as 'hard' and 'difficult' can also be read as reflecting broader popular gendered constructions of science as 'more important' than the arts. In other words, the boys could be drawing on popular discourses within which it is more acceptable to say that they find Science difficult and hard, as opposed to finding, say, arts or languages hard, because arts are traditionally regarded as 'soft' or 'easy' subjects.

Boys' choices, aspirations and ambitions

> In traditional analyses of young people's career choice and gender it has largely been the career choices of *girls* which has provided cause for concern ... However, more recently a concern with 'boys' under-achievement' has lead some researchers to focus on *boys*' career aspirations and perceptions of the adult labour market
>
> (Francis 2002: 76)

As illustrated above, Francis argues that, historically, girls' aspirations have been positioned as more problematic than boys' aspirations. I would agree, but would also add that until recently within the field of 'race' and education, greater attention was given to Muslim girls' educational and careers aspirations and choices (which have been assumed to be problematically low due to family and cultural restrictions and taboos). As detailed earlier in the book, however, Muslim boys are now being increasingly targeted by educational policy discourses that seek to raise their 'low aspirations'. This 'raising aspiration' discourse is closely linked with popular concerns to 'raise achievement', and both have been keenly applied to working class (minority ethnic) boys.

When they were asked about their educational ambitions, just over half of the Muslim boys (at least one boy in each group) suggested that they expected to continue in education after their GCSEs. An almost equal number of boys were unsure as to what they wanted to do after their GCSEs and a few talked about working or undertaking other forms of training.

LA: What do you all want to do after you er finish?
Mehmet: Go to college [LA: college]
Ashav: College [LA: college]
Jahed: College
LA: uh ... what you gonna do ... like A-levels or –
Mehmet: Yeah A-levels
Ashav: YTS

```
LA:       YTS? Yeah? What you wanna do?
Ashav:    [inaudible] engineer
```

(Eastfield School, LA)

A popular view expressed among the boys was that their future plans would depend upon how they did in their GCSE examinations, which I would suggest echoes Ball *et al.*'s (2000) model of working class pupils as 'contingent' educational choosers. Themes of uncertainty, risk and contingency were evident throughout the boys' constructions of their potential post-GCSE pathways. For example, Rakim suggested that his A Level subject choices would be determined by his GCSE results ('Depends what results we get in the GCSE's, innit?'), and so had not yet made any specific plans, preferring to 'wait and see' what happened ('I'm not sure what I want to do'). Boys at the other schools also felt that their future progression routes would depend upon their degree of success in their GCSE examinations, and thus had equally vague ideas about the specific form that their post-16 routes might take:

```
TD:       I mean do you all want to go to college – ?
Sham:     College, yeah
All:      Yeah
TD:       Why? Why do you all want to go to college? Why do you think
          it's important?
Jagdip:   Get a good qualification ... umm, try and get a good career –
Sham:     Yeah
TD:       Uh – what [subject] do you all want to do?
Jagdip:   Don't know yet really!
```

(Lowtown School, TD)

```
LA:       What do you all wanna do when you leave here? cos you're
          gonna be doing GCSEs next year ... what you gonna do after
          that?
Wajit:    Go to college [LA: college?]
Kabir:    College ... sixth form
```

(Westfield School, LA)

```
LA:       What do you wanna do when you leave here? ... Have you
          thought about it?
Gufter:   I wanna go to college
LA:       College?
Gufter:   Sixth form
Jamil:    I want to go to sixth form ... and then carry it on to Uni
LA:       What about you two? Do you wanna go to college or?
```

Imran:	College yeah
Sarfraz:	Wanna go to college
LA:	What do you wanna do at college? What do you wanna study?
Gufter:	I haven't really thought about it much but … I wanna take up engineering
LA:	uh huh
Jamil:	Business
LA:	What about you?
Imran:	I don't know! hh!

(Lowtown School, LA)

'Having a plan', or more precisely, having a clearly mapped out plan for progressing into higher education, has been identified as a characteristically middle class discourse (Ball *et al.* 2000). Yet 'planning' may also be gendered. On the whole, the Muslim boys' aspirations appeared to be vaguer, less specific and not as carefully considered as the Muslim girls' responses (see Archer 2002a). Various reasons have been put forward to account for the perceived lower, and vaguer, educational and occupational aspirations that have been noted among working class boys. As Francis (2002) summarizes, some people have argued that working class boys may not apply themselves so much at school because they assume jobs will be waiting for them (Pickering 1997). Others have suggested that these boys may make less effort to achieve qualifications because they imagine that their futures will be spent 'on the dole' (claiming unemployment allowances) because there are so few (manual) jobs remaining (Arnot *et al.* 1999). Some of the Muslim boys in this study were clearly confident that there would always be unskilled jobs (that do not require a qualification) open to them within family businesses (in restaurants and shops), and thus may not have felt an urgency to develop a detailed alternative plan of action.

Overall, most of the boys expressed a general interest in continuing into post-compulsory education (GCSE results 'permitting'). This broadly reflects the generally higher rates of progression into FE and HE that have been noted among British minority ethnic groups in comparison to white working class rates of participation (Modood 1993). These proportionally higher levels of post-compulsory participation might be linked to the prevalence of family and community discourses among British minority ethnic groups which value further/higher education as a means for improving social mobility (see, for example, Archer and Leathwood 2003). Indeed, Rakim hinted that his family not only expected, but demanded, him to stay on into sixth form:

LA:	What are you gonna do when you leave here next year – oh no – I mean, are you gonna leave here next year?

Rakim: I'd *like* to, but ... I think we've got to err do our A-levels
Ali: Sixth form

(Hightown School, LA)

This theme – of strong parental encouragement of children into post-compulsory education – has been identified a characteristic discourse not only of middle class families but also *minority ethnic* working class families (Francis 1999; Archer and Hutchings 2000). I also found evidence of a typical working class discourse of 'keeping close' (Pugsley 1998) within the boys' constructions of higher education. As Gufter said, if they were to progress into HE, they would not live away from home and would 'mainly just stick around this area'. As Pugsley and others detail, this is a prevalent finding within working class respondents' views on higher education.

In terms of their occupational aspirations, as illustrated within the preceding interview extracts, 'engineering' was a popular choice among the boys. Six boys mentioned that they would like to do 'engineering' as a future job and four mentioned that they would be happy with office or 'business' jobs. Three boys wanted to work with computers. A striking finding across the groups was the number of boys who claimed that their ambition is to 'earn a lot', 'get rich quick', or be 'the richest man in the world', 'an entrepreneur' or to 'own my own airline' or to be a 'gangster leader'. These views reflect an interplay between discourses of 'laddishness' and 'gangsta' masculinities. Other aspirations included: to be a footballer; to do something related to sports or art/drawing; to undertake a YTS scheme; to work in my father's shop; to join the armed forces and, as detailed below, to do 'dirty/scruffy work'.

LA: What do the rest of you wanna do after your exams? (..) what sort of jobs do you wanna do? ... you wanna be an engineer ... what sorts of things do the rest of you wanna do?
Jahed: Wanna earn a lot!
Mehmet: Summit that's dirty
LA: Dirty work?
Mehmet: Something that's scruffy work

(Eastfield School, LA)

The boys' occupational aspirations appeared to contain a mixture of classed aspirations. Francis (2002) found that the jobs favoured by boys in the top/middle ability band were 'footballer', 'businessman', 'solicitor' and 'architect'. These preferences reflected differences between the social class of respondents in Francis' sample and the Muslim boys in this study. Mehmet and some of the other boys expressed preferences for manual jobs, particularly jobs that involve being 'dirty' and 'scruffy' (see Archer *et al.* 2001b). Such perceptions echo the views of the white working class 'lads' whom Willis (1977) wrote about. Willis argued that processes of schooling prepare working class boys for the factory floor, and more recent work (Mac an Ghaill 1996) suggests that these processes largely continue to operate despite the decline in heavy industry work in Britain. It has been suggested that most pupils, but especially working class boys, are not sufficiently aware of the changing nature of the modern employment market and thus many unrealistically expect to work within 'traditional' male manual industries. For example, Pickering (1997) suggests that boys are largely not aware of the wide-scale decline in manual jobs. Rees and Delamont (1999) also argue that girls in particular are not aware of, or are not encouraged into, shortage areas like engineering. In this respect, the popularity of engineering as a career aspiration among Muslim boys may be read as a potentially fruitful choice.

Francis (2002) argues that both boys' and girls' aspirations reflect gender dichotomies but she also points to evidence which suggests that pupils' aspirations (but particularly those of girls) are becoming ever more diverse. In general, she proposes that boys are becoming more 'gender conservative' than girls in their career aspirations, tending towards scientific, technical and business jobs (Francis 1996; 2002). Muslim boys in this study were no exception:

TD: I mean have you all got like ... goals and ambitions that you wanna – things you wanna do? ... I mean what do you all wanna be? ... what career do you wanna get into?
Yasser: Wanna be a business man
TD: Wanna be a business man – what about the rest of you?
Shabid: Wanna get into um ... computer business ... [inaudible] learning about how computers are run ... umm using them
TD: What about you two?
Abdul: Wanna be an engineer
TD: An engineer?
Yasser: I wanna do something in computing

(Eastfield School, TD)

LA: Yeah ... what do you wanna do like ... job-wise? What do you reckon you're gonna do? Or [what] do you wanna do?
Rahan: Mechanical engineering
LA: Yeah?
Wajit: Well-paid job
LA: Well-paid, like?
Wajit: Manager – no, not manager – you know like ... something! Like in an office or something! ... Like an office

(Westfield School, LA)

As indicated earlier, in addition to the popularity of 'business' and engineering, individual boys aspired to careers associated with sport, civil engineering and the armed forces. Naseem (from Lowtown School) was unique, however, in his stated ambition of becoming good at drawing ('to be a good drawer').

TD:	What about you? Have you got a career in mind, or something you really want to do?
Naseem:	Company job
Said:	Mmm, I don't really be sure yet
TD:	No? All of you? You're not sure?
Jagdip:	Not sure
Naseem:	Not sure
TD:	I mean, is there nothing you – you' d *like* to do? If you *could* do anything?
Sham:	um … uh – I wanted to be a footballer! [laughing] but it didn't work out! hh! But I'm too much of a – you know – didn't work out! I don't know! I don't really … I don't know yet – I mean … I like stuff to do with sport – so … become like a sports teacher or-or a physiologist or something like that – I'm not really sure yet

(Lowtown School, TD)

NS:	What do you want to do when you're say a bit older?
Nazir:	I want to go – I was hoping to go into civil engineering or summit like that but … uh … I'm not sure – it depends … on the grades
//	
NS:	Yeah … how about you two – what do you want to do when you're a bit older? What kind of career would you like to have? Ambitions – have you got any ambitions? What do you wanna *do* with your life? Do you wanna work not work? If you wanna work – why do you wanna work? What do you wanna do?
Imtaz:	I don't know now
NS:	You – you're not sure?
Imtaz:	No
NS:	What about you?
Majid:	I wanna join the armed forces
NS:	You wanna join the armed forces? [Majid: yeah] mmm why's that?
Majid:	Just because I like it!

(Westfield School, NS)

The boys' views of girls' choices[1]

The boys discussed not only their own aspirations but those of their Muslim female peers. As discussed earlier, Muslim girls have been identified as educational causes for concern due to their low post-compulsory partici- pation rates (Modood 1993; Coffield and Vignoles 1997). For example, Muslim women have been highlighted as 'disappearing' from post-com- pulsory education: 'Women from certain ethnic groups between the ages of 16 and 24 tend to "disappear" from participation in the preparatory stages of progression to Higher Education' (Rabiee and Thompson 2000: 6). Within the popular imagination, issues of 'culture' have been identified as the source of Asian women's problems, and Muslim femininity has been popularly stereotyped as 'ruthlessly oppressed and in need of liberation' (Brah 1994: 158). Policy discourses have thus explained Muslim girls' exclusion from post-compulsory education as due to their oppression by authoritarian, patriarchal home 'cultures'. However, feminists and critical theorists have identified such stereotypes as racist discourses, and have attempted to shift attention onto the detrimental effects of institutional racisms and sexisms upon Asian/Muslim girls' aspirations and attainment. For example, emphasis has been placed on the ways in which professionals' stereotypes of Asian girls can close down particular opportunities and routes to them (Brah and Minhas 1986; Brah 1994; Basit 1997b; Shain 2000). As Brah writes,

> The social imagery of Asian women as hapless dependents who would most likely be married off at the earliest possible opportunity has played an important role in shaping the views that teachers or careers officers might hold of young Muslim women's education and employment prospects. Such professionals have an important role to play in encouraging or discouraging young Muslim women from pursuing certain types of education or employment
>
> (Brah 1994: 156)

Brah also found that:

> it was clear that low expectations and stereotyped perceptions of Asian girls, their aspirations, abilities and cultures on the part of educational professionals were seen by the women as a major obstacle to Asian girls' success in the labour market
>
> (Brah 1994: 167–8)

The case of Muslim girls provides an additional important caveat to the popular assumption that 'girls = success' and 'boys = failure' within the 'boys' under-achievement' debate. In other words, some girls (namely those from white middle class backgrounds) seem to achieve much better than others. This implicit association (between white middle class girls and educational success) may explain some teachers' stereotypically lower expectations of Asian and African/Caribbean girls. Research has found that minority ethnic girls feel that their teachers expect less of them both academically in class and in relation to their future ambitions and careers (Mirza 1992; Basit 1997a; Parker-Jenkins *et al.* 1997; Archer *et al.* 2001b). Indeed, feminist scholarship has drawn attention to various ways in which girls' educational choices may be constrained by wider popular notions of what is 'acceptable', in terms of girls' subject choices and career aspirations (see Stone 1994).

Across the discussion groups Muslim boys constructed Muslim girls as lacking agency and choice in their post-16 decisions, and proposed that girls' participation in post-compulsory education was solely a matter of parental choice. As Yasser told Tamar (the Asian interviewer), it all 'depends on their parents really'. Several boys who talked with the white interviewer described how some Muslim girls are forced to leave education at the age of 16 in order to get married and/or fulfil domestic roles. This stereotype is illustrated by the extract below, in which girls are portrayed as staying at home and 'watching the tea', rather than pursuing careers. These examples were related jokingly by the boys and, interestingly, were often not actually borne out in respondents' accounts of their own family relations:

LA: Do you think the girls in your year will be getting jobs like you or not?
Rakim: Well some of them
Mushtak: Some won't be allowed to –
Rakim: [inaudible]
Mushtak: Some will go on to do further education, soon as you're sixteen that's –
Rakim: Yeah, you getting married now! (laughs)
LA: Do you know people who are getting married at sixteen?
Rakim: I don't know anyone
LA: What sort of jobs do you think the girls you know will be doing?
Rakim: Some of them, like the ones that do well, they'll just be the same as, you know um, boys. But some of them won't even – they'll just stay at home
Mushtak: Watching the tea!

(Hightown School, LA)

I would suggest that the boys reproduced a patriarchal discourse in which public and private social spheres are understood through a gender binary, in which the (female) home and the (male) workplace are positioned as mutually exclusive and oppositional spheres. The boys located 'normal' Muslim femininity within the domestic sphere, suggesting that girls' lives were characterized by responsibility for the family, housework, cooking and childcare. They suggested that only those girls who 'do well' academically are able to enter the world of further education and work, earning the chance to 'be the same as ... boys'. The young men's suggestion, that only *some* girls attain sufficiently high grades to warrant continuing in post-16 education, is interesting given the widespread public concerns with boys' under-achievement. It is also pertinent given that young men and women (in this study and in other research) are widely aware of this 'crisis' and are familiar with the notion of male under-achievement (for example, Francis 1999). In this respect, the Muslim boys' views illustrate the limits of the boys' under-achievement discourse: they are aware both that some boys achieve better than others, and that some girls achieve less well than others. As indicated earlier within the chapter, the boys positioned themselves as able to exercise choice over their post-16 routes, and they took it for granted that they would 'naturally' continue into either education or work after their GCSEs. In contrast to their constructions of Muslim girls' choices, the boys' unquestioning assumption that they themselves would work in the future might be interpreted as revealing the integral role played by the notion of work within boys' constructions of future masculine identities. In other words, the association between masculinity and paid employment was 'too true to warrant discussion' (Douglas 1964). The boys automatically, and unquestioningly, assumed that they would be able to make their own choices but, in contrast, they suggested that young Muslim women's choices are dependent upon a mixture of internal and external factors such as culture, circumstance and/or attainment.

Shain (2000) found that Asian girls with low levels of attainment tended to expect to drop out of school, whereas those in higher sets tended to aim to stay on. However, her explanation for this occurrence differs considerably from the views of the young men cited above. The boys suggested that the likelihood of a girl staying in, or leaving, education at the age of 16 will relate to her parents' gendered cultural expectations for their daughter. Conversely, Shain (2000) argues that the expectation of leaving school, among lower-attaining Asian girls, is a strategy through which girls actively resist the school system. She suggests that these girls draw upon ethnicized and gendered cultural discourses to resist schooling. Furthermore, Mushtak and Rakim thought that high-attaining Muslim girls were trying to earn the privilege to be free 'like boys' in their post-16 options. Shain, however, views such girls as adopting a strategy that enables them to survive the *education system* (as opposed to, say, seeking refuge from 'oppressive' home cultures).

I would also interpret the interview extract above as illustrating how the boys use humour to bond together in the discursive production of Muslim/Asian masculine identities. The boys' constructions of 'passive' Muslim girls (who are largely confined to the domestic sphere) constitute discursive points against which the boys can assert and create hegemonic masculinities, as the boys attempt to 'defend' their 'traditional' Muslim male spheres from female 'invasion'. As Gilroy (1993) and Alexander (1996) have both argued, masculine identities are negotiated within specifically racialized contexts and may centre on struggles over the control of 'our' women and specific symbols of masculinity. The boys' talk may thus be read as demonstrating the ways in which they attempt to carve out a specifically Muslim male arena of dominance in relation both to white society/ men *and* Muslim women through the assertion of these particular masculine identities (Archer 2001). In other words, by positioning Muslim girls as lacking agency and restricted by 'traditional' feminine roles of domesticity and marriage, boys were able to assert strong masculine identities and defend positions of male privilege.

The extract can also be read as drawing upon, and reproducing, a popular 'common sense' discourse in which Muslim girls are represented as oppressed and restricted in their educational choices. Boys drew on additional themes of 'danger', 'change', 'culture' and 'tradition' to justify their views, and they placed the blame for the causes of this restriction within white/British society. Generally, the boys suggested that British society has become increasingly dangerous for women, who therefore require more 'protection' and guidance from men. The main source of danger was framed in terms of the difficulty of upholding women's 'honour' when they participate in comprehensive (mixed sex) education:

TD: Do you think your sisters should go to college?
Naseem: No
Sham: No I think she – cos my sister – your sister's clever! [Jagdip: you know] thing is –
Jagdip: If you're like somewhere like ... Pakistan like Bangladesh they'll probably be OK, but here –
Sham: Yeah but here! You know like –
Jagdip: Cos they're more like lessons you go to your college and [Sham: you're mixing with boys] and go to college and how are we supposed to know what's happening and what's not!
Sham: So uh ... they won't let 'em ... it's the way we've been brought up really, I mean.

(Lowtown School, TD)

As illustrated by the above example, the boys used a notion of 'protection' to argue that many Asian women are (and indeed should be) restricted from continuing in education. The need for this protection was justified in terms of 'culture' to both the white interviewer ('it's tradition') and the Asian interviewer ('it's the way we've been brought up'). Yuval-Davis and Anthias (1989) argue that within discourses of culture, women are often positioned as 'cultural carriers' and embodiments of cultural differences. As Anthias suggests, 'gender relations are important boundary markers between one ethnic group and another. The "true" ethnic subject is often defined through conformity to gender stereotypes' (Anthias 1996: 18). I suggest that the young men in this study defined their Muslim masculine identities in relation to women, through the 'protection of femininity' (Wetherell 1993). This duty involves the policing of women's behaviour and 'knowing what's going on'. I interpret the boys' use of the 'protection of femininity' (as a defining feature of Muslim masculinity and 'tradition') as enabling them to both assert and maintain positions of hegemonic privilege, as they construct themselves as powerful by virtue of their 'caring' for women (see Wetherell and Potter 1992).

Boys drew on themes of culture and tradition in discussions with both the Asian and white interviewers. It was notable, however, that the transcripts produced with Asian interviewers were suffused with accounts of racism, unlike the texts produced with the white interviewer. Although the boys did not explicitly link the 'protection' of Muslim girls to protection from racism, some of the boys who talked to Tamar did suggest that some parents may not let their daughters continue in education because western society is becoming more dangerous and violent. As Yasser (from Eastfield School) suggested:

> Yeah, it's just that some parents don't let their daughters come to high school either [Abdul: yeah] cos you know ... their ... their reputation these days is going bad [Abdul: is going bad] innit? There are *guns* now, people have got *guns* in Mill Town so ... when we were little kids there weren't even one cop car, we didn't even know what coppers *were*! I mean apart from on TV ... but now you see coppers every-where and its gone badder.

This invocation of an increasingly 'dangerous' western/British society also constitutes an important element of the boys' constructions of racialized masculinities, because such representations enable the boys to justify their continued positions of power and privilege in relation to girls. The boys' invocation of 'worsening' times in Mill Town also challenges popular western liberal ideals of women's equal participation in education (meaning that potential feminist counter-discourses can be dismissed as 'irrespon-sible' or untenable within this 'unsafe' environment). Thus this portrayal of the 'dangerous' local conditions can be mobilized to justify the tightening of 'protective' patriarchal relations.

It is important to note, however, that constructions of 'dangerous wes-tern society' were predominantly produced in conversations with Tamar and, as such, I would suggest that the author's whiteness may have had a 'silencing' effect upon the articulation of comparable discourses. There might be various reasons for this silence within the white interviewer transcripts: it might reflect the boys' desire to avoid moments of conflict or it may reflect a perceived lack of any meaningful, shared discursive context between interviewer and respondents. However, it is also possible that the boys' use of such discourses is an example of their 'doing', or performance, of racialized masculinity, in which they are actively asserting their identities, and justifying their views, in relation to the Asian woman researcher.[2]

The boys were keen to justify, and excuse, themselves from any responsibility for intervening to redress sexual inequalities. They achieved this by drawing upon a discourse of 'culture as tradition'. As Sham claimed, 'what can we do? It's tradition':

TD: I mean do you think you would go – do you think some of the girls would go as far as maybe you would go? you would go?

Sham: They *could* – if they got given the *chance* ... cos like some of the girls are really bright – like Eri [J: Eri] she's good – so ... if-if they got given the chance to go ahead with a career

TD: But ... do you think they *will*?

Sham: I don't reckon ... but I don't know

Jagdip: Some of them

Sham: Depends who – what their parents like – we don't really know 'em

Jagdip: yeah, we don't really know 'em

TD: Depends on the parents ... What do you think should be done? ... do you think things should – do you think should change it?

Sham: Yeah but – what can we do? It's tradition.

Jagdip: Yeah

TD: Yeah – but like you're all the next generation – [Sham: but –] so you *could*! You *could* change it!

Sham: That wouldn't solve it! Cos could either be – change it and be heroes for some of them, but we would still have hell of a – [Jagdip: yeah and we wouldn't like –] like our forefathers – [TD: so –] just – carry on with the tradition!

TD: So you'd carry on and just leave it?

Sham: Yeah!

All: Yeahh! [laughs]

TD: [Laughs] So you w- do you reckon the girls will change it?

Sham: They *could* –

Jagdip: Yeah, yeah

Sham: I mean there's been like- like in Bangladesh ... but – did y- that, that woman ... she was almost killed because err- she produced this book about women ... in Bangladesh – what was she called?

Jagdip: Uma summit –

Sham: Uma- pretty name, Uma, that ... and they were *calling* her! ...

	didn't even know what she did! So – my dad's like that, you know. He believe that –
Jagdip:	Yeah! A bit like what Salman Rushdie did!
Sham:	Yeah! But it wasn't like – it was about *sexism* – it was about women should have more jobs and they should be allowed what they do ... what – to do what ... I mean it was *against* Islam ...

(Lowtown School, TD)

The topic of Muslim girls' educational and occupational choices evoked considerable emotional responses and debate among the boys. I suggest that these reactions reflect the ways in which such issues provided a key context for boys to engage in the re/production of identities and inequalities. Sham's concluding sentences (in the above interview extract) also indicate an element of confusion among the boys regarding what they felt to be acceptable or not acceptable behaviours.

The girls' own views of their choices and aspirations are detailed more fully in Archer (2002b), but to summarize, Muslim girls suggested that their fathers and parents generally supported them in their educational choices and aspirations. For example, one girl was adamant that her father would support her decisions irrespective of whether she chose to work or continue in post-compulsory education. As I have argued elsewhere (Archer 2002b), the boys' constructions of girls' choices thus reveal more about their own construction of racialized, patriarchal masculinities than they do about the 'reality' of many Muslim girls' lives.

In this chapter I have argued that analysis of Muslim pupils' educational 'choice(s)' reveals a complexity of inter-related themes concerning identities and inequalities of 'race', class and gender. Choice is a medium of both power and stratification (Giddens 1995), and educational choices are never rational or neutral individual cognitive processes. Unequal patterns of choice between different social groups reflect patterns of social injustice (Reay 1998). Differential patterns of educational preference and decision-making between social groups thus reflect the particular social relations and location from which they are asserted, and mirror unequal opportunities to access to privileged forms of cultural, social and economic capital (Reay *et al.* 2001).

Bourdieu (for example, 1986, 1990) has been very influential in drawing attention to classed inequalities in relation to processes of 'choice' and he details the ways in which choices and aspirations are embedded in common sense, tacit knowledges of 'what is appropriate for people like me/us'. Research by Diane Reay and Stephen Ball and colleagues has also detailed the ways in which working class educational choices and aspirations are unequally located in relation to middle class choices. For example, attention has been drawn to inequalities between middle class and working class families in relation to choosing secondary schools (Ball and Vincent 1998;

Reay and Lucey 2001), further education colleges (Maguire *et al.* 1999) and universities (Reay 1998). This chapter has attempted to develop this theorization further to explore some of the ways in which social class interacts with 'race', ethnicity and gender within Muslim boys' notions of their own, and Muslim girls' post-16 choices and in relation to their own subject preferences.

For example, I have drawn attention to the ways in which boys' views of possible and/or desirable options are bound up within notions of what might be appropriate, usual, possible and 'safe' for 'people like me', and more specifically, for Muslim girls or boys. Pupils' aspirations and choices are also limited by their unequal possession of the cultural and economic 'capital' that is required to negotiate educational routes and to be aware of, and take advantage of, a range of post-16 possibilities. As such, it is suggested that the boys occupied disadvantaged positions in relation to post-16 'choices' and decision-making, and had unequal access to social, economic and/or cultural capital and resources that would have enabled them to increase their horizons of possibility of choice.

Summary

In this chapter I have argued that Muslim boys drew on discourses and identities of 'race', class and gender within their constructions of educational preferences and (post-16) choices. Themes of culture, change, identity and tradition were mobilized by the boys when they talked about Muslim girls' choices, and I suggested that these negotiations represent some of the ways in which boys 'do' (racialized) masculinity. Inequalities of social class were apparent within boys' contingent choosing of post-16 routes and their preferences for 'secure' and 'safe' jobs. The boys also identified how racism can constitute a barrier to achieving well at school and later securing employment.

As also argued by Ball *et al.* (2000), the understandings that have been put forward in this chapter stand in stark contrast to popular policy conceptualizations of young people's post-16 educational/occupational decision-making, which are based on notions of rationality and assume that post-16 decision-making is necessarily informed and logical. In her critical examination of young people's views and aspirations, Francis found that pupils' belief in discourses of educational meritocracy masked their ability to perceive how structural inequalities might impact upon their lives:

A direct link between academic achievement and future job prospects was presented by many of the students and this was constructed as straightforward and unproblematic ... there appeared little awareness among the students that factors beyond their control such as discrimination might impact upon their job prospects

(Francis 1999: 313)

Ainley and Bailey (1997) also found evidence of the ways in which discourses of meritocracy are employed by young people, who commonly think that success in one's career is 'up to you', and thus solely the result of individual effort and ability. As Francis discusses, however, this individualistic, meritocratic belief is problematic because it places the burden of responsibility upon individuals rather than structures of inequality.

Inter-connecting themes of gender, social class and ethnicity were all evident within the Muslim boys' discussions of their post-16 choices and options, demonstrated, for example, through their associations between Muslim masculinity and a 'breadwinner' identity and through their denial of Muslim girls' 'choices'. Implications for practice will be taken up and considered further within the next, final chapter of the book.

Notes

1 This section is rewritten and drawn from Archer (2002b).
2 Remember that, as a young Pakistani woman interviewer, Tamar was occupying a position that was very different from, and thus challenged, the boys' constructions of 'normal' and 'proper' Asian femininity.

chapter eight

Conclusion: Muslim boys and schooling

Introduction

This concluding chapter requires a brief preface. Convention has it that the author concludes by offering practical recommendations for teachers, researchers and policy-makers, based on his or her research findings. This convention is problematic on a number of levels, not least because there is no simple or straightforward way in which research findings can be translated into practice (see Davies 2003 and Fox 2003 for excellent reviews of these arguments). In fact, within academic circles the very nature of the theory–practice divide itself is contested and subject to multiple, competing forces (Archer and Leathwood 2003). These wider debates aside, it should be stated that the original study did not contain the perspective of practitioners within its scope.

Nonetheless, the book has been written with an audience of teachers and educators, as well as researchers, in mind and I do believe that the issues raised are pertinent to the research and practice of all these constituencies. For example, in her research on teachers' life histories, Raphael Reed found that respondents continually drew attention to the 'difficulties and tensions experienced around working with boys, particularly in working-class and multiethnic contexts' (Raphael Reed 1999: 106). From this point of view, I hope that the book should be of use, and of interest, to those who currently (or who may in the future) work with Muslim boys. However, the issue of *how* the book might be of use will need to be considered (and indeed could form the basis of more detailed consideration than issues of time and space will allow here).

On one level, this book could be read as providing an insight into Muslim boys' identities, views and experiences in order to provide the practitioner, policy-maker or researcher with 'less oppressive' knowledges and understandings of Muslim masculinity. I feel, however, that such an approach depends upon a fixed and reductive notion of knowledge and 'truth' – a position that has been consistently argued against throughout the text. Furthermore, this type of approach can be critiqued for representing an imperialist or colonialist desire for 'knowing' and 'understanding' black youth (Alexander 2000: 225). Indeed, the associated acts of naming and appropriation that this knowledge production involves can in themselves constitute a practice through which Other(s) are colonized within academic theory and practice (Werbner 1996; S. Ahmed 1999). The framing of knowledge and research is of crucial importance: for example, white HE students in Alison Jones' research (2003) on diversity and equality expressed their desire to 'know' and 'be told' about their Maori peers. However, these students only wanted to know about particular non-threatening differences between themselves and Maoris (such as aspects of culture and tradition) but not experiences of inequalities and racism which, as Jones points out, would threaten the status quo and challenge white students' hegemony within the classroom.

Consequently, it must be emphasized that this book will not provide teachers and researchers with a clear, defined knowledge of 'Muslim boys'. Nor will it necessarily render Muslim boys more 'known' or 'knowable' within readers' classrooms and/or research projects. The text has a different aim, which is to help readers to rethink and challenge both their own, and dominant/popular, ways of understanding British Muslim masculinity. In this respect, the book attempts to create room for alternative ways of representing and engaging with issues concerning Muslim pupils within schools. Mirza and Reay (2000: 21) propose a similar discursive arena in their notion of a 'third space', which they identify as a point from which to highlight 'other worlds'. My own aim is thus to open up space for a range of non-hegemonic, 'other' readings of Muslim masculinity, while fore-grounding a theorization of masculinity as inherently racialized and classed (or conversely, gendered, racialized ethnicities and racialized, gendered class identities). Academically and politically I wish to focus attention on representations of Muslim boys as thinking, agentic, complex human beings, rather than the simplistic, homogenized, negative stereotypes which currently abound in the popular imagination.

This is not to say that the book is not 'useful', or simply an academic, blue skies exercise. In fact, it is precisely by charting 'other worlds' that both the potential and the limits of gender, 'race' and class school reform policies come sharply into focus (Mirza and Reay 2000: 21). As Lyn Raphael Reed (1999) emphasizes, it is vitally important to explore alternative forms of practice that engage with issues of masculinity (to which I would also add issues of 'race' and class) within schools.

> This is not a theoretical debate alone; it is a challenge to each and every teacher who daily inhabits and contests the patriarchal spaces of our

educational institutions. It is a matter of ideas and actions. It is an issue of *discourse* and *praxis*

(Raphael Reed 1999: 94)

Indeed, throughout the book, attention has been drawn to the ways in which particular discourses, conceptualizations, assumptions and stereotypes about Muslim boys can have 'real' effects and implications for pupils within schools. These effects span multiple sites, locations and social levels and they are evident within academic theory, in educational policy and practice and within the everyday lives of the boys. In other words, I would emphasize that the question of how we represent and talk about issues of Muslim masculinity is of vital importance and has far-reaching consequences.

With these thoughts in mind, the final following sections detail ways forward for addressing inequalities of 'race', gender and social class within schools, policy and research (although, of course, it is acknowledged that this task is highly complex and will require a holistic model of action). The issues addressed are: overhauling concepts and terminology; tackling racisms in school; addressing class inequalities in education; engaging with masculinity in schools.

Overhauling concepts and terminology: opening up the language of difference, identity, race, class and gender

I have argued throughout the book that identities and inequalities of 'race', class and gender are not discrete, mutually exclusive entities. In other words, 'difference' is not fixed or static; it is constantly shifting and evolving across time and context. Similarly, the boundaries of social differences are not fixed or definitive; differences are relational and intermesh with one another, occupying complex and overlapping relations with other forms of loosely bounded 'difference'. Differences are never total or complete: they are always partial, reworked and in process. At the same time they are embodied, follow discernible patterns and are enduring: some forms of difference can also be difficult to 'escape' (Archer 2003). Thus, as Stuart Hall (1992) astutely notes, difference is indeed a slippery and contested concept that is difficult to define and pin down.

So why should teachers and researchers need to immerse themselves in this conceptual quagmire? I would like to suggest that the importance of engaging in this (admittedly difficult and perhaps frustrating) theoretical venture is the need to strive towards producing meaningful and emancipatory (non-oppressive/non-exclusionary) research and knowledge that can help effect social change. Sara Ahmed similarly argues that

Unless we begin to ask questions about how differences and ambi-guities get re-incorporated, then I think the feminist consideration of (the impossibility of) identity will remain inadequate to the task: that is, it will not be able to engender a transformative politics

(S. Ahmed 1999)

Thus, I would suggest that a critical/feminist approach to research within schools can be usefully guided by Haraway's (1990: 191) argument 'for pleasure in the confusion of boundaries and for responsibility in their construction'. That is, we should embrace the multiplicity, complexity and fluidity of social phenomena, while also retaining an awareness of how, first, our own social positions interact within the research process to pro-duce these knowledges and, second, the knowledges and understandings we produce are never 'value neutral'.

Therefore we need to be able to move beyond narrow conceptualizations of *identity*, *'race'/ethnicity* (and associated concepts of racism, 'culture', 'community' and 'Muslim'), *gender* (specifically masculinity/masculinities) and *social class*. Suggestions are made below as to how these concepts might be opened up within educational discourses.

Identity

Previous chapters have illustrated the complexity of British Muslim boys' identities. Issues of 'race', religion, class and gender all structured the boys' sense of who they are and their experiences of being Muslim, British and male. Identity was also a central element within the boys' negotiations of post-16 choices and options, the ways in which they lived their everyday lives inside and outside of school, and formed the lens through which they interpreted the world and events around them. In order to engage with issues of identity within schools therefore, we need to be able to attend to its multifarious nature. I have suggested that identity can be usefully con-ceptualized as both embodied *and* 'performed', constructed and asserted by agentic individuals *and* constrained and structured by structural inequal-ities. In other words, identities are constructed through and within language and discourse, but they are also structured by material factors and inequalities. Equally, identities are not just consciously articulated, argued and asserted – they have an unconscious, emotional and psychic dimension. Furthermore, identity is relational, defined through other relationships: in addition to being articulated through a notion of what 'I am' or who 'we are', it can be constructed through a sense of what we are 'not',[1] and how others see us and indeed how we *think* others see us.

Throughout the book I have argued against an 'identity politics' approach to the study of racialized masculinities within schools. I have suggested that it is not necessarily desirable, or indeed possible, to 'match' the identities of the interviewer or researcher with those of the participants. I have proposed instead that attention might more usefully be given to analysing the complex ways in which identities and inequalities of 'race', class, gender and age interact between respondents and interviewers within the production of the research. We need to critically engage with issues of power and identity if we want to produce more egalitarian knowledge(s) and representations in relation to Muslim pupils. This means that teachers and researchers (especially those from dominant and privileged backgrounds) have a particular responsibility to critically examine their own roles within the classroom and in research processes alike. This process can be achieved by engaging critically with issues of representation.

In my study of Muslim masculinity, I have questioned how to theorize multiple identities comprising social class, gender, sexuality, 'race', religion and ethnicity. Some sociologists (such as Bradley 1996) favour a model of 'hybrid' or 'fragmented' identities as a means for engaging with this multiplicity in a way that moves beyond homogenized and static notions of 'cross-cutting' or 'intersecting' social categories. However, I would suggest that notions of 'hybrid' identities nonetheless need to be used with care, because, like the conceptualizations they claim to displace, they are still subject to the potential danger of slipping into essentialism (Yuval-Davis 1997). In other words, while there are no easy solutions to these ongoing questions, it is useful to keep these theoretical tensions as a constant presence within our research and practice to ensure that we are always mindful of the complexity of identities and inequalities.

'Race' and racism

I have attempted to draw attention to the powerful impact of racist discourses (and narrow, dominant notions of racism and race) on the lives of the young men. In order to engage effectively with issues of 'race' and racism we need to address the ways in which these concepts are framed and understood. Racialized ethnic identities and inequalities are complex and shifting phenomena. Muslim boys do not construct and inhabit neatly bounded 'Muslim' identities, but perform, enact, challenge and resist a range of identities that are 'culturally entangled' (Hesse 2000). For example, Chapter 3 charted the ways in which boys shifted across and between 'black', 'Asian', 'English', 'Bangladeshi/Pakistani' and 'British' identities. These slippages were not random or meaningless – they were located and strategic elements (operating on both conscious and unconscious levels) within the boys' processes of 'doing' identity.

I have argued that educational theory, policy and practice should utilize a circumscribed notion of '*race*', in line with the sociological and feminist rejection of biological conceptualizations of race. As Rattansi (1995) details, biological conceptualizations of race posit that bodies are racialized, that particular populations share biological/physiological traits and that people/groups can be organized into a racial hierarchy. These views have been called a discourse of 'scientific racism', which, while at the height of popularity in the nineteenth and early twentieth centuries, carry a degree of currency in the contemporary world.

Theories of 'new' and 'modern' *racism* have since been proposed. 'Modern' racism encapsulates the subtle, contemporary manifestations of racism. The concept of 'new' racism reflects how dominant racist discourses now focus on themes of 'culture' (rather than biology), naturalizing 'cultural differences' and 'ethnic groups', rather than biological racial categories. The emphasis upon 'cultural differences' (rather than racial hierarchies) within discourses of new racism, constitute as potent a force as 'old' racism, because racial/cultural differences are still subjected to processes of inferiorization, discrimination and exclusion (Rattansi 1992). In Britain attention has been drawn to the ways in which contemporary understandings of 'race' are constructed through multiple discourses of 'patriotism, nationalism, xenophobia, Englishness, Britishness, militarism and gender difference' (Gilroy 1987: 43). Thus (new) racist discourses focus on issues of inclusion and exclusion, questioning who may/may not 'belong' to the national (and local) community. I have attempted to show how these themes and concerns structure Muslim boys' everyday lives, with (new and old) racism(s) constituting a daily presence. Thus, I would argue, the study draws attention to the need for teachers and researchers to be able to engage with the invidious, subtle, covert knowledges that are embedded in 'our' everyday thinking and language.

Ethnicity, culture and community

I would suggest that attention must also be drawn to tensions and contradictions within conceptualizations of ethnicity. The popularity, and usage, of the concept of 'ethnicity' has increased in response to the problematic terminology of race. Indeed, Stuart Hall proposed a radical reworking of 'ethnicity' precisely as a means for challenging contemporary racist discourses around nationhood and race. As Oommen (2001) argues, the concept of ethnicity needs to be treated with care, particularly to ensure that it is not collapsed into notions of nationality, community and culture. As Alexander (2000) notes, 'new' sociological models of ethnicity emphasize the importance of 'hybrid', creative identities, acknowledging the role of interconnecting and competing discourses of social class and gender. In contrast, 'old' models of ethnicity revolved around more static notions of homogenous 'communities'. While the conceptualization of 'new' ethnicity is not in itself problematic, it does raise particular issues in relation to Asian groups, who have tended to be closely associated with notions of *culture* and *community* within the dominant imagination (Benson 1996; Alexander

2000). Indeed, racist discourses have precisely seized upon the supposed threat to the British way of life posed by the (assumed) strength and cohesion of Asian culture and community (see Gilroy 1987).

Notions of 'culture' and 'family' were central themes within boys' constructions of Muslim identities. However, I have attempted to emphasize the fluidity and contingency in the boys' use of these concepts. For example, I illustrated how they drew on transnational and local discourses that were redefined across time, generation and context (Eade 1989; Werbner 1990; Shaw 1988) and were structured by discourses of gender and social class. In the discussion groups, the boys drew on themes of 'culture' within their constructions of patriarchal masculinities, particularly in relation to their conceptualizations of Muslim femininity. Culture provided a site for engaging in struggles over meanings, and for asserting powerful masculine identities in relation to girls. Thus, conceptually it has been suggested that 'ethnicity cannot be reduced to culture and . . . "culture" cannot be seen as a fixed, essentialist category' (Yuval-Davis 1994: 183). 'Culture' refers to the 'processes, categories and knowledges through which communities are defined as such: that is, how they are rendered specific and differentiated' (Donald and Rattansi 1992: 4). Culture is thus a site for where power is exercised/negotiated (Bourdieu 1990).

Just as issues of 'culture' require careful conceptualization, I would suggest that teachers and researchers should pay due consideration to their understandings of 'community'. Alexander's (1998, 2000) studies of black and Bangladeshi young men demonstrated how notions of community are actively constructed between Asian boys. She demonstrates that discourses of 'community' may be bound up with, and negotiated in relation to, shifting discourses of the family, politics, age, gender and territory. Similarly, young men in this study were also seen to utilize shifting notions of Asian and Muslim 'community' within their discussions.

A conceptualization of 'imagined' communities and 'shifting' identities does not imply that these identities are in any way unreal or without effect or consequence. As I have attempted to argue, the (complex, multiple) ways in which pupils understand these relations are necessary bases for their sense of who they are, and impact upon pupils' actions, behaviours and aspirations (albeit in complex ways). Thus, rather than attempting to uncover a singular objective 'truth' about Muslim boys, it is more useful and valid to explore the complexity within their experiences and representations of self, and the relationship between these and boys' experiences within schools.

Muslim identity

I also suggest that 'Muslim' identity is a contested concept. Muslim communities may be strongly internally differentiated, for example, by language, region and religious practices/values, all of which are 'in process', debated and contested social divisions. The meanings and boundaries of the boys' Muslim identities were constantly negotiated, debated and reconfigured across personal, community and national spheres. Thus, the boys' Muslim identities, and their construction of Muslim brotherhood, might be better conceptualized as 'imagined communities' (Anderson 1993). I noted that the boys' constructions of Muslim identities were grounded within struggles around 'authenticity' and the assertion of patriarchal discursive power both within their male peer groups and in relation to the Asian and white female interviewers. As such, I would like to foreground an interpretation of Muslim masculinity as inherently relational and shifting, constructed in relation to a range of other identities, and as contested and constantly renegotiated across different times and contexts. This perspective stands in stark contrast to current popular notions of a unitary (and often demonized) Muslim masculinity.

In practice, I suggest that Muslim pupils should be recognized as constituting a diverse and provisional (in other words, not fixed or simplistically definable) 'group'. The differences between Muslim pupils are as 'real' and valid as their similarities because the Muslim identity itself is a political and contested category. Teachers and researchers need to be careful not to interpret the actions and views of particular individuals or groups (whether high or low profile) as characteristic of a particular community.

Gender

Gender (and indeed, all other social identities) is similarly shifting and 'in process'. I have attempted to delineate the ways in which masculinity is shifting, contested and relational, drawing attention to the ways in which the boys negotiated, constructed and challenged various possible versions of what it means to be a (Muslim) man. To this effect, I have drawn upon a notion of relational and contextual 'masculinities', suggesting, for example, that the boys' performances of popular, 'laddish' masculinities are organized in relation to discourses of racialized masculinity and femininity and are differently enacted between home and school.

I have also suggested that gender identities cannot be separated from discourses of 'race' and class. For example, the boys idealized particular symbols of black US working class African/Caribbean masculinity within their constructions of 'hyper-masculine' male identities. The boys' attempts to assert patriarchal, hegemonic masculinities were intimately intermeshed with their constructions of (passive, domestic and docile) Muslim femininity and in this respect, they manoeuvred to produce 'locally' hegemonic identities. For example, they presented themselves as powerful, agentic individuals via their representations of Muslim girls as weak, passive and restricted by 'traditional' cultural norms and values. The boys also defined themselves through the 'protection' of Muslim femininity, which researchers and teachers might wish to examine further within the context of anti-sexist work.

Social class

As I have argued elsewhere (Archer 2003), social class is a prime concern within any discussion of issues of identity and education, and a conceptualization of racialized, classed masculinities is useful in this respect. Figures suggest that many of the schools with higher than average proportions of Muslim pupils may also be institutions with greater percentages of working class pupils in general. These are more likely to be urban institutions that enjoy fewer resources and have lower than average levels of achievement. Thus issues of poverty, social class, 'race' and exclusion are frequently inter-related – indeed, minority ethnic graduates also record lower average earnings than their white counterparts.

Traditional sociological theories and definitions of social class have focused primarily on economic and occupational criteria. Such models have been critiqued for their failure to account for gender and other social identities and inequalities: for example, collapsing 'race' into social class and/or reading social class within an assumed white context. Accordingly, I have attempted to illustrate the various ways in which the boys' working class locations structured, and impacted on, their identities and experiences. For example, I have drawn attention to the subtle ways in which social class inequalities may structure and constrain Muslim boys' educational horizons. I have also attempted to trace the ways in which classed identities have psychic, as well as material, dimensions and consequences (for example, Lucey and Reay 2000; Reay and Lucey 2000; Walkerdine *et al.* 2001), and would suggest that the intersection of class and gender dimensions within constructions of racism constitutes an interesting further avenue for exploration.

Addressing racism(s) and racialized masculinities in schools

The question remains, however, as to what can, or might, we actually *do*? Strong criticisms have been levelled at multiculturalist and anti-racist approaches to addressing inequalities of 'race'. Partly these criticisms have suggested that the measures adopted have had little impact on levels of racism and racial incidents in classrooms and schools. For example, 'consciousness raising' has been critiqued as patronizing and implicit in maintaining the overall societal status quo (for example, Wetherell and Potter 1992). Critiques have also been levelled at strategies that position 'race' as a marginal, not a mainstream, issue, particularly those which position minority cultures as both the cause of the pathology and its cure. They fail to acknowledge the role of societal institutions, seeking instead to create 'liberated enclaves' (see Cohen and Taylor 1992). Furthermore, such approaches tend to rest on the assumption that there is 'a reality that has to be discovered and then changed, rather than a reality which is being created and re-created when practised and discussed' (Yuval-Davis 1994: 190).

In order to effectively engage with racism(s) within schools, pupils' (and indeed teachers') *emotional attachments* to racist discourses must also be considered. In contrast to previous rationalistic psychological and positivistic theories of prejudice, I have drawn attention to the ways in which racism(s) also comprise 'non-rational', emotional and identity-related elements. Racist discourses may be highly contradictory, seemingly inconsistent, contextual and inter-linked with wider social discourses, identities and inequalities. The embedded assumptions within institutional cultures also require careful critical inspection. Given the complexity of the task in hand, it is perhaps over-ambitious to expect the individual school or teacher to address all potential sources and aspects of racism(s). Indeed, irrespective of educational level or sector, it can be incredibly difficult to address inequalities in the classroom because majority group students are often highly resistant to any initiative or change in culture that appears to 'favour' other pupils. Thus we need to understand the ways in which Muslim/minority ethnic *and* white pupils *and* staff can all resist educational discourses and particular social relations through their racialized, gendered and classed identities.

I would argue that an awareness of this complexity can be invaluable in the design and implementation of egalitarian strategies and practices. In particular, teachers and researchers can usefully pay attention to *processes of racialization* within their work, attending to these as they occur both in the imagination of the dominant society and as they are contested from within particular ethnic collectivities (Anthias and Yuval-Davis 1992). The task thus becomes to understand the differences that our differences make (to paraphrase Diane Reay 1996a). Teachers and researchers are part and parcel of pupils' production of identities (of 'race', class and masculinity) within the classroom and the research context. We need to engage with our own various, and multiple, roles within the reproduction of identities and inequalities. Injustices are not solely 'out there', they are also produced through what we say and do.

Addressing 'taken for granted', common sense views of particular groups or communities is key in attempts to address *institutional racism(s)*. The Macpherson Report, published following the murder of the young black student Stephen Lawrence, defined institutional racism as:

> The collective failure of an organisation to provide an appropriate and professional service to people because of their colour, culture or ethnic

origin. It can be seen or detected in processes, attitudes and behaviour which amount to discrimination through unwitting prejudice, ignorance, thoughtlessness and racist stereotyping which disadvantage minority ethnic people

(Macpherson 1999: 28)

It may be useful to consider what is meant, and conveyed, by references to pupils' 'home culture(s)'. We may want to re-examine and question which elements are being selectively highlighted within celebrations of 'Asian culture' and whose values we are normalizing and/or stereotyping when referring to particular 'cultural' phenomena. Teachers and researchers need to be very wary of 'culture' discourses; we need to ensure that they are not used to represent 'natural' group differences or to 'impose stereotypic notions of "common cultural need" upon heterogeneous groups with diverse social aspirations and interests' (Brah 1992: 129).

Exclusionary school hierarchies can be formed through complex racialized and gendered interactions and processes, thus schools may also find it useful to critically re-examine some of the assumptions underpinning 'normal' practices and activities. For example, the location, timing and musical slant of school discos emerged as a divisive practice within some of the discussion groups. Asian girls rarely attended, some of the Muslim boys' parents did not want their sons to take part, and some of the boys who did go were unhappy with the balance of music played (which they felt reflected the white pupils' tastes more than their own). Bringing such practices into an open forum for discussion and debate might help to address imbalances between dominant assumptions of 'normal' adolescent identity, and minority counter-discourses of risk, safety, ownership and control. These issues do not only impact on after school and social activities, but are important concerns in relation to the development and delivery of school curricula. For example, I would suggest that current policy drives to promote citizenship education raise important questions in relation to discourses of culture. It is not surprising that the ideal of citizenship (which conveys a notion of national belonging and participation) is being promoted during a time in which there are also widespread popular concerns about 'British identity' in relation to Muslim fundamentalism, European Union and globalized, ethnically 'hybridized' (black) youth cultures. In other words, I would suggest that it is crucially important to interrogate the norms and values underpinning such strategies in order to ensure that they do not become forms of social control.

I would strongly argue that to effectively (and better) engage with equality issues in schools will require a 'repoliticization' of the educational policy agenda. This would be no mean feat within the current 'new managerialist' climate, which places emphasis on issues of 'quality', accountability, audit and testing as opposed to 'equality'. Teachers and researchers can provide an important critique to counter-balance dominant new managerialist discourses: it is vital that we continue to question our common sense terminology and understandings, and make spaces for critical representations and pupils' experiences.

In terms of addressing issues of gender in the classroom, teachers and researchers may wish to examine further the ways in which 'race' interacts with masculinity among pupils. Focusing on 'race', religion and ethnicity can contribute a valuable extra dimension to existing debates on boys and schooling. For example, while we know that boys tend to dominate teacher attention in mixed sex schools (Howe 1997; Younger and Warrington 1999; Francis 2000a; Warrington and Younger 2000), the ways in which this may, or may not, be played out in relation to minority ethnic and Muslim boys is less clear.

It has been popularly suggested that one solution to the 'boys in crisis' debate might be to increase the numbers of male 'role models' within schools. It is of little surprise that this suggestion has been advocated most vigorously in relation to African/Caribbean boys, reproducing racist stereotypical notions of problematic black masculinity as characterized by absent fathers and overbearing mothers. Given the growth of popular concerns with Muslim male identities, it would be of little surprise if strategies were to emerge promoting the potential utility of 'positive' Muslim male role models for improving Muslim boys' behaviours and achievement. However, the idea of using such role models is highly problematic because it relies upon an over-simplification and essentialization of (black) male identities, and is often proposed in a way that fails to question the 'type' of masculinity that is being promoted or resisted. The use of role models as a strategy in schools also diverts attention away from institutional racism(s) and undermines women teachers (see Epstein *et al.* 1998; Raphael Reed 1999).

Instead, I would second Lyn Raphael Reed's (1999: 104) call for further feminist analyses and accounts of the production of sexualized identities in school, 'looking at the relationship between adult and child processes across the masculine/feminine divide and including the complexities of the unconscious'. This is a useful and interesting direction which could facilitate an understanding of the 'circulation of sexualised power in classroom spaces and would allow a different reading of the significance male and female teachers bring to their interactions with and interpretations of both boys and girls' (Raphael Reed 1999). Skelton (2001) similarly proposes that teachers and researchers need to consider which versions of masculinity are being generally encouraged and promoted within schools. I would like to extend this question further to encourage reflection upon which versions of *ethnic* and *racial* (masculine) identity are encouraged, promoted and (most importantly) normalized within schools. Thus, teachers and researchers may wish to examine 'the different versions of masculinity which are open to and taken up by boys in schools; how they may work to produce problems for educators and for boys themselves; and how boys come to inhabit them' (Epstein *et al.* 1998: 4). For readers wishing to engage further with a critical examination of 'normal' educational discourses and practices, I would also recommend Bronwyn Davies' (1997) notions of 'critical literacy' and her work on the operation of (symbolic) violence in schools. While Davies writes primarily within the context of gender, her arguments can also be usefully brought to bear upon racialized masculinities and femininities.

Conclusion

The purpose of this project has been an ambitious one: I have tried to produce an account of a group of boys' constructions of Muslim masculinities that opens up, rather than closes down, potential avenues of interpretation. Within this work, I have inevitably subjugated individual differences in favour of identifying patterns of meaning, but I have also focused intently on individuals and their words and accounts, while attempting to convey broader ideas and arguments about wider societal discourses and inequalities. I have had to negotiate the tightrope between claiming and privileging particular circumspect/provisional 'truths' while vigorously denying the truth of other discourses (namely those which I perceive to be pathologizing and negative). Not least, my aim has been to strive towards that impossible dream of producing a text that is both 'properly' theoretical *and* 'useful' at the same time. And yet the research discussed within this book remains inherently problematic and emblematic of wider social inequalities. For example, it is as a white, middle class researcher that I have exercised control over the study and have retained the authorial power to determine whose voices are represented, in what ways and for which ends and purposes. Furthermore, the boys and the Asian interviewers who took part in the study (both of whose labour and experiences I have benefited from and exploited) have not had the opportunity to strongly influence or determine the ways in which they have been represented. In this respect, the book occupies an uneasy political and ethical space.[2]

I would like to conclude by summarizing a few of the key arguments and messages that arise from the book. First, it is vital that educational research, policy and practice is able to engage with the diversity of social inequalities which currently permeate and structure pupils' experiences of schooling because theoretical/conceptual and practical issues are closely linked. Second, there is still much work to be done to encourage the recognition that issues of 'race', racism and ethnicity are mainstream concerns, for example, issues in relation to Muslim masculinity are issues for *everyone*, not just for particular groups or communities. Third, the current popular demonization of Muslim masculinity should be seen as a contemporary twist on the 'old' racist rhetoric as voiced in the 1970s by Enoch Powell, with the claim that:

> the nation has been and is still being, eroded and hollowed out from within by implantation of unassimilated and unassimilable populations … alien wedges in the heartland of the state
>
> (Enoch Powell, 9 April 1976, cited in Gilroy 1987)

We need to be able to identify and target the ways in which such views continue to be played out in social and educational discourses.

As a fourth point, I would argue that addressing multiple identities and inequalities in 'race', class and gender in our work is a hard task, but this does not absolve us of the responsibility of trying. Irrespective of whether we work within the context of research, policy or practice, issues of gender and 'race'/ethnicity should be addressed in a holistic, inter-linked way. For this, we need to have a conceptual framework within which to engage with multiple inequalities in order to work 'across' differences of 'race', class and gender between educators/researchers and, in this instance, young ethnic minority men.

And finally, I would like to conclude by suggesting that what is at stake is the dismantling of unequal social privileges. To paraphrase and extend the words of Diane Reay (1997), the solution to social and educational inequalities does not lie in making working class pupils more middle class, nor is it about rendering Muslim pupils more like white pupils. It is not even a case of trying to get Muslim boys to behave and think more like white boys or like girls. Instead, we need to grapple with inequalities as they are played out within social and educational systems, within the ways we think about and conceptualize the world around us and within our many and varied professional practices. Tackling inequalities of 'race', ethnicity, gender and social class within schools requires us to re/connect our political and theoretical beliefs with our professional experiences, or, to put it another way, we need to engage in a dual process of grounding our politics and politicizing our practices. In this way we might work towards creating positive changes in schools and society that will benefit not only Muslim boys but also the lives of all pupils.

Notes

1 Said (1978) cited in Wetherell and Potter (1992)
2 It is also notable that I have not attempted to engage with particular 'difficult differences', such as issues of 'forced marriage' and other problematic and oppressive practices. This omission is largely due to my wish to focus on 'mainstream' Muslim identities and such issues did not constitute the everyday

experiences of the pupils in question, and thus did not strictly fall within my specific remit. I acknowledge, however, that there are still a number of important issues outstanding that deserve further attention and consideration in future work.

References

Aboud, F. (1988) *Children and Prejudice*. Oxford: Blackwell.

Adelman, C. (1985) Who are you? Some problems of ethnographer culture shock, in R.G. Burgess (ed.) *Field Methods in the Study of Education*. Brighton: Falmer Press.

Afshar, H. (1989) Education: hope, expectations and achievements of Muslim women in West Yorkshire, *Gender and Education*, 1: 261–72.

Ahmed, B. (1996) The social construction of identities and intergroup experiences: the case of second generation Bangladeshis in Britain. Unpublished PhD thesis, University of Sheffield.

Ahmed, S. (1999) 'She'll wake up one of these days and find she's turned into a nigger': Passing through hybridity, *Theory, Culture and Society*, 16(2): 87–106.

Ainley, P. (1994) *Degrees of Difference: Higher Education in the 1990's*. London: Lawrence and Wishart.

Ainley, P. and Bailey, W. (1997) *The Business of Learning*. London: Cassell.

Alexander, C. (1996) *The Art of Being Black*. Oxford: Oxford University Press.

Alexander, C. (1998) Re-imagining the Muslim Community, *Innovation*, 11(4): 439–50.

Alexander, C. (2000) *The Asian Gang*. Oxford: Berg.

Anderson, B. (1993) *Imagined Communities* (London, Verso)

Anthias, F. (1996) *Rethinking Social Divisions: Or What's So Important About Gender, Ethnicity, 'Race' and Class?* Inaugural Lecture Series. London: Greenwich University Press.

Anthias, F. (2001) New hybridities, old concepts: the limits of 'culture', *Ethnic and Racial Studies*, 24(4): 619–41.

Anthias, F. and Yuval-Davis, N. (1992) *Racialized Boundaries: Race, Nation, Gender, Colour and Class and the Anti-racist Struggle*. London: Routledge.

Anwar, M. (1979) *The Myth of Return: Pakistanis in Britain*. London: Heinemann Press.

Archer et al. 2001a: Published in: *International Studies in Sociology of Education*, Vol. II No.1. pp.41–62

Archer, L. (1998) The social construction of identities by British Muslim pupils aged 14–15 years. Unpublished PhD thesis, University of Greenwich.

Archer, L. (2000) Social class and access to higher education. Report from the Social Class and Widening Participation to Higher Education project, Institute for Policy Studies in Education, University of North London, October.

Archer, L. (2001) Muslim brothers, black lads traditional Asians: British Muslim young men's constructions of 'race' religion and masculinity, *Feminism and Psychology*, 11(1): 79–105.

Archer, L. (2002a) 'It's easier that you're a girl and that you're Asian': interactions of 'race' and gender between researchers and participants, *Feminist Review*, 72: 108–32.

Archer, L. (2002b) Change, culture and tradition: British Muslim pupils talk about Muslim girls' post-16 'choices', *Race, Ethnicity and Education*, 5(4): 359–76.

Archer, L. (2003) Social class and higher education, in L. Archer, M. Hutchings and A. Ross (eds) *Higher Education and Social Class*. London: Routledge Falmer.

Archer, L. and Hutchings, M. (2000) 'Bettering yourself'? Discourses of risk, cost and benefit in ethnically diverse, young working-class and non-participants' constructions of higher education, *British Journal of Sociology of Education*, 21(4): 555–74.

Archer, L. and Leathwood, C. (2003) Identities, inequalities and higher education, in L. Archer, M. Hutchings and A. Ross (eds) *Higher Education and Social Class*. London: Routledge/Falmer.

Archer, L., Hutchings, M. and Leathwood, C. (2001a) Engaging with commonality and difference: theoretical tensions in the analysis of working-class women's educational discourses Publication details?

Archer, L. and Yamashita, H. (2003a) 'Knowing their limits?' Identities, inequalities and inner city school leavers' post-16 aspirations, *Journal of Education Policy*, 18(1): 53–69.

Archer, L. and Yamashita, H. (2003b) Theorising inner-city masculinities: 'race', class, gender and education, *Gender and Education*, 15(2): 115–32.

Archer, L., Pratt, S.D. and Phillips, D. (2001b) Working-class men's constructions of masculinity and negotiations of (non) participation in higher education, *Gender and Education*, 13(4): 431–50.

Archer, L., Hutchings, M. and Ross, A. (2003) *Higher Education and Social Class. Issues of Exclusion and Inclusion*. London: Routledge/Falmer.

Arnot, M., Gray, J., James, M., Ruddock, J. and Duveen, G. (1998) *Recent Research on Gender and Educational Performance*. London: Office for Standards in Education.

Arnot, M., David, M. and Weiner, G. (1999) *Closing the Gender Gap?* Cambridge: Polity.

Back, L. (1996) *New Ethnicities and Urban Culture: Racisms and mulitculture in young lives*. London: UCL Press.

Baker, H.A., Best, S. and Lindeborg, R.H. (1996) Representing blackness/representing Britain: cultural studies and the politics of knowledge, in H.A. Baker, M. Diawara and R.H. Lindeborg (eds) *Black British Cultural Studies*. Chicago: University of Chicago Press.

Ball, S. (2003) *Class Strategies and the Education Market: The Middle Class and Social Advantage*. London: Routledge Falmer.

Ball, S. and Vincent, C. (1998) 'I heard it on the grapevine': 'hot' knowledge and schools choice, *British Journal of Sociology of Education*, 19: 377–400.

Ball, S., Maguire, M. and Macrae, S. (2000) *Choice, Pathways and Transitions Post–16: New Youth, New Economies in the Global City*. London: Routledge Falmer.

Ballard, R. (1994) *Desh Pardesh: The South Asian Presence in Britain*. London: Hurst.

Bannerjea, K. (2000) Sounds of whose underground? The fine tuning of diaspora in an age of mechanical reproduction, *Theory, Culture and Society*, 17(3): 64–79.

Barbour, R. and Kitzinger, J. (eds) (1999) *Developing Focus Group Research: Politics Theory and Practice*. London: Sage.

Basit, T. (1996) I'd hate to be just a housewife: career aspirations of British Muslim girls, *British Journal of Guidance and Counselling*, 24(2).

Basit, T. (1997a) *Eastern Values, Western Milieu: Identities and Aspirations of Adolescent British Muslim Girls*. Aldershot: Ashgate.

Basit, T. (1997b) 'I want more freedom but not too much': British Muslim girls and dynamism of family values, *Gender and Education*, 9(4): 425–40.

Bauman, Z. (1996) From pilgrim to tourist: on a short story of identity, in S. Hall and P. du Gay (eds) *Questions of Cultural Identity*. London: Sage.

Benson, S. (1996) 'Asians have culture, West Indians have problems': discourses on race inside and outside anthropology, in T. Ranger, Y. Samad and O. Stuart (eds) *Culture, Identity and Politics*. Aldershot: Avebury Press.

Berry, J.W., Kim, U., Minde, T. and Mok, D. (1987) Comparative studies of acculturative stress, *International Migration Review*, 21: 491–511.

Betancourt, H. and Regeser Lopez, S. (1993) The study of culture, ethnicity and race in American psychology, *American Psychologist*, 48(6): 629–37.

Bhavnani, K. (1988) Empowerment and social research: some comments, *Text*, 8: 41–50.

Bhavnani, K. and Phoenix, A. (eds) (1994) *Shifting Identities, Shifting Racisms. A Feminism and Psychology Reader*. London: Sage.

Biddulph, S. (1994) *Manhood: A Book about Setting Men Free*. Sydney: Finch Publishing.

Billig, M. (1988) The notion of 'prejudice': some rhetorical and ideological aspects, *Text*, 8: 91–111.

Billig, M. (1991) *Ideology and Opinions: Studies in Rhetorical Psychology*. London: Sage.

Billig, M. (1995) *Banal Nationalism*. London: Sage.

Billig, M. and Cochrane, R. (1984) 'I'm not National Front, but . . .', *New Society*, 68.

Billig, M., Condor, S., Edwards, D. *et al.* (1988) *Ideological Dilemmas: A Social Psychology of Everyday Thinking*. London: Sage.

Bird, J. (1996) *Black Students in Higher Education: Rhetorics and Realities*. Buckingham: Open University Press.

Blair, M. (1995) 'Race', class and gender in school research, in J. Holland, M. Blair and S. Sheldon (eds) *Debates and Issues in Feminist Research and Pedagogy*. Clevedon: Open University.

Bly, R. (1990) *Iron John: A Book About Men*. Reading, MA: Addison-Wesley.

Boaler, J., Wiliam, D. and Brown, M. (2000) Students' experiences of ability grouping – disaffection, polarisation and the construction of failure, *British Educational Research Journal*, 27(4).

Bourdieu, P. (1986) *Distinction: A Social Critique of the Judgement of Taste.* London: Routledge.

Bourdieu, P. (1990) *The Logic of Practice.* Cambridge: Polity.

Bradley, H. (1996) *Fractured Identities: Changing Patterns of Inequality.* Cambridge: Polity.

Brah, A. (1992) Difference, diversity and differentiation, in D. James and A. Rattansi (eds) *'Race', Culture and Difference.* London: Sage.

Brah, A. (1994) 'Race' and 'Culture' in the gendering of labour markets: south Asian young Muslim women and the labour market, in H. Afshah and M. Maynard (eds) *The Dynamics of 'Race' and Gender: Some Feminist Interventions.* London: Taylor and Francis.

Brah, A. (1996) *Cartographies of Diaspora: Contesting Identities.* London: Routledge.

Brah, A. and Minhas, R. (1986) Structural racism or cultural difference? Schooling for Asian girls, in G. Weiner (ed.) *Just a Bunch of Girls.* Milton Keynes: Open University Press.

Brewer, R. (1993) Theorizing race, class and gender: the new scholarship of black feminist intellectuals and black women's labour, in S.H. James and A.P.A. Busici (eds) *The Black Feminisms: The Visionary Pragmatism of Black Women.* London: Routledge.

Brittan, A. (1989) *Masculinity and Power.* New York: Cassess.

Brod, H. (1994) Some thoughts on some histories of some masculinities: Jews and other others, in H. Brod and M. Kaufman (eds) *Theorizing Masculinities.* London: Sage.

Brown, L.M. (1998) Voice and ventriloquation in girls' development, in K. Henwood, C. Griffin and A. Phoenix (eds) *Standpoints and Differences: Essays in the Practice of Feminist Psychology.* London: Sage.

Brown, R. (1988) *Group Processes: Dynamics Within and Between Groups.* Oxford: Blackwell.

Brown, R. (1995) *Prejudice: Its Social Psychology.* Oxford: Blackwell.

Buckingham, D. (1993) *Children Talking Television: The Making of Television Literacy.* London: Falmer.

Burman, E. (1994) Jewish feminism and feminist theory, in K. Bhavnani and A. Phoenix (eds) *Shifting Identities, Shifting Racisms. Feminism and Psychology Reader.* London: Sage Publications.

Burman, E. and Parker, I. (1993) Introduction – discourse analysis: the turn to the text, in E. Burman and I. Parker (eds) *Discourse Analytic Research: Repertoires and Readings of Texts in Action.* London: Routledge.

Butler, J. (1990) *Gender Trouble: Feminism and the Subversion of Identity.* London: Routledge.

Calhoun, C., Yuval-Davis, N., Oommen, T.K. *et al.* (2001) Symposium on ethnicity, *Ethnicities*, 1(1): 9–23.

Carrigan, T., Connell, R. and Lee, J. (1985) Towards a new sociology of masculinity, *Theory and Society*, 14: 551–604.

Cealey Harrison, W. and Hood-Williams, J. (1998) More varieties than Heinz: social categories and sociality in Humphries, Hammersley and beyond, *Sociological Research Online*, 3(1). www.socresonline.org.uk/3/1/contents

Cheng, Y. and Heath, A. (1993) Ethnic Origins and Class Destinations, *Oxford Review of Education*, 19 (2): 151–65.

Clark, J. and Newman, J. (1997) *The Managerial State*. London: Sage.

Clatterbaugh, K. (1990) *Contemporary Perspectives on Masculinity: Men, Women and Politics in Modern Society*. Washington, DC: Westview.

Coffield, F. and Vignoles, A. (1997) *Widening Participation in Higher Education by Ethnic Minorities, Women and Alternative Students*. National Committee of Inquiry into Higher Education, Report 5. London: The Stationery Office.

Cohen, P. (1988) The perversions of inheritance: studies in the making of multi-racist Britain, in P. Cohen and H.S. Bains (eds) *Multi-Racist Britain*. London: Macmillan.

Cohen, P. (1989) *The Cultural Geography of Adolescent Racism*. Centre for Multicultual Education: University of London Institute of Education.

Cohen, P. (1997) *Rethinking the Youth Question*. London: Macmillan.

Cohen, S. and Taylor, L. (1992) *Escape Attempts: The Theory and Practice of Resistance to Everyday Life*, 2nd edn. London: Routledge.

Coltrane, S. (1994) Theorizing masculinities in comtemporary social science, in H. Brod and M. Kaufman (eds) *Theorizing Masculinities*. London: Sage.

Connell, R.W. (1987) *Gender and Power*. Cambridge: Polity.

Connell, R. (1989) Cool guys, Swats and wimps: the interplay of masculinity and education, *Oxford Review of Education*, 15: 291–303.

Connell, R.W. (1995) *Masculinities*. Cambridge: Polity.

Connell, R.W. (1996) Teaching the boys: new research on masculinity, and gender strategies for schools, *Teachers College Record*, 98(2): 206–35.

Connell, R.W. (1997) The big picture: masculinites in recent world history, in A.H. Halsey, H. Lauder, P. Brown and A. Stuart Wells (eds) *Education: Culture, Economy and Society*. Oxford: Oxford University Press.

Connolly, P. (1998) *Racism, Gender Identities and Young Children: Social Relations in a Multi-ethnic, Inner-city Primary School*. London: Routledge.

Connolly, P. and Neill, J. (2001) Constructions of locality and gender and their impact on the educational aspirations of working class children. Paper presented at Addressing Issues of Social Class and Education: Theory into Practice Conference, University of North London, London, June.

Constantinou, S. and Harvey, M. (1985) Dimensional structure and intergenerational differences in ethnicity: the Greek Americans, *Sociology and Social Research*, 69: 234–54.

Cooper, C. (1993) *Noises in the Blood: Orality, Gender and the 'Vulgar' Body of Jamaican Culture*. London: Macmillan.

Corrigan, P. (1979) *Schooling the Smash Street Kids*. London: Macmillan.

CVCP (1998a) *From Elitism to Inclusion: Good Practice in Widening Access to Higher Education*, Main Report. London: CVCP.

CVCP (1998b) *Workshops on Widening Participation in Higher Education*. Paper Vc/98/29, September. London: CVCP.

Davies, B. (1989) *Frogs and Snails and Feminist Tales*. London: Allen and Unwin.

Davies, B. (1997) Constructing and deconstructing masculinities through critical literacy, *Gender and Education*, 9(1): 9–30.

Davies, B. (2003) Death to critique and dissent? The policies and practices of new managerialism and of 'evidence–based practice', *Gender and Education*, 15(1): 91–103.

Davies, P., Williams, J. and Webb, S. (1997) Access to higher education in the late twentieth century: policy, power and discourse, in J. Williams (ed.) *Negotiating Access to Higher Education: The Discourse of Selectivity and Equity*. Buckingham: SRHE and Open University Press.

Delamont, S. (2000) The anomalout beasts: hooligans and the sociology of education, *Sociology*, 34: 95–111.

DES (Department of Education and Science) (1985) *Education for All*, the Swann Report. London: HMSO.

Deshpande, P. and Rashid, N. (1993) Developing equality through local education authority INSET, in I. Siraj-Blatchford (ed.) *'Race', Gender and the Education of Teachers*. Buckingham: Open University Press.

DfEE (1999) *Participation Rates in Higher Education by Social Class 1991–2/ 1997–8* September, Dataset ST29313, www.statistics.gov.uk/statbase/xdataset.asp.

Donald, J. and Rattansi, A. (eds) (1992) *Race, Culture and Difference*. London: Sage.

Douglas, J.W.B. (1964) *The Home and the School*. London: McGibbon and Kee.

Duelli Klein, R. (1983) How to do what we want to do: thoughts about feminist methodology, in G. Bowles and R. Duelli Klein (eds) *Theories of Women's Studies*. London: Routledge and Kegan Paul.

Eade, J. (1989) *The Politics of Community: The Bangladeshi Community in East London*. Avebury: Aldershot.

Edley, N. and Wetherell, M. (1995) *Men in Perspective: Practice, Power and Identity*. London: Prentice Hall/Harvester Wheatsheaf.

Edley, N. and Wetherell, M. (1997) Jockeying for position: the construction of masculine identities, *Discourse and Society*, 8: 203–17.

Edwards, R. (1990) Connecting method and epistemology: a white woman interviewing black women, *Women's Studies International Forum*, 13(5): 477–90.

El-Solh, C.F. and Mabro, J. (eds) (1992) Muslim women's choices: religious belief and social reality, *Cross Cultural Perspectives on Women*, Vol.12. Oxford: Berg.

Ellis, J. (1991) Local government and community needs: a case study of Muslims in Coventry, *New Community*, 17(3): 359–76.

Epstein, D., Elwood, J., Hey, V. and Maw, J. (1998) *Failing Boys? Issues in Gender and Achievement*. Buckingham: Open University Press.

Essed, P. (1990) *Everyday Racism: Reports from Women of Two Cultures*. Alameda, CA: Hunter House.

Finch, J. (1993) It's great to have someone to talk to: ethics and politics of interviewing women, in M. Hammersley (ed.) *Social Research: Philosophy, Politics and Practice*. London: Sage.

Fine, M., Weis, L., Powell, L. and Wong, L.M. (1997) *Off White: Readings on Race, Power and Society*. London: Routledge.

Fox, N.J. (2003) Practice-based evidence: towards collaborative and transgressive research, *Sociology*, 37(1): 81–102.

Francis, B. (1996) Doctor/nurse, teacher/caretaker: children's gendered choice of adult occupation in interviews and role plays, *British Journal of Education and Work*, 9(3): 47–58.

Francis, B. (1998) *Power Plays*. Stoke-on-Trent: Trentham

Francis, B. (1999) Lads, Lasses and (New) Labour: 14–16 year old students' responses to the laddish behaviour of boys and boys' under-achievement debate, *British Journal of Sociology of Education*, 20: 355–71.

Francis, B. (2000a) *Boys, Girls and Achievement*. London: Routledge/Falmer.

Francis, B. (2000b) The gendered subject: students' subject preferences and discussions of gender and subject ability, *Oxford Review of Education*, 26(1): 35–48.

Francis, B. (2001) Men teachers and the construction of heterosexual masculinity in the classroom, *Sex Education*, 1(1): 9–21.

Francis, B. (2002) Is the future really female? The impact and implications of gender for 14–16 year olds' career choices, *Journal of Education and Work*, 15(1): 75–88.

Francis, B., Hutchings, M., Archer, L. and Melling, L. (forthcoming) Subject-choice and occupational aspirations among pupils at girls' schools, *Pedagogy, Culture and Society*.

Frosh, S., Phoenix, A. and Pattman, R. (2002) *Young Masculinities*. Basingstoke: Palgrave.

Furlong, A. and Cartmel, F. (1997) *Young People and Social Change: Individualization and Risk in Late Modernity*. Buckingham: Open University Press

Gardner, K. and Shukur, A. (1994) 'I'm Bengali, I'm Asian and I'm living here': the changing identity of British Bengalis, in R. Ballard (ed.) *Desh Pardesh: The South Asian Presence in Britain*. London: Hurst and Company.

Gerwitz, S. (2000) Social justice, New Labour and school reform, in S. Gerwitz, G. Lewis and J. Clarke (eds) *Rethinking Social Policy*. London: Sage and The Open University.

Ghuman, P.A.S. (1991) Have they passed the cricket test?: A qualitative study of Asian adolescents, *Journal of Multilingual and Multicultural Development*, 17(3): 457–66.

Giddens, A. (1995) *Politics, Sociology and Social Theory: Encounters with Classical and Contemporary Social Thought*. Stanford, CA: Stanford University Press.

Gill, R. (1995) Relativism, reflexivity and politics: interrogating discourse analysis from a feminist perspective, in S. Wilkinson and C. Kitzinger (eds) *Feminism and Discourse: Psychological Perspectives*. London: Sage.

Gillborn, D. (1990) *'Race', Ethnicity and Education: Teaching and Learning in Multi-Ethnic Schools*. London: Unwin Hyman.

Gillborn, D. and Gipps, C. (1996) *Recent Research on the Achievements of Ethnic Minority Pupils*. London: HMSO.

Gilligan, C. (1982) *In a Different Voice: Psychological Theory and Women's Development*. Cambridge, MA: Harvard University Press.

Gilroy, P. (1987) *Problems in Anti-Racist Strategy*. London: Runnymede Trust.

Gilroy, P. (1991) *There Ain't No Black in the Union Jack*. Chicago: University of Chicago Press.

Gilroy, P. (1993) *Small Acts*. London: Serpent's Tail.

Gilroy, G. and Lawrence, E. (1988) Two-tone Britain: white and black youth and the politics of anti-racism, in P. Cohen and H.S. Bains (eds) *Multi-racist Britain*. London: Macmillan.

Gough, B. (1998) Men and the discursive reproduction of sexism: repertoires of difference and equality, *Feminism and Psychology*, 8(1): 25–49.

Gough, B. and Edwards, G. (1998) The beer talking : four lads, a carry out and the reproduction of masculinities, *Sociological Review*, 46(3): 409–35.

Gramsci, A. (1971) *Selections from the Prison Notebooks*. London: Lawrence and Wishart.

Guardian (1999) Rites and wrongs. We have done away with hereditary peers. Now we should face up to the need for a secular state, *Guardian*, 29 October: http://www.guardianunlimited.co.uk/Archive/Article/0,4273,3922496,00.html

Guardian (2002) Tenuous thread of suspicion that leads to Chatty, *Guardian*, 3 September: http://www.guardian.co.uk/uk_news/story/0,3604, 785150,00.html

Hall, S. (1992) New ethnicities, in J. Donald and A. Rattansi (eds) *'Race', Culture and Difference*. London: Sage.

Hall, S. (1993a) What is this 'black' in black popular culture?, *Social Justice* 20(1–2): 101–14.

Hall, S. (1993b) For Allon White: metaphors of transformation, *Carnival, Hysteria, Writing*. Cambridge: Cambridge University Press.

Hall, S. (1996) Introduction: who needs 'identity'? in S. Hall and P. du Gay (eds) *Questions of Cultural Identity*. London: Sage.

Halliday, F. (1999) 'Islamaphobia' reconsidered, *Ethnic and Racial Studies*, 22(5): 892–902.

Hammersley, M. and Atkinson, P. (1987) *Ethnography Principles in Practice*. London: Routledge.

Haraway, D. (1990) A manifesto for cyborgs: Science, technology and socialist feminism in the 1980s, in L.J. Nicholson (ed.) *Feminism/Postmodernism*. London: Routledge.

Harding, S. (1987) *Feminism and Methodology*. Milton Keynes: Open University Press.

Haywood, C. and Mac an Ghaill, M. (1996) Schooling masculinities, in M. Mac an Ghaill (ed.) *Understanding Masculinities*. Buckingham: Open University Press.

Haywood, C. and Mac an Ghaill, M. (2001) *A Sociology of Men and Masculinities*. Buckingham: Open University Press.

Head, J. (1999) *Understanding the Boys*. London: Falmer.

Hearn, J. (1996) The organisation(s) of violence: men, gender relations, organisations and violences, in B. Fawcett, B. Featherstone, J. Hearn and C. Toft (eds) *Violence and Gender Relations: Theories and Interventions*. Thousand Oaks, CA: Sage.

Hearn, J. and Collinson, D.L. (1994) Theorizing unities and differences between men and between masculinities, in H. Brod and M. Kaufman (eds) *Theorizing Masculinities*. London: Sage.

Hebdige, D. (1996) Digging for Britain: an excavation in seven parts, in H.A. Baker, M. Diawara and R.H. Lindeborg (eds) *Black British Cultural Studies*. Chicago: University of Chicago Press.

Henwood, K. and Pidgeon, N. (1995) Grounded theory and psychological research, *The Psychologist*, 8(3): 115–18.

Hesse, B. (2000) *Un/settled Multiculturalisms. Diasporas, Entanglements, Transruptions*. New York: Zed Books.

Hiro, D. (1991) *Black British, White British: A History of Race Relations in Britain*. London: Grafton.

Hogg, M., Abrams, D. and Patel, Y. (1988) Ethnic identity, self-esteem and occupational aspirations of Indian and Anglo-Saxon British adolescents, *Genetic, Social and General Psychology Monographs*, 113: 487–508.

hooks, b. (1982) *Ain't I a Woman?: Black Women and Feminism*. London: Pluto Press.

hooks, b. (1992) *Black Looks*. London: Turnaround Press.

House of Commons, Home Affairs Select Committee (1986) *Bangladeshis in Britain*. London: HMSO.

Howe, C. (1997) *Gender and Classroom Interaction: A Research Review*. Edinburgh: SCRE.

Hurtado, A. and Stewart, A.J. (1997) Through the looking glass: inplications of studying whiteness for feminist methods, in M. Fine, L. Weis, L. Powell and L. Mun Wong (eds) *Off White: Readings on Race, Power and Society*. London: Routledge.

Hutnik, N. (1991) *Ethnic Minority Identity: A Social Psychological Perspective*. Clarendon Press: Oxford.

Jackson, C. (2002a) Can single-sex classes in co-educational schools enhance the learning experiences of girls and/or boys? An exploration of pupils' perceptions, *British Educational Research Journal*, 28: 37–48.

Jackson, C. (2002b) 'Laddishness' as a self-worth protection strategy, *Gender and Education*, 14(1): 37–51.

Jones, A. (2003) Talking cure: the desire for dialogue, in M. Boler (ed.) *Troubling Speech, Disturbing Silence*. New York: Peter Lang.

Kahani-Hopkins, V. and Hopkins, N. (2002) 'Representing' British Muslims: the strategic dimension to identity construction, *Ethnic and Racial Studies*, 25(2): 288–309.

Kehily, M. and Nayak, A. (1997) 'Lads and laughter': humour and the production of heterosexual hierarchies, *Gender and Education*, 9(1): 69–87.

Kelly, A.J.D. (1989) Ethnic Identification, association and redefinition: Muslim Pakistanis and Greek-Cypriots in Britain, in K. Liebkind (ed.) *New Identities in Europe: Immigrant Ancestry and the Ethnic Identity of Youth*. Aldershot: Gower.

Kenway, J. (1995) The information superhighway and postmodernity: the social promise and the social price, *Comparative Education*, 32(2): 17–231.

Kenway, J. and Fitzclarence, L. (1997) Masculinity, violence and schooling: challenging 'poisonous pedagogies', *Gender and Education*, 9(1): 117–33.

Kimmel, M.S. (1994) Masculinity as homophobia: fear, shame and silence in the construction of gender identity, in H. Kaufman and M. Brod (eds) *Theorizing Masculinities*. London: Sage.

Kitwood, T. and Borrill, C. (1980) The significance of schooling for an ethnic minority, *Oxford Review of Education*, 6(3): 241–53.

Kysel, F. (1988) Ethnic background and examination results, *Educational Research*, 30(2): 83–9.

Lather, P. (1988). Feminist perspectives on empowering research methodologies, *Women's Studies International Forum*, 11: 569–81.

Lewis, G. (2000) Discursive histories, the pursuit of multiculturalism and social policy, in G. Lewis, S. Gerwitz and J. Clarke (eds) *Rethinking Social Policy*. London: The Open University and Sage.

Lewis, G., Gewirtz, S. and Clarke, J. (eds) (2000) *Rethinking Social Policy*. London: The Open University and Sage.

Lewis, P. (1994). 'Being a Muslim and being British': the dynamics of Islamic reconstruction in Bradford', in R. Ballard (ed.) *Desh Pardesh: The South Asian Presence in Britain*. London: Hurst and Co.

Lightbody, P. and Durndell, A. (1996) Gendered career choice: is sex-stereotyping the cause or the consequence? *Educational Studies*, 22(2): 133–46.

Lingard, B. and Douglas, P. (1999) *Men Engaging Feminisms*. Buckingham: Open University Press.

Lloyd, T. (1999) *Young Men, the Job Market and Gendered Work*. York: York Publishing Services.

Lucey, H. and Reay, D. (2000) Social class and the psyche, *Soundings*, 15: 139–54.

Lucey, H., Melody, J. and Walkerdine, V. (2003) Uneasy hybrids: psychosocial aspects of becoming educationally successful for working class young women, *Gender and Education*, 15 (3).

Lydon, N. (1996) Man trouble, *Guardian*, 14 May.

Mac an Ghaill, M. (1988) *Young, Gifted and Black*. Milton Keynes: Open University Press.

Mac an Ghaill, M. (1994) The making of black English masculinites, in H. Brod and M. Kaufman (eds) *Theorizing Masculinities*. London: Sage.

Mac an Ghaill, M. (1996) 'What about the boys?': schooling, class and crisis masculinity, *The Sociological Review*, 44(3): 381–97.

Majors, R. and Billson, J. H. (1992) *Cool Pose: The Dilemmas of Black Manhood in America*. New York: Lexington Books.

McGivney, V. (1999) *Excluded Men: Men Who are Missing from Education and Training*. Leicester: National Institute of Adult Continuing Education.

McKellar, P. (1994) Only the fittest of the fittest will survive: black women and education, in L. Stone (ed.) *The Education Feminism Reader*. London: Routledge.

Macpherson, W. (1999) *The Stephen Lawrence Inquiry: Report of an Inquiry by Sir William Macpherson*. London: The Stationery Office.

Maguire, M., Ball, S.J. and Macrae, S. (1999) Promotion, persuasion and class-taste: marketing (in) the UK post-compulsory sector, *British Journal of Sociology of Education*, 20: 291–308.

Mahony, P. and Zmroczek, C. (eds) (1997) *Class Matters: 'Working Class' Women's Perspectives on Social Class*. London: Taylor and Francis.

Mama, A. (1995) *Beyond the Masks: Race, Gender and Subjectivity*. London: Routledge.

Marcia (1980) Identity in adolescence, in J. Adelson (ed.) *Handbook of Adolescent Psychology*. New York: Wiley.

Marland, M. (1995) *Further Improving Examination Results*, Special Governors Meeting Report. Reproduced in Raising Achievement in Inner City Schools. London: Education Magazine Seminar Series.

May, S. and Modood, T. (2001) Editorial, *Ethnicities*, 1(1): 5–7.

Maynard, M. and Purvis, J. (1994) Doing feminist research, in M. Maynard and J. Purvis (eds) *Researching Women's Lives from a Feminist Perspective*. London: Taylor and Francis.

Messner, M.A. (1997) *Politics of Masculinities: Men in Movements*. London: Sage.

Michael, M. (1996) *Constructing Identities*. London: Sage.

Mies, M. (1993) Towards a methodology for feminist research, in M. Hammersley (ed.) *Social Research: Philosophy, Politics and Practice*. London: Sage.

Mirza, H.S. (1992) *Young, Female and Black*. London: Routledge.

Mirza, H.S. (1999) Black masculinities and schooling: a black feminist response, *British Journal of Sociology of Education*, 20(1): 137–47.

Mirza, H.S. and Reay, D. (2000) Spaces and places of black educational desire: rethinking black supplementary schools as a new social movement, *Sociology*, 34(3): 521–44.

Modood, T. (1992) *Not Easy Being British*. Stoke-on-Trent: Trentham.

Modood, T. (1993) The number of ethnic minority students in British higher education: some grounds for optimism, *Oxford Review of Education*, 19: 167–82.

Modood, T. (1994) The end of a hegemony: the concept of 'Black' and British Asians, in J. Rex and B. Drury (eds) *Ethnic Mobilisation in a Multicultural Europe*. Aldershot: Avebury Press.

Modood, T. (1997) *Ethnic Minorities in Britain: Diversity and Disadvantage – Fourth National Survey of Ethnic Minorities in Britain*. London: Policy Studies Institute.

Modood, T. and Shiner, M. (1994) *Ethnic Minorities and Higher Education: Why are there Differential Rates of Entry?* London: Policy Studies Institute.

Morawski, J.G. (1997) White experimenters, white blood and other white conditions: locating the psychologist's race, in M. Fine, L. Weiss, L.C. Powell and L.M. Wong (eds) *Off White: Readings on Race, Power and Society*. London: Routledge.

Morgan, D.H.J. (1992) *Discovering Men*. London: Routledge.

Morgan, D.L. (1997) *Focus Groups as Qualitative Research*. Thousand Oaks, CA: Sage.

Morgan, D.L. (1998) *The Focus Group Guidebook*. Thousand Oaks, CA: Sage.

Morley, L. (1997) A Class of One's Own: women, social class and the academy, in P. Zmroczek and C. Mahony (eds) *Class Matters: 'Working Class' Women's Perspectives on Social Class*. London: Taylor and Francis.

Mullard, C. (1985) Multiracial education in Britain: from assimilation to cultural pluralism, in M. Arnot (ed.) *Race and Gender: Equal Opportunities Policies in Race and Gender*. Milton Keynes: The Open University and Pergamon Press.

Munt, S.R. (ed.) (2000) *Cultural Studies and the Working Class: Subject to Change*. London: Cassell.

Murphy, P. and Elwood, J. (1998) Gendered learning outside and inside school: influences on achievement, in D. Epstein, J. Elwood, V. Hey and J. Maw (eds) *Failing Boys?* Buckingham: Open University Press.

Nagel, C. (2002) Constructing difference and sameness: the politics of assimilation in London's Arab communities, *Ethnic and Racial Studies*, 25(2): 258–87.

NCIHE (National Committee of Inquiry into Higher Education) (1997) *Higher Education in the Learning Society*, the Dearing Report. London: The Stationery Office.

Newton, J. (1998) White guys, *Feminist Studies*, 24(3): 574–98.

Noble, D. (2000) Ragga music: dis/respecting black women and dis/reputable sexualities, in B. Hesse (ed.) *Un/Settled Multiculturalisms: Diasporas, Entanglements, Transruptions*. London: Zed Books.

Oakley, A. (1981) Interviewing women: a contradiction in terms, in H. Roberts (ed.) *Doing Feminist Research*. London: Routledge and Kegan Paul.

Oliver, M. (1992) Changing the social relations of research production, *Disability, Handicap and Society*, 7(2): 101–14.

Omi, M. and Winant, H. (1983) By the Rivers of Babylon: race in the United States, Parts 1 and 2, *Socialist Review*, 13(5) and 13(6).

Omi, M. and Winant, H. (1986) *Racial Formation in the United States*. London: Routledge.

Oommen, T.K. (2001) Situating ethnicity conceptually, *Ethnicities*, 1(1): 13–15.

Padilla, A.M., Alvarez, M. and Lindholm, K.J. (1986) Generational status and personality factors as predictors of stress in students, *Hispanic Journal of Behavioural Sciences*, 8(3): 275–88.

Paechter, C. (1998) *Educating the Other: Gender, Power and Schooling*. London: Falmer Press.

Parker-Jenkins, M., Hawe, K., Barrie, A. and Khan, S. (1997) Trying twice as hard to succeed: perceptions of Muslim women in Britain. Paper presented at the British Educational Research Association Annual Conference, University of York, September.

Pettigrew, T.F. (1971) *Racially Separate or Together?* New York: McGraw-Hill.

Phinney, J. (1989) Stages of Ethnic Identity Development, *Journal of Early Adolescence*, 9(1–2): 34–49.

Phinney, J. (1990) Ethnic identity and adolescents and adults: review of research, *Psychological Bulletin*, 108(3): 494–514.

Phinney, J. and Alipuria, L. (1990) Ethnic identity in older adolescents from four ethnic groups, *Journal of Adolescence*, 13.

Phinney, J., Chavira, V. and Tate, J.D. (1992) The effect of ethnic threat on ethnic self-concept and own-group ratings, *Journal of Social Psychology*, 133(4): 469–78.

Phoenix, A. (1994) Practising feminist research: the intersection of gender and 'race' in the research process, in M. Maynard and J. Purvis (eds) *Researching Women's Lives from a Feminist Perspective*. London: Taylor and Francis.

Phoenix, A. (1997) The place of 'race' and ethnicity in the lives of children and young people, *Educational and Child Psychology*, 14(3): 5–24.

Phoenix, A. (1998) Dealing with difference: the recursive and the new, *Ethnic and Racial Studies*, 21(5): 859–80.

Phoenix, A. (2000) Constructing gendered and racialized identities: young men, masculinities and educational policy, in G. Lewis, S. Gerwitz and J. Clarke (eds) *Rethinking Social Policy*. Buckingham: Open University Press.

Pickering, J. (1997) *Raising Boys' Achievement*. London: Network Educational Press.

Powell, E. (1968) Rivers of Blood, speech given at the Annual General Meeting of the West Midlands Area Conservative Party, 20 April.

Pugsley, L. (1998) 'Throwing your brains at it': higher education, markets and choice, *International Studies in Sociology of Education*, 8(1): 71–90.

Rabiee, F. and Thompson, D. (2000) *Widening Participation Increasing Access to Higher Education for Muslim Women*, internal report. Birmingham: UCE/ University of Birmingham Westhill.

Raphael Reed, L. (1999) Troubling boys and disturbing discourses on masculinity and schooling: a feminist exploration of current debates and interventions concerning boys in school, *Gender and Education*, 11(1): 93–110.

Rassool, N. and Morley, L. (2000) School effectiveness and the displacement of equity discourses in education, *Race, Ethnicity and Education*, 3(3): 237–58.

Rattansi, A. (1992) Changing the subject? Racism, culture and education, in J. Donald and A. Rattansi (eds) *Race, Culture and Difference*. London: Sage.

Rattansi, A. (1995) Forget postmodernism? Notes from de Bunker, *Sociology*, 29(2): 339–49.

Rattansi, A. and Westwood, S. (eds) (1994) *Racism, Modernity and Identity: On the Western Front*. Cambridge: Polity.

Reay, D. (1990) Working with boys, *Gender and Education*, 2(3): 269–82.

Reay, D. (1996a) Insider perspectives or stealing the words out of women's mouths: interpretation in the research process, *Feminist Review*, 53: 57–73.

Reay, D. (1996b) Dealing with difficult differences: reflexivity and social class in feminist research, *Feminism and Psychology*, 6(3): 443–56.

Reay, D. (1997) The double-bind of the 'working class' feminist academic: the success of failure or the failure of success? in P. Mahony and C. Zmroczek (eds) *Class Matters: 'Working Class' Women's Perspectives on Social Class*. London: Taylor & Francis.

Reay, D. (1998) 'Always knowing' and 'never being sure': familial and institutional habituses and higher education choice, *Journal of Education Policy*, 13: 519–29.

Reay, D. and Lucey, H. (2000) 'I don't like it here, but I don't want to be anywhere else': children living on inner-London council estates, *Antipode*, 32(4): 410–28.

Reay, D. and Lucey, H. (2001) Stigmatised choices: social class and local secondary school markets. Paper presented at Addressing Issues of Social Class and Education: theory into practice, University of North London, London, June.

Reay, D and William, D. (1999) 'I'll be a nothing': structure, agency and the construction of identity through assessment, *British Educational Research Journal*, 25(3): 343–54.

Reay, D., Davies, J., David, M. and Ball, S.J. (2001) Choices of degree or degrees of choice? Class, race and the higher education choice process, *Sociology*, 35(4): 855–74.

Rees, G. and Delamont, S. (1999) Education, in D. Thomson and A. Dunkerley (eds) *Wales: The State of the Nation*. Cardiff: University of Wales Press.

Reynolds, T. (1997) Class matters, 'race' matters, gender matters, in P. Mahony and C. Zmroczek (eds) *Class Matters: 'Working Class' Women's Perspectives in Social Class*. London: Taylor and Francis.

Rhodes, P.J. (1994) Race-of-interviewer effects: a brief comment, *Sociology*, 28(2): 547–58.

Ross, M. (1998) In search of black men's masculinities, *Feminist Studies*, 24(3): 599–626.

Rushdie, S. (1988) *The Satanic Verses*. New York: Viking Penguin.

Samad, Y. (1992) Book burning and race relations: the political mobilisation of Bradford Muslims, *New Community*, 18(4): 507–19.

Samad, Y. (1996) The politics of Islamic identity among Bangladeshis and Pakistanis in Britain, in T. Ranger, Y. Samad and O. Stuart (eds) *Culture, Identity and Politics*. Aldershot: Ashgate Publishing.

Sewell, T. (1997) *Black Masculinities and Schooling: How Black Boys Survive Modern Schooling*. Stoke-on-Trent: Trentham Books.

Sewell, T. (1998) Loose canons: exploding the myth of the 'black macho' lad, in D. Epstein, J. Elwood, V. Hey and J. Maw (eds) *Failing Boys?* Buckingham: Open University Press.

Shain, F. (2000) Culture, survival and resistance: theorizing young Asian women's experiences and strategies in contemporary British schooling and society, *Discourse: Studies in the Cultural Politics of Education*, 21(2): 155–74.

Shain, F. (2003) *The Schooling and Identity of Asian Girls*. Stoke-on-Trent: Trentham Books.

Sharma, A., Hutnyk, J. and Sharma, S. (1996) *Dis-Orienting Rhythms*. London: Zed Press.

Shaw, A. (1988) *A Pakistani Community in Oxford*. Oxford: Basil Blackwell.

Shaw, A. (1994) The Pakistani community in Oxford, in R. Ballard (ed.) *Desh Pardesh: The South Asian Presence in Britain*. London: Hurst and Company.

Skelton, C. (2000) 'A passion for football': dominant masculinities and primary schooling, *Sport, Education and Society*, 5(1): 5–18.

Skelton, C. (2001) 'Real Men' or 'New Men'? Changing images of male primary teachers. Presented at British Educational Research Association Conference, University of Leeds, 14–16 September.

Solomos, J. (1993) *Race and Racism in Britain*, 2nd edn. London: Macmillan.

Solomos, J. and Back, L. (1995) *Race, Politics and Social Change*. London: Routledge.

Spivak, G. (1990) *The Post-Colonial Critic: Interviews, Strategies, Dialogues*. London: Routledge.

Stanley, L. and Wise, S. (1990) Method, methodology and epistemology in feminist research processes, in L. Stanley (ed.) *Feminist Praxis*. London: Routledge.

Stanley, L. and Wise, S. (1993) *Breaking Out Again: Feminist Ontology and Epistemology*. London: Routledge.

Stone, L. (ed.) (1994) *The Education Feminist Reader*. London: Routledge.

Stopes-Roe, M. and Cochrane, R. (1990) *Citizens of this Country*. Philedelphia: Multilingual Matters.

Thomas, K. (1996) 'Ain't nothing like the real thing': black masculinity, gay sexuality and the jargon of authenticity, in M. Blount and G.P. Cunningham (eds) *Representing Black Men*. London: Routledge.

Tomlinson, S. (1984) *Home and School in Multicultural Britain*. London: Batsford.

Trow, M. (1994) *Managerialism and the Academic Profession: Quality and Control*. Milton Keynes: The Open University.

Van Dijk, T.A. (1984) *Prejudice and Discourse: An Analysis of Ethnic Prejudice in Cognition and Conversation*. Amsterdam: Benjamins.

Verma, G., Zec, P. and Skinner, G. (1994) *The Ethnic Crucible: Harmony and Hostility in Multi-Ethnic Schools*. London: Falmer Press.

Walkerdine, V. (1990) *Schoolgirl Fictions*. London: Verso.

Walkerdine, V., Lucey, H. and Melody, J. (2001) *Growing Up Girl. Psychosocial Explorations of Gender and Class*. Basingstoke: Palgrave.

Warrington, M. and Younger, M. (2000) The other side of the gender gap, *Gender and Education*, 12(4): 493–507.

Watkins, C. (1998) Trends in Exclusion. Paper presented at the BPS Annual Conference, Brighton, March.

Weiner, G., Arnot, M. and David, M. (1997) Is the future female? Female success, male disadvantage, and changing gender patterns in education, in A. Halsey, H.

Lauder, P. Brown and A. Stuart Wells (eds) *Education: Culture, Economy, Society*. Oxford: Oxford University Press.

Weinreich, P. (1983) *Identity, Personal and Sociocultural*. Stockholm: Almqvist and Wiskell.

Werbner, P. (1990) *The Migration Process: Capital, Gifts and Offerings Among British Pakistanis*. Oxford: Berg.

Werbner, P. (1991) Shattered bridges: the dialectics of progress and alienation among British Muslims, *New Community*, 17: 331–46.

Werbner, P. (1996) Essentialising the other: a critical response, in T. Ranger, Y. Samad and O. Stuart (eds) *Culture, Identity and Politics*. Alderslot: Ashgate Publishing.

Werbner, P. and Modood, T. (eds) (1997) *Debating Cultural Hybridity, Multi-Cultural Identities and the Politics of Anti-Racism*. London: Zed Books.

West, C. (1993) The new cultural politics of difference, in S. During (ed.) *The Cultural Studies Reader*. London: Routledge.

West, J. and Lyon, K. (1995) The trouble with equal opportunities: the case of women academics, *Gender and Education*, 7(1): 51–68.

Westwood, S. (1990) Racism, black masculinity and the politics of space, in J. Morgan and D. Hearn (eds) *Men, Masculinities and Social Theory*. London: Unwin Hyman.

Wetherell, M. (1987) Unequal equalitarianism: a preliminary study of discourse concerning gender and employment opportunities, *British Journal of Social Psychology*, 26: 59–71.

Wetherell, M. (1993) Masculinity as constructed reality. Paper for the plenary in feminist issues in research and theory presented at the Conference on Constructed Realities: Therapy, Theory and Research, Lofoten, Norway, June.

Wetherell, M. (1994) The knots of power and negotiation, blank and complex subjectivities, *Journal of Community and Applied Social Psychology*, 4(4): 305–8.

Wetherell, M. and Edley, N. (1998) Gender practices: steps in the analysis of men and masculinities, in K. Henwood, C. Griffin, and A. Phoenix (eds) *Standpoints and Differences: Essays in the Practice of Feminist Psychology*. London: Sage.

Wetherell, M. and Potter, J. (1986) Discourse analysis and the social psychology of racism, *British Psychological Society Section Newsletter*, 15.

Wetherell, M. and Potter, J. (1992) *Mapping the Language of Racism: Discourse and the Legitimation of Exploitation*. London: Harvester Wheatsheaf.

Whitehead, S. (1999) Hegemonic masculinity revisited, *Gender, Work and Organization*, 6(1): 58–62.

Willis, P. (1977) *Learning to Labour: How Working Class Kids Get Working Class Jobs*. Farnborough: Saxon House.

Wilson, A. (1984) *Finding a Voice: Asian Women in Britain*. London: Virago.

Yip, A.K.T. (2002) Negotiating space with family and kin in identity construction: the narratives of non-heterosexual Muslims in the UK. Paper presented at the annual conference of the British Sociological Association 'Reshaping the Social', University of Leicester, 25–27 March.

Younger, M. and Warrington, M. (1999) The gender gap in classroom interactions: reality or rhetoric? *British Journal of Sociology of Education*, 20: 327–43.

Yuval-Davis, N. (1994) Women, ethnicity and empowerment, *Feminism and Psychology*, 4(1): 179–97.

Yuval-Davis, N. (1997) Ethnicity, gender relations and multiculturalism, in P. Werbner and T. Modood (eds) *Debating Cultural Hybridity: Multi-Cultural Identities and the Politics of Anti-Racism*. London: Zed Books.

Yuval-Davis, N. (2001) Contemporary agenda for the study of ethnicity, *Ethnicities*, 1(1): 11–13.

Yuval-Davis, N. and Anthias, F. (eds) (1989) *Woman – Nation – State*. London: Macmillan.

Index

n indicates a note.

BOYS, LITERACIES AND SCHOOLING
THE DANGEROUS TERRITORIES OF GENDER-BASED LITERACY
REFORM

Leonie Rowan, Michele Knobel, Chris Bigum and Colin Lankshear

Current debates about boys and schooling in many Western nations are increasingly characterized by a sense of crisis as government reports, academic research and the day to day experiences of teachers combine to indicate that:

- boys are consistently underperforming in literacy
- boys are continuing to opt out of English and humanities
- boys represent the majority of behaviour problems and counselling referrals
- boys receive a disproportionate amount of special education support

This book responds to the complexity of the current debates associated with boys, gender reform, literacy and schooling by offering a clear map of the current context, highlighting the strengths and weaknesses of the various competing solutions put forward, and outlining a range of practical classroom interventions designed for dealing with the boys/literacy crisis. The authors consider the ways in which particular views of masculinity, gender reform, literacy, technology and popular culture can either open up or close down new conceptualizations of what it means to be a boy and what it means to be literate.

Contents

Introduction – Dangerous places: debates about boys, girls, schooling and gender based literacy reform – What about the boys?: the rhetoric and realities of the new gender crisis – How, who, where, when, why and what way? Mindsets on gender reform in schools – Some really useful theoretical company for transforming and transformative literacy education – Mindsets matter: an overview of major literacy worldviews – Making it not so transformative: literacy practices for girls and boys – Exorcising digital demons: information technology, new literacies and the de/re-construction of gendered subjectivities – From Pacman to Pokemon: cross generational perspectives on gender and reform in a 'post-feminist' age – Conclusion – Bibliography – Index.

256pp   0 335 20756 1 (Paperback)   0 335 20757 X (Hardback)

CHALLENGING VIOLENCE IN SCHOOLS
AN ISSUE OF MASCULINITIES

Martin Mills

Finally! A book that not only shows how the problem of 'school violence' is really a problem of boys' violence, but also a book that offers concrete, gender-based interventions to help all of us – parents, teachers, community – work to reduce it. It is not an overstatement to say that this book will save lives.

Professor Michael Kimmel, SUNY Stony Brook.

● Why are boys the major perpetrators of violence in schools?
● What are the significant issues which schools need to take into account when dealing with boys' violence?
● What are some practical strategies for addressing these issues?

This book explores the relationship between violence and masculinity within schools. There is a clear need to explore this relationship. A substantial amount of evidence exists which demonstrates how boys are the major perpetrators of violence in schools – from extreme acts of violence such as school shootings in the US to more common forms of schoolyard bullying – and that both girls and boys are their victims. The book suggests that violence has been 'masculinized' in such a way that boys often perpetrate violence as a means of demonstrating their perception of what counts as a valued form of masculinity. This masculinization of violence has often meant that girls experience violence from boys who are seeking to demonstrate their superiority over girls, and it has also meant that some boys often experience violence due to their non-conformity to dominant images of masculinity. In order to support these arguments the book draws on extensive interview data collected from boys and teachers who were involved in anti-violence programmes in their schools.

Contents

192pp   0 335 20584 4 (Paperback)   0 335 20585 2 (Hardback)